THE GREAT
CONSPIRACY

THE GREAT CONSPIRACY

BRITAIN'S SECRET
WAR AGAINST
REVOLUTIONARY FRANCE
1794–1805

Carlos de la Huerta

AMBERLEY

Dedicated to my mother, Carmen Luz Castellon

First published 2016

Amberley Publishing
The Hill, Stroud
Gloucestershire, GL5 4EP

www.amberley-books.com

Copyright © Carlos de la Huerta, 2016

The right of Carlos de la Huerta to be identified
as the Author of this work has been asserted in
accordance with the Copyrights, Designs and
Patents Act 1988.

ISBN 978 1 4456 5948 0 (hardback)
ISBN 978 1 4456 5949 7 (ebook)

British Library Cataloguing in Publication Data.
A catalogue record for this book is available
from the British Library.

Typesetting and Origination by Amberley
Publishing.
Printed in the UK.

CONTENTS

LEADING FIGURES

Paul Barras (1755–1829) Jacobin politician, regicide and one of the most powerful members of the Directory.

Napoleon Bonaparte (1769–1821) Revolutionary general, First Consul and Emperor of France.

Louis Antoine Henri de Bourbon-Condé (1772–1804) Grandson of the Prince de Condé and last Duke d'Enghien.

Georges Cadoudal (1771–1804) Breton general, leader of the chouans and political assassin.

Antoine Balthazar Joseph D'André (1759–1825) French politician and royalist agent in the service of England.

Philippe d'Auvergne, Prince de Bouillon (1754–1816) Vice-Admiral of the British Navy and governor of the island of Jersey.

Pierre Marie Desmarest (1764–1832) Head of Napoleon's secret police.

Francis Drake (1764–1821) British Diplomat and spy, he was accredited to the court of Genoa and Munich during the revolutionary and Napoleonic wars.

Louis Bayard Lewis Duval (1769–1844) Royalist spy and perhaps the real-life inspiration behind Baroness d'Orczy's fictional creation, the Scarlet Pimpernel.

Louis Fauche-Borel (1762–1829) Swiss bookseller and royalist agent in the service of England.

Louis Stanislas Xavier de France, King of France and Navarre (1755–1824) Younger brother of Louis XVI, head of the emigration 1789–1814 and claimant to the throne.

Marie Pierre Louis de Frotté (1766–1800) Soldier and leader of the Norman rebels.

Balthazar François, Marquis de Barthélemy (1747–1830) French diplomat and elected member of the Directory for a few months.

Joseph Fouché, Duc d'Otrante (1759–1820) French Politician, regicide and Minister of Police under the Directory and Napoleon.

James Harris, 1st Earl of Malmesbury (1746–1820) Career diplomat, Minister Plenipotentiary and twice Britain's peace envoy.

Louis Joseph, Prince de Condé (1737–1818) Only son of the Duke of Bourbon, *Prince du Sang* and commander-in-chief of the émigré army.

Frédéric Michel de Lajolais (1765–1808) Revolutionary general and diplomatic emissary.

Louis-Alexandre de Launay, Comte d'Antraigues (1753–1812) Pamphleteer, diplomat and royalist spy.

Jacques Pierre Lemaître (1742–1795) Advocate, royalist agent and founding member of the Paris Agency.

General Jean Victor Marie Moreau (1763–1813) Esteemed republican general and Victor of Hohenlinden.

Jean Guillaume Hyde de Neuville (1776–1857) Aristocrat of English descent, French diplomat and royalist agent for the exiled Bourbon princes.

Jacques Mallet du Pan (1749–1800) Career journalist and one of the most respected contemporary observers of the French Revolution.

Charles Maurice de Talleyrand-Périgord, Prince de Talleyrand (1754–1838) Master diplomat and statesman, Foreign Minister from 1797 to 1807.

Louis Edmond Antoine le Picard de Phélippeaux (1767–1799) Engineer, royalist agent and former classmate of Napoleon Bonaparte.

Jean Charles Pichegru (1761–1804) Celebrated Revolutionary general and Conqueror of Holland.

William Pitt the Younger (1759–1806) Britain's youngest serving Prime Minister, led the country's war effort against revolutionary France.

Thomas Laurent Madeleine Duverne de Presle (1763–1814) Naval officer, royalist agent and one of the leading members of the Paris Agency, Louis XVIII's principal spy network in the capital.

Pierre François Réal (1757–1834) Politician, jurist, policeman and Councillor of State.

Claude Ambroise Régnier, Duke de Massa (1746–1814) Lawyer and politician, served as *Grand Juge* and Minister of Justice under Napoleon.

Jean Gabriel Maurice Rocques, Comte de Montgaillard (1761–1841) Adventurer, royalist spy and double agent.

Anne Jean Marie René Savary, 1st Duke of Rovigo (1774–1833) General and Commandant of Napoleon's special bodyguard, he later served as Minister of Police.

Sir William Sidney Smith (1764–1840) British Admiral and Spy, he served in a number theatres during the revolutionary and Napoleonic wars.

Jean-Claude Hippolyte Méhée de la Touche (1762–1826) French Jacobin and spy.

Jacques Jean Marie Francois Boudin de Tromelin (1771–1842) French émigré and counter-revolutionary, he later became a general under Napoleon, his former enemy.

Charles Whitworth, 1st Earl of Whitworth (1752–1825) British diplomat, ambassador to Paris and later Lord Lieutenant of Ireland.

William Wickham (1761–1840) Police magistrate, minister plenipotentiary to the Helvetic Body and Britain's spymaster on the Continent.

William Windham (1750–1810) Whig politician and Secretary of War, he was one of the staunchest advocates of the counter-revolution.

John Wesley Wright (1769–1805) Gallant naval commander and intelligence officer.

PROLOGUE

At five o'clock in the evening on Tuesday 28 January 1794, a dark, unmarked carriage pulled up before a small white house in London's fashionable Kensington Square and two men wrapped in plain frock coats clambered down. Ringing the bell, the pair stood in the cheerless winter cold as the resident of the building shuffled slowly to the door, his right foot dragging behind his left due to a congenital defect which he otherwise ascribed to a childhood fall. Moments later, the door swung open and an unpleasant-looking individual of medium height with a high forehead, pale blue eyes and a nose slightly *retroussé* appeared.[1] Recognising him instantly as the notorious Bishop of Autun, the two men identified themselves as 'Messengers of the State'. Serving him with a deportation order, they declared that he had five days to leave the country or face repatriation back to France.[2] In protest, he addressed himself to Britain's king, George III, and William Pitt, his prime minister, defying them to present proof or justification for his removal from the realm; to his irritation, he received no reply. Under the summary provisions of the Alien Act, which was passed into law just over a year earlier, the government was under no obligation to provide any explanation.[3]

After a brief respite, during which time he was permitted to arrange his affairs, he quit England, his country of exile since September 1792. He had originally thought of seeking asylum in Geneva or Florence but was made to understand that his appearance in either city would not be welcomed on account of his early support of the Revolution. So, equipped with letters of introduction to George Washington and Alexander Hamilton, he set sail on the *William Penn* for America. The departure of the vessel was delayed by a storm in the English Channel, forcing her captain to seek repairs in Falmouth, and it was not until 28 April 1794 that she docked in the port of Philadelphia, after a pleasant and uneventful crossing lasting thirty-eight days.[4]

This exile, Charles Maurice de Talleyrand-Perigord, was just one of the many émigrés who were expelled from Britain during this great and turbulent period in history. On 29 January 1794, a day after Talleyrand received the summons, *The Times* reported how two French agents, operating under assumed names, had been arrested in Dover on government orders and dispatched to Ostend. Among their papers were discovered 'the most convincing proofs of their having carried on correspondence with the Jacobins in France'.[5] The Home Office was not being overly suspicious; there was good reason to believe that as war with revolutionary France intensified, the republican government would employ rogue elements among the émigré community to exploit increasing leftist radicalism in Britain.

Scores of clubs and societies agitating for parliamentary reform had appeared in Britain since the fall of the Bastille, the most influential of which was the London Corresponding Society. Despite the harassment of press gangs and attacks in Parliament, the LCS had managed to retain its membership and on 14 April 1794, following a number of gatherings that had taken place throughout the country, it hosted an open-air festival at Chalk Farm in North London at which between 2,000 and 3,000 people gathered to petition for reform and a dissolution of Parliament. The proceedings of these clubs were mostly nonviolent but their depiction in the police reports suggested a shadowy underworld group in which dangerous fanatics were conspiring to subvert the social and political institutions of the country.[6]

The man charged with their surveillance was William Wickham, a suave and talented magistrate who would rapidly rise to become Britain's spymaster on the European continent. Born in

October 1761 at Cottingley in the West Riding of Yorkshire, he was the eldest son of Henry Wickham Esq., a lieutenant-colonel in the 1st Regiment of Foot Guards and Justice of the Peace. After attending Harrow School, Wickham was sent to Christ Church, Oxford where he obtained a studentship and formed a lifelong friendship with future prime minister Lord Grenville, one that would eventually exercise a huge influence on his career in the diplomatic service. On 16 April 1794, Wickham instructed a recent recruit to the LCS, Edward Gosling, to discover whether radicals 'were serious in their conversation and really intended to procure arms'.[7] From these findings Wickham drafted a report that was laid before the cabinet. Its effect was immediate. On 12 May the papers of the LCS were seized and the leaders, an obscure cobbler named Thomas Hardy and the writer John Thelwall, were apprehended and taken into custody. The Home Office had expected to find evidence of arms procurement and correspondence with Jacobin agents, but scrutiny of the papers by the Privy Council revealed only that the members planned to collect en masse should anything resembling a 'national uprising' occur. Despite the absence of treasonous evidence, Britain's Home Secretary, Henry Dundas, presented the House of Commons with a note from King George III demanding the introduction of repressive measures. The government, still convinced that a French conspiracy was involved, sharpened its focus on the émigré population, and on 23 May, the day that habeas corpus was suspended, Pitt authorised their removal from Winchester to Reading, Farnham and Stockbridge because, as he cynically claimed, 'he had taken an interest in the welfare of these people'. The government widened its net of arrests to the provinces in an attempt to unravel this purported conspiracy. In his speech, Pitt explained that the LCS and its fellow radical clubs had formed a plan for a 'Convention for all England' which spelled the 'total subversion of the Constitution, the annihilation of Parliament and the destruction of the King himself'.[8] Faced with the spectre of a revolution in their homeland, only a few dissenting voices were raised in objection to this gross abrogation of justice.

In reward for his service Wickham was invested with the direction of the Alien Department, a bureaucratic branch of the Home Office which had been created to administer the Alien Act.[9] The Act was designed to place tight restrictions on the movements of all foreigners either entering the country or already resident there. Specifically, it made it a legal requirement that all foreigners register their name and rank upon entering the country, render their arms to the control of customs and be issued a mandatory passport by a magistrate. It also enabled any foreigner to be imprisoned for refusal to leave the country if so demanded.[10] The severity of these measures naturally disquieted France's émigré community. Each day, from his second-floor office at No. 20 Crown Street, Westminster, where the Foreign and Commonwealth Office stand today, scores of refugees filled the public waiting room in order to raise a complaint of some description. Despite the weight of work, Wickham discharged his duties without complaint and with his customary zeal. However, he occupied this position for only a few months, as in mid-October he was entrusted with a confidential mission to Switzerland, where Lord Robert Stephen Fitzgerald, the fifth son of the 1st Duke of Leinster, was at that time Envoy Extraordinary and Minister Plenipotentiary.[11]

A couple of weeks before, Fitzgerald had transmitted to Downing Street a secret plan for the restoration of the Bourbon monarchy that he had received from a celebrated journalist, Mallet du Pan, and his good friend Jean Joseph Mounier, constitutional royalists claiming to be in covert communications with Jean Lambert Tallien, the President of the National Convention in Paris. Du Pan, Swiss by birth, had previously addressed a note to Pitt and Grenville pointing out that Britain's failure to support the counter-revolutionary movement in France would result in the consolidation of the republican government. The English ministers consequently judged that the overtures deserved attention; however, George III did not think that Lord Fitzgerald was qualified to handle complex negotiations with men 'of superior talents' and stipulated that a replacement be found. 'For the business in hand,' he wrote, 'let Lord Grenville find some very wary man.'[12] The choice thus fell on Wickham. As Superintendent of Aliens, he had acquired strong ties with the émigré community in Britain and had, from the discreet confines of his office, carried out a clandestine correspondence with royalists in the French interior. He also possessed an intimate knowledge of Switzerland, having studied at the University of Geneva, and had on several preceding occasions procured information useful to the government thanks to his marriage to Mademoiselle Eleanor Madeline Bertrand, the beautiful eldest daughter of a professor in the University of Geneva's mathematics faculty. Finally, being a relatively obscure minister, it was thought that his sudden departure would not excite comment or arouse much public attention.[13]

Little was it supposed that the mission he was about to embark upon would have an immediate and profound impact on the course of the French counter-revolution.

I

PICHEGRU'S TREASON

On 15 October 1794, William Wickham bade farewell to his charming wife and set off from his residence in London, arriving at Harwich approximately twelve hours later. His mission was considered so confidential that it was kept secret from the staff at the Foreign Office and only communicated to the chief members of the cabinet. Boarding a packet with a passport issued from the Alien Office, he set sail for Helvoetsluys, a sea port on the island of Voom off the coast of Holland. A dense grey fog hung in the air, blanketing the horizon and rendering it difficult for the vessel's captain to spot French privateers lurking in the distance. Throughout the crossing Wickham remained below deck, studying a transcript of Grenville's instructions that he had copied at his home before tossing the original in the fireplace. He was to ascertain whether the royalists' overtures were genuine and to discuss the broad terms upon which a Bourbon restoration might be effected. They included the re-establishment of the Catholic religion, the repeal of the proscription laws against the émigrés and the proclamation of a general amnesty for political offences except for the 'authors and principal actors' of the massacres perpetrated in Paris, Lyons and throughout the provinces.[1]

At approximately ten o'clock at night, after a safe passage lasting fifty-four hours, the English packet entered the harbour by way of the great sluice from which Helvoetsluys derives its name. Having passed the customs control without delay, Wickham climbed into a gaudy coach waiting to convey the passengers to Brill, a fortified seaport in the mouth of the Meuse, six miles distant. The countryside resembled the fens of Lincolnshire, studded with tall trees and dotted with pretty farmhouses and windmills.[2] Wickham unfortunately did not keep a detailed record of his impressions, at least none that can be imputed to him. From Brill he switched transport and continued twelve miles to the great port of Rotterdam. For ten more days his lonely carriage trundled through the Low Countries and the western fringes of Germany, dodging the conquering French armies, before finally crossing the Swiss frontier near Rheinfelden. After staying overnight in the ancient bishopric of Basle, he headed southwards through the beautiful Moutier valley. Eventually, on 1 November 1794, his carriage emerged from a fine and ancient forest. After crossing the River Aar on a long wooden bridge half a league distant, his carriage pulled up before the gates of Berne.

At the barricades, Wickham was subjected to a rigorous interrogation by sentinels who examined his passport suspiciously before searching the luggage strapped to the roof of his carriage. They also questioned him on his name, his profession, his place of origin and the motives for his visit, all of which he answered to their apparent satisfaction. The sentinels thereupon entered Wickham's particulars in their register and, returning his passport to him, coldly waved his carriage through.

The atmosphere in Berne during these troubled days was fraught with tension. Just a few months before, Swiss Jacobins had seized control of the neighbouring city state of Geneva. As streams of terrified refugees came straggling across the frontier, the ruling oligarchy, which controlled the Senate, introduced a series of measures to arrest the perceived spread of subversive republican activities. They censored the circulation of revolutionary pamphlets, employed spies all over and ordered the 'police supervision of foreigners'.[3] They also published a proclamation violently denouncing the late proceedings in Geneva, warning citizens against similar practices and strictly forbidding all involvement with any man 'sullied with crimes'.[4]

Among the men who were the subject of strict surveillance, not only from the Bernese police but from French diplomatic agents, was the famed pamphleteer Mallet du Pan. Despite frequent visits from royalists and politicians of every stripe, he had kept aloof as far as possible from the intrigues of which Berne, and the neighbouring cantons, had become the centre. He was nevertheless repeatedly denounced by François Barthélemy, the French ambassador to what the French named the Helvetic Cantons, who tried to have him expelled from Switzerland on the grounds that he was an avowed enemy of the Republic.[5] Wickham was well aware that du Pan was the object of suspicion but, despite the attendant risks, he made contact with him within days of his arrival. His first interview, however, revealed to him that matters were not as advanced as claimed. Not only were du Pan and Mounier unable to provide evidence of their relations with any prominent members of the National Convention in Paris, but the claims that they had received personal assurances of support from Tallien himself collapsed after a few probing questions. Moreover, in the course of the discussions, it was inferred that the British government would have to expend large sums of money just to pursue these pretended negotiations. In these circumstances, Wickham decided that it would be inappropriate to proceed any further and declined to advance any funds, making no attempt to conceal his suspicion that a gross deception had been practised upon the British government. But while expressing his annoyance and disappointment, he told the two constitutionalists that it would not be altogether inadvisable to break off relations and that an opportunity to resume talks may arrive at some future time.[6]

Grenville was nevertheless completely satisfied with Wickham's management of the affair and, following Lord Fitzgerald's request to be granted leave, charged his friend with assuming responsibility for Britain's diplomatic affairs in Switzerland. From Dover Street, on 9 December 1794, the Foreign Minister wrote:

I cannot let this Messenger go without adding to my public despatch a few words to express to you how completely satisfied all the King's servants with the delicate transaction which you were entrusted. Hope not inconvenience to remain a few more months, as your presence may be of the greatest use. We receive little intelligence from France, from which much reliance can be placed, respecting the general disposition of the country or the events in the inland and southern provinces, except what comes through Switzerland. It would therefore be extremely material to exert yourself to the utmost to procure constant and detailed information from thence. Be upon your guard with Mounier and du Pan, but a communication with them may be rendered useful.[7]

In spite of every precaution, Barthélemy was immediately informed of the interview by his agents. Although the secrets of the meeting were unknown, Barthélemy supposed that the English cabinet had dispatched Wickham to confer with du Pan and Mounier on the subject of the re-enactment of the constitution of 1791 and that given Grenville's well-known confidence in his friend, and the pecuniary resources made available to him, his installation in Switzerland would lead to an altogether more aggressive mission than the languid one discharged by his ineffectual predecessor. As Barthélemy informed his masters in Paris, Wickham's commission signalled a redoubled effort by England to accelerate the war and try and push the Court of Vienna to *'un parti extrême'*.[8] He was not altogether wrong.

On 16 March 1795, a special messenger arrived on Wickham's doorstep bearing a confidential despatch from the Foreign Office. The message, once deciphered, revealed that the Imperial Court of Vienna had formulated a plan to attack France by way of the Franche-Comté and that the Habsburg Emperor intended to avail himself of the support of the émigré army, then strung out on the right bank on the Rhine. In execution of this plan, Wickham's position as chargé d'affaires in Switzerland was to be of 'material service', not least for procuring and collecting information. He was instructed by Lord Grenville to cooperate with the Austrian army, offer the émigrés assistance in conducting auxiliary operations and prepare the ground for a royalist insurrection.[9] The émigré army was under the command of Louis Joseph de Condé, a Prince du Sang and only son of the Duke de Bourbon. At this time, his headquarters was a pleasant country house formerly belonging to the bishops of Spire in Bruchsal, a village in Baden, near Karlsruhe. His army was a 'strange spectacle', numbering no more than 4,000–5,000 half-starved, ill-clad volunteers, mainly French ex-officers, magistrates and German mercenaries.[10] Despite his terrible misfortunes, he enjoyed a preeminent position among the pure royalists, who since the fall of the Bastille had dreamt of nothing but the return of the *ancien régime* in its 'purest' form. Condé was a hero's name, and though nearing his sixtieth year his courage and skill on the battlefield were never questioned.[11] These qualities invested him with a degree of prestige that the claimant of the throne, Louis XVIII, the unwieldly brother of France's deceased king, could never hope to enjoy. The Pretender had, during his unhappy exile in Coblentz, made a demonstration of his authority, arraying himself in military uniform and imbuing the court with a martial spirit, but in the eyes of the émigrés Condé was incontestably their leader, the very man from whom the strength of the reactionary movement emanated, the man for whom they would sacrifice all.

In his instructions, Lord Grenville authorised Wickham to make 'secret advances' of up to £30,000 to the prince if the distress of his army had not been alleviated.[12] The Imperial Court of Vienna had thus far devoted a paltry 200,000 florins a month to its maintenance, and as an inevitable consequence Condé's troops had suffered terribly during the bleak winter. The situation was so dire that the Princess of Monaco, his mistress, was forced to hock her diamonds in order to supply the needs of his little court.[13] From his headquarters Condé alerted the Duke d'Harcourt, his intermediary in London, to his grave financial difficulties, warning that they would invariably lead to the dissolution of his army. The cabinet therefore proposed that Condé put his army under British pay after the expiration of the last campaign. Condé was open to the suggestion but, being timorous in matters of diplomacy, stipulated that the consent of the emperor must first be obtained. The Austrians, however, were disinclined to agree to the proposal, being only too happy to see the royalists' prominence in the forthcoming campaign diminished, especially as it was their intention to obtain territorial compensation from France. The English cabinet therefore dispatched Sir Morton Eden, a distinguished diplomat and brother of Lord Auckland, to the Court of Vienna to press the subject but was told that with the plan of operations on the side of Franche-Comté in motion, the Habsburg emperor was determined to retain the direction of the army of Condé in its present condition. This being the case, Eden pressed upon the emperor the absolute necessity that urgent measures be taken to provide for the material wants of that army. Eventually, on 4 May 1795, a conference was held in which it was agreed that England would guarantee the interest of an Austrian loan and that in return the emperor would deploy 200,000 men upon the Rhine. Furthermore, it was resolved to render the émigré army effective in the field. The British government accordingly dispatched the Scottish military attaché Colonel Charles Gregan Craufurd to the prince's camp in order to impart the pleasing news that he would receive £140,000 for this purpose.[14]

Whilst Condé put his army on a surer footing, Wickham prepared the ground for a royalist insurrection in France. To harness disaffection in the southern and eastern regions he focused on Lyons, the most counter-revolutionary city in France. One of his first acts was to solicit the support of the Comte de Precy, a tall and lanky royalist with bright white teeth who led the retreat from the city when it had risen up against the Convention in 1793.[15] Precy was at this time employed in the service of the Kingdom of Sardinia but readily agreed to give Wickham the benefit of his advice and experience. He cautioned England's minister that, following the city's dreadful experience at the hands of the Jacobins, anti-Convention forces in Lyons would not risk an uprising unless they were fully supported by their allies. He advised Wickham that the chief royalists in the town should first be supplied with arms and with money. However, the insurrection could only begin once the Austrians had crossed the Rhine and Condé had penetrated Franche-Comté at the head of his army. Precy's plan was accordingly sent to London, where it was subsequently approved without great revision.[16]

For the purpose of strengthening lines of communication with Lyons, Precy recommended the employment of Louis Bayard, an intrepid young engineer who had served under him during the city siege.[17] In the beginning of May Bayard had returned from Lyons where, concealed in Wickham's house and recovering from fatigue, he gave his English host a first-hand account of the slaughter of ninety-two prison inmates at which he was a bystander. The prison massacre was perpetrated by anti-revolutionary 'murder gangs' which terrorised the provinces in the late winter and early spring of 1795 in the name of the king. The gangs called themselves the 'Companies of Jesu' or 'Companies of the Sun' but were, according to one republican agent, nothing more than 'royalist death squads' composed of '*muscadins*, returned émigrés, deserters and foreigners'.[18] Wickham wanted nothing to do with these gangs, believing that their disorganised anti-revolutionary violence would only bring the full weight of the Convention to bear down on Lyons before it could defend itself with outside help. Hoping, however, that they 'be directed to better purposes', Wickham directed Bayard and the chevalier Louis Gabriel d'Artez, a former navy officer, to persuade the extremists to curb their excesses until the time was ripe for the émigrés to lead the rebellion.[19] From Bayard's account, the 'decided and pronounced opinion of the very great majority' of Lyons was in favour of monarchy, unlike during the troubles of 1793 when there were scarcely a hundred real royalists in place. He attributed this shift in sentiment to the 'extreme ability and good conduct' of Precy, who, thanks to 'clever politicking', was able to win over the goodwill of the population.[20]

Besides deploying agents along the south-eastern frontier of France and maintaining a correspondence with Lyons, Wickham also dispatched emissaries to Paris and entered into relations with the rebel leaders in the west. However, his first effort to carry out this task on a large scale was less successful. With the support of his secretary, a French émigré by the name of Le Clerc de Noissy, he entered into communications with a royalist agent named Joseph Vincent in Paris. The latter, formerly a post office employee under the *ancien régime*, claimed to have successfully suborned several officials in various government departments and also to have established an understanding with the chief architect of Robespierre's fall, Jean Lambert Tallien. For several weeks he claimed that Tallien would pronounce himself in favour of a Restoration and that a *coup d'état* was imminent. But it soon became evident that Vincent's promises were delusory, forcing Wickham to concede that he had been deceived and that the £1,200 which he had advanced to finance the scheme had been needlessly squandered.[21]

Despite the failure of this démarche, Wickham was not without hope of seducing from the Republic an even more important figure than Tallien. For months he had been entertaining the idea of winning over to the service of the monarchy the most esteemed of republican generals, the celebrated conqueror of Holland, General Jean Charles Pichegru.

* * * *

Pichegru was then in his thirty-fifth year, and although he owed his rank and honours to the Republic he was known to harbour a deep mistrust of its institutions. It was possible that this wariness was rooted in his semi-clerical upbringing.[22] When he was young he professed a longing to enter a Franciscan monastic order, but like many boys of his age he decided on a military education. In the spring of 1795, the Convention appointed him Commandant of Paris and charged him with suppressing the insurrection known as 12 *Germinal* an III. Afterwards, he repaired to Alsace to assume his new command upon the Rhine. In his letter of service he was notified that should the armies of the north and of the Sambre and Meuse be combined to the Rhine, the supreme command would devolve upon him.

Wickham received reports which made him doubt Pichegru's allegiance to the Republic. They related how he had treated émigrés who fell in his captivity in Holland with great care and distinction and that during the suppression in Paris he reportedly indicated in private his contempt for the Jacobins. Similar impressions had been reported by republican spies who, at Pichegru's command headquarters on the left bank of the Rhine, observed how the general was openly indignant at the Convention's neglect to victual his troops. Yet, according to one intelligence brief, the chances of 'tampering' with the general successfully were small.[23] One of the obstacles was that Pichegru was notoriously principled, uncompromising and 'not in the least accessible to persuasion or influence'. So, any attempt to win him over would fail unless he already held royalist convictions of his own. Like many disaffected soldiers, Pichegru believed that the Republic could not endure; but, being of a cautious and sedate nature, he would need sufficient inducement to risk openly switching sides. Wickham, however, did not want to make direct overtures to Pichegru himself, believing that his proposals would more likely meet with a favourable reception if they were made by the Prince de Condé and not an Englishman. Both he and Craufurd therefore pressed upon the prince the necessity of embarking upon the negotiation without delay, offering also to supply whatever money would be necessary to facilitate the negotiations. Wickham proposed employing a Swiss officer or the royalist agent d'Artez to make the overture, but raised no objection when Condé evinced his preference for appointing an agent himself, intimating that it would be one of his officers. However, he told Wickham that he needed to refer the matter to his sovereign first and it was not until 26 July, after having been empowered to promise a royal pardon and confer rewards, that the prince summoned his agent to his headquarters and charged him with opening communications with Pichegru.

Condé's appointment could not have fallen on a more implausible figure – a short, tubby bookseller with a cleft chin from Neuchâtel, Switzerland, by the name of Louis Fauche-Borel.[24] A professed royalist, Borel was unquestionably intelligent, but like many adventurers of this age he was rash, excessively vain and prone to illusion. The plan was that he would enter France, solicit an interview with the general and then report back immediately. The reward for his services was substantial. Besides the promise of adventure he would receive 1,000 *Louis*, but in the event of the Restoration he would also be awarded the payment of 1 million *Louis*, the directorship of the Royal Press, the position of Inspector General of the Libraries of France and the Order of St Michel.[25]

On 19 August 1795, Borel presented himself at Pichegru's headquarters at Illkirch, a small market town in the neighbourhood of Strasbourg. Concealed in the sleeve of his coat was a letter written on plain paper without seal or coat of arms but signed Louis Joseph de Bourbon. The prince could not stomach to address Pichegru by the title of general as conferred upon him by the Republic and therefore couched the letter in the following stiff terms:

> Seeing that M Pichegru is in the mind which I expected, he should send me a line in his own hand and some person in his confidence to whom I may explain all the advantages which I can guarantee to M Pichegru and his friends, provided he will combine with me for the purpose of saving France and of restoring our sovereign to his throne; failing the measure which I have suggested, all sorts and ways and means might be devised, and yet precious time might be lost and an important secret compromised.[26]

To the communication was affixed a document containing the conditions under which the restoration was to be carried out and the union of the two armies effected. Pichegru was to proclaim Louis XVIII under the title of King of France and Navarre. Once his army swore their oath of allegiance, the Bourbon flag would be hoisted at Strasbourg and Hüninguen. A trumpeter would thereupon be sent across the Rhine to announce to Condé that Louis XVIII had been proclaimed king and to invite him to join forces with Pichegru and the republican camp. He was also promised, should he agree to the above conditions, to 'the staff of a Marshal of France; The Château de Cambord; A House in Paris; A gratuity of a million *livres*; A yearly pension of two hundred *thousand livres*.'[27] A monument was also to be erected bearing the inscription, 'Pichegru saved the French monarchy and gave peace to Europe.'[28] Furthermore, his native town of Arbois would be granted exemption from taxation for a period of ten years and be renamed in his honour. Folding the note, Pichegru nodded in assent. He was prepared to initiate negotiations after some preconditions were first met. Borel could scarcely contain his delight. The bookseller from Neuchâtel was poised to become a millionaire.

The negotiations, however, stumbled from the first. To Pichegru, the plan was impractical in that it was on the right bank of the Rhine and not on the left that the royalists and republicans should proclaim the king. Condé, however, rejected the counterproposals, arguing that the Austrians would never permit the republicans to cross the Rhine unopposed. He also added a further measure. He demanded the surrender of the German town of Hüninguen to convince the Austrians of Pichegru's good faith. Borel returned to Alsace on 25 August and handed Pichegru the signed letter that Condé had written on 22nd with these amendments. At the sight of this letter Pichegru supposedly promised to send a confidential agent immediately to Basle. He also entrusted to Borel a note containing two lines in his own hand: 'Y. has received X.s letters and will consider them with the object of making use of them at the proper time. He will be careful to give X. due warning.'[29]

Despite his apparent openness to a *rapprochement*, Pichegru refused to commit to any action until he had first crossed the Rhine and entrenched himself firmly on the right bank. No doubt he was undecided. Although he staked his reputation on the eventual demise of the Republic, he did not want to commit himself to such a dangerous venture until the fate of the Convention had been decided. For as he knew at this time, Paris was in a state of foment. On 22 August 1795, the same day that Condé signed his letter, the Convention approved a new constitution to replace the Jacobins' discredited one. The constitution promised to create a political middle way, one which favoured the propertied classes but also appealed to the many moderates in the interior who remained undecided about the choice between a limited monarchy and a limited republic.[30] The constitution was to be liberal and embody the separation of powers. The legislature would consist of two houses – a Council of Five Hundred, which proposed new legislation, and a Council of *Anciens*, which transformed bills into laws. The *Anciens* was also invested with powers to choose a Directory of five members which would be vested with executive authority. However, the Convention also proposed passing the 'Two Thirds Law' which stipulated that two-thirds of the membership of the new legislative councils was to be chosen from the sitting members of the convention. This decision to prolong the monopoly of power in the hands of men who belonged to their number proved unwise, for its immediate effect was to give new impetus to the growing movement that was in favour of a moderate, monarchical settlement.[31]

At first, reports from the capital were encouraging. The rebels appeared well organized and in command of widespread support across all the sections (subdivisions of revolutionary Paris). But on 5 October 1795 (13 *vendémiaire* in the revolutionary calendar), in another historic *journée*, they were mercilessly crushed by government troops on the front-steps of the church of St Roch.

2

RECALLED

One week after the failed uprising, police stormed the Café de Valois on the rue des Bons-Enfants and arrested a fifty-three-year-old lawyer from Honfleur whilst he sat discreetly reading the *Journal de Paris*. Upon raiding his apartment on the rue Sainte-Croix-de-la-Bretonnerie, near the Faubourg Saint-Antoine, they found a bundle of correspondence stashed away in the kitchen. The letters apparently dealt with innocuous matters, but between the lines, in sympathetic ink, were concealed coded messages between the exile court at Verona, the insurgents in La Vendée and a number of royalist agents operating in Paris. The lawyer, whose name was Pierre Jacques Lemaître, had been under surveillance for a number of days after having been denounced to the police by a double agent from Caen. Before the storming of the Tuileries he had occupied the office of *Secrètaire des Finances*, but in 1791, with the consent of the late king, Louis XVI, he formed the 'Paris Agency', a spy network which had been established for the purpose of gathering intelligence, corrupting officials and training public opinion for the restoration of the monarchy.[1]

Lemaître was an unlikely agent. A decade earlier, on 5 December 1785, while the French public was fixated on the century's greatest scandal, the affair of the Cardinal de Rohan and the Diamond Necklace, police agents arrested him as he tried to sneak through the city gates. Out from under his redingote tumbled a bundle of clandestine political literature. During a search of his apartment in Belleville two days later they discovered a stack of illegal pamphlets criticising the Controller General of Finances, Charles Alexandre de Calonne, and other important political and financial figures.[2] In their dossier, the police described him as possessing an 'old fashioned wig, gloves, spectacles, glossy dress coat, back biter and sardonic smile'. He was also arrested following the deposition of the king but was released thanks to the intercession of his neighbour Jean Lambert Tallien, who certified that Lemaître was a gentleman who led a very secluded life and knew only good patriots.[3]

In the days leading up to the uprising Lemaître had been clamouring in the streets, distributing incendiary pamphlets and bribing journalists to speak out against the Revolution. He had hoped to turn the rebellion in the royalists' favour, but despite his indefatigable efforts he was unable to exert any real influence on the evolution of events. The reality was that the sections' opposition to the Convention arose not from any attachment to the 'pure' principles of royalism but from a fervent determination to prevent the prolongation of the Convention's powers. As he well knew, it was the constitutionalists, not the partisans of the king, who were the real impulse behind the movement.[4]

Lemaître's correspondence nevertheless furnished the National Convention with the names of the deputies whom his agents claimed to have converted, as well as the details of the many intrigues and deceptions that had been practiced in order to solicit money from the English government. Worse still, it betrayed the names of the agents employed in obtaining these funds from Wickham who, as they could now prove, headed a 'secret committee' of émigrés in Switzerland and was subsidising Condé's army in order to excite counter-revolutionary movements throughout the provinces.[5]

Despite these startling revelations, no violent repression ensued after the uprising. The Convention, not wanting to draw undue attention to the popularity of the movement, contented itself with purging the staff of the National Guard and placing it under the direction of the general commanding the army of the interior. The sections were disarmed and commissions were formed to try the leaders of the rebellion, most of whom were nevertheless allowed to slip through the city barriers unmolested. In the days that followed only ten death sentences were pronounced, among them one for Pierre Jacques Lemaître himself. He was brought before a military council in the Lepeletier Section, the epicentre of revolt, and charged with crimes against the state. On 11 November, he was guillotined at the Place de Grève. His fellow Paris agent, the Abbé André Charles Brottier, a crabbed and sullen character, was also apprehended but was released, purportedly due to lack of evidence.[6]

Back in Paris, the new government took its seat of power. Between nine and ten o'clock on the morning of 2 November 1795 France's appointed rulers met at the headquarters of the Committee of Public Safety. As they rode in their carriage to the Petit Luxembourg accompanied by 400 footmen and 40 horsemen, one of the five, Louis Marie de la Révellière Lépeaux, an unrepentant atheist, noticed that their cavalry escort all wore battered shoes over woollen socks replete with holes. They arrived at the Petit Luxembourg 'without great fanfare', where they found bare palatial rooms devoid of furniture or fixtures. The concierge Dupont hastily found them a rickety table, of which the foot was timeworn, and four creaking chairs. He then brought in a few wooden logs and lit a fire before which they sat and warmed their hands. The Directory was installed.[7]

Having assumed power, the Directory was immediately presented with the obvious difficulty of restoring order in the interior. To meet this enormous challenge, it took prompt measures to strengthen its means of internal security by reorganising, and expanding, the apparatus of the state itself. Within days, it began to issue a set of directives designed not only to centralise key governmental bodies but also to arrogate greater powers to itself. The Directory decreed that the Bureau de Surveillance and police organs established by the Committee of Public Safety be placed under the supervision of the newly appointed Minister of the Interior, Pierre Bénézech, an apparently malleable creature who was expected to adapt his 'language and conduct' according to the principles enunciated by France's new government. Bénézech was to answer directly to the wonderfully debauched Paul Barras who, in turn, assumed personal control of the country's security apparatus whilst the third director, Lazare Carnot, the celebrated 'organiser of victory' in the Committee of Public Safety, took the reins of the army.[8]

Among Barras' first actions was to petition the Council of Five Hundred for the creation of a seventh ministry, the Ministry of Police. Speaking before the assembly, the forty-year-old regicide justified the ministry's foundation on account of the many counter-revolutionary plots which had 'sought to lead astray the people of Paris'.[9] He identified these enemies of the Fatherland as returned émigrés 'in the pay of the foreigner' and claimed that it was only with 'an active police force that their intrigues could be thwarted'. The ministry's objective was to centralise police operations and mount rigorous surveillance in the interior and the danger zones contiguous to its borders in order to foil the 'destructive plots' which they attributed, as one proclamation to the population of Marne read, to 'the intrigues of the Cabinet of St James' and its 'perfidious ministers'.[10]

To gather information in the interior, the Directory also appointed commissaries to oversee the administration of each *département* and to report back to the newly appointed Minister of Police, Merlin de Douai, on the arrests of émigrés and the seizure of any papers compromising the Republic. It was estimated that their presence would be instrumental to the system of surveillance within the interior. In their capacity as government-appointed agents, the commissaries were deemed 'vigilant sentinels' and active agents who were expected to have 'precise knowledge' of all that happened in their departments.[11] As one circular read, a commissary 'should see all, know all'. Each of them was handed a manual stipulating in detail their intended functions. The parameters of their surveillance, as prescribed in this manual, were wide-ranging. They were instructed to keep all foreigners under surveillance and deport any person they judged to be a menace to security.[12] They were also expected to inspect all vessels entering and leaving ports and ensure that all individuals arriving from England be furnished with an approved passport and placed under the surveillance of the municipality before being allowed to continue their route within the interior. The commissaries assigned to the port cantons were furthermore required to oversee the transmission of all papers, letters, gazettes and packets arriving from abroad to the local commandant or naval administrators for examination. The evident success with which the Directory organised its security apparatus was soon acknowledged by William Wickham himself. As he would write to Lord Grenville, the Minister of Foreign Affairs, 'The Directory are in possession of a regular, established government, that they have the direction of a powerful machine, most skilfully framed and put together to which they have added violence.'[13]

A week earlier, on 5 November, Condé had been waiting impatiently at Mullheim in Breisgau when he received a secret order to cross the Rhine and penetrate into the Franche-Comté in concert with an Austrian division commanded by General Michael Melas. It was expected that his appearance on French soil would then trigger popular insurrections at Lyons, the Jura and at Besançon. Wickham was delighted by the news, confiding to Lord Grenville that he harboured the 'most sanguine hopes' that the prince's passage through the Rhine would meet with unqualified success.[14] From his official residence in Berne, he issued a flurry of instructions to his agents throughout the region. The Comte de Precy was to set off at once to Lyons to take command of the royalist forces, where the city's former mayor, the elderly Jacques Pierre Imbert Colomès, a former botanical scientist and rector of the Hospital General for the poor, reassured him that the local population would declare in their favour. Wickham estimated that £60,000 would be sufficient to sustain the insurrections, with two-thirds of the share devoted to Lyons, £10,000 for suborning the French forces at Besançon and the remaining £10,000 to be held in readiness for 'unforeseen expenses'.[15]

While Wickham occupied himself in preparing Lyons and the eastern provinces for insurrection, Francis Drake, the thirty-one-year-old British Minister Plenipotentiary to the Republic of Genoa and the Court of Milan, was busy rousing the south. For the past three months, his emissaries in Provence had been recruiting volunteers for a royalist offensive. He had been allocated six aliases to use with his own agents and six for reporting to Wickham, as well as instructions on the ingredients for making 'sympathetic' ink. The royalists of Provence, he reported to Lord Grenville, 'would not move unless the signal be given at Lyons and the operations at Lyons will, in their turn, depend upon the amount of support which the Prince de Condé receives from the Court of Vienna'.[16] But with regard to the dispositions of Austria, the news transmitted to him by his colleague at Turin, John Trevor, an effete career diplomat, did not give him any cause for satisfaction. As Drake warned Wickham, Louis XVIII's restoration to the French throne 'did not make any part of the System of the House of Austria and that, provided any sort of monarchy was established, it imported little to the interests of that House upon whose head the crown was placed'.[17]

The British military attaché, Colonel Charles Gregan Craufurd, shared these apprehensions too. At the time when Condé had received his orders to prepare to cross the Rhine, he was assigned to the headquarters of General Cleyfart who was advancing against the positions which Pichegru had taken up near Worms. He suspected that the Austrians intended Condé's penetration into the Franche-Comté to be a diversion and that its real object was to assist their military operations in the Palatinate. But he was doubtful whether, having affected their purpose, they intended to countermand the expedition at the last moment or whether they proposed that the royalist contingent should advance unsupported into Franche-Comté and court certain destruction. He therefore took leave of Cleyfart and immediately raced to Switzerland, where he planned to impart his suspicions to Wickham.

When Craufurd arrived in Lausanne on the evening of 24 November he found Wickham visibly perturbed by news from the frontier. Among the many adventurers who enjoyed the confidence of the Prince de Condé was Pierre Charles Marie Joseph Duclos, the Marquis de Bésignan. A former seigneur in the department of the Drôme, Bésignan had escaped to Switzerland in 1792 after armed peasants and local Jacobins had laid his château under siege. Since then, he had frequently returned to his homeland where, together with Dominique Allier, one of the leaders of the notorious 'murder gangs', and the latter's sadistic lieutenant Guillaume Fontanieu, alias Peg-Leg, he recruited guerrilla bands and staged nuisance attacks against the republican authorities.[18] His plotting drove him far afield, from the deep and narrow valley of the Rhône to the hill villages of the Monts du Forez, and though he was undoubtedly courageous his projects were nevertheless half-baked, more the hare-brained schemes of an adventurer than the calculated machinations of a conspirator. Wickham had long complained of Bésignan's imprudence and refused to entrust him with confidential missions, but despite his best precautions, including trying to prevent his entry into France, Bésignan managed to learn many details of the plot, and set out in person for Lyons, bringing with him a bundle of highly incriminating documents.

Bésignan was stopped by customs officials at the frontier station of Megrin, in the *département* of Aix, and an attempt was made to detain him. He had entrusted a child to smuggle his papers across the frontier but when the officials discovered them on her person Bésignan fled into the neighbouring woods, shooting a gendarme in the ensuing chase. The newly installed Directory, at any rate, scored a major intelligence coup with the interception of his papers. As Wickham complained to Lord Grenville, the capture of Bésignan's papers was a 'disaster', compromising 'almost every well-disposed person in the interior'.[19]

The volume of correspondence was 'immense', numbering more than 500 items. They provided the government with a full list of names of the royalist conspirators including Jacques Pierre Imbert Colomès and Nicolas Dutheil, the intermediary between the French prince and King George III's ministers. Also, not only were a number of Bésignan's letters written in his own hand but many of the conspirators signed their letters without taking the elementary precaution of using anagrams or pseudonyms. As a consequence, the Directorial police was able to identify a number of émigrés who, though unnamed, were associated with the conspirators. In the report on the conspiracy, the Directory was presented with the powers that Louis XVIII had given to raise soldiers, the orders for them to serve under the Comte de Precy and copies of the plans to raise Lyon and the Midi. It also gave lists of the military leaders from each *arrondissement*, the dispositions of the mobile columns and their operational plans and the names of the diocese and parish leaders who had worked together to reunite as many citizens under the 'flags of the throne and altar'. Armed with this intelligence, the Directory ordered the search and seizure of every named conspirator as well as instructed the police to place all known acquaintances under surveillance.[20]

The news of Bésignan's misadventure plunged Lyons into a state of profound confusion. Imbert Colomès and his chief accomplices took to flight. Though Wickham was careful not to have communicated directly with him, he was certain that his name would be mentioned in a number of these letters, putting him in awkward difficulty with the Helvetic Cantons. To his chagrin, he also learned that Condé's projected passage of the Rhine had been countermanded. The prince had received orders to dismantle his armed camp at Mullheim, trek down the right bank of the Rhine and set up new quarters at Wisloch, a small German city thirteen kilometres south of Heidelberg. But as he was about to quit he received intelligence from his agents that the garrison of Strasbourg was poorly protected and that many of the townsfolk were not unfriendly to the prince. Condé imparted the news to Wickham and dispatched an emissary to Mannheim to update the Austrian General Würmser on the news and to entreat him to make 10,000–12,000 troops available to support storming the fort. The success of the enterprise, however, depended on Pichegru's favourable disposition.

Pichegru, however, obfuscated. In a private interview with Demougé, a spy in the pay of the Austrian Imperial Staff, he refused to proffer assistance or engage in such precipitate action, employing evasive language about his true intentions towards Strasbourg. The Austrians too were unreceptive, claiming that they had no troops to spare for the venture. Condé was nevertheless undeterred and dispatched Demougé to Pichegru's headquarters for a second interview. Pichegru knew that the Directory was keeping him under close observation and was reluctant to receiving visitors. He had already forbidden Louis Fauche-Borel's presence at his headquarters on the grounds that his repeated visits would excite the suspicion of the Directory's agents. Nevertheless, on 9 December he agreed to a private audience with the Austrian spy. On this occasion, Demougé kept a transcript of their conversation. The Directory, Pichegru declared, would self-destruct under the weight of its own unpopularity. Only military victories would prolong its existence. He also recommended that Condé abandon the plan of storming the garrison as any loss of life would shake public opinion in the favour of the Directory and assuredly strengthen its position. He suggested instead that the prince cross the Rhine and make contact with his outposts along the Queich, a tributary of the river which rises in the southern part of the Palatinate forest. From there, he should make preparations for combination of their two forces under the same flag. 'We are all Frenchmen, let us unite,' he declared.[21]

Würmser, however, refused to grant the émigrés passage on the Rhine and directed Condé to remain at his quarters at Bühl, a quiet village sitting in the valley of the Lauch, conveniently situated for carrying on a correspondence with Strasbourg. Unfortunately, his plans were derailed by the arrest of Borel, his chief agent in that town. Borel had arrived in Strasbourg at the beginning of November and immediately devoted himself to gathering intelligence and suborning the republican defenders. In accordance with Wickham's instructions, he had opened communications with Demougé and the other spies in the pay of Austria. However, on the night of 21 December, Borel was arrested at his inn by the town major and charged with perpetrating acts of espionage. His papers were confiscated, except for one compromising letter from the Prince de Condé which remained concealed in a secret compartment of his writing case. He was conveyed to the military prison by an escort of gendarmes who, during the journey, taunted him with the grisly spectre of the guillotine. Upon arriving at the Pont Couvert he was cast into a damp and malodorous dungeon before being interrogated by the investigating magistrate who promptly discharged him, having satisfied himself of the prisoner's answers. He later assured Wickham and Craufurd that his release from prison was owed to Pichegru's intervention, a claim that had no probable foundation other than being the assurance of an accomplished storyteller.[22]

On the same day that Borel was arrested, the Austrian generals Cleyfart and Würmser submitted a proposal to General Jean Baptiste Jourdan for a temporary suspension of hostilities. Having achieved many of their tactical objectives, both were disposed to believe that the moment had arrived for their withdrawal into winter quarters to recover from their exertions and take shelter from the inclemency of the weather. Despite his secret designs, Pichegru agreed to the Austrian proposal with noted relief. The Directory itself was less than satisfied with his conduct during the Palatinate campaign. It had decided to supersede him as far back as November after having received news of the loss of the lines at Mainz. The Directory's mediation on the subject reached the notice of Craufurd. On 9 December, he reported to Lord Grenville that Pichegru was to be replaced by General Kléber, thus depriving the British government 'of the important services he seemed disposed to render us'.[23] Although Kléber declined the position, Pichegru submitted a request to be relieved from his command on the grounds of ill health and ill fortune. It was not until 23 December that the Directory decided to accept his resignation, but news then arrived that Pichegru and Jourdan had concluded the armistice on New Year's Eve. With hostilities being temporarily suspended, the Directory rescinded its decision to recall him and retained him in his position of command.

Two weeks into his seclusion at Illkirch, Pichegru received word of an event which appears to have deeply troubled him. He learned that the commandant of 6th division in Besançon, General Ferrand, had just been arrested and conveyed under armed escort to Paris to answer to charges of sedition brought before him. Ferrand, like Pichegru, had entered into secret negotiations with agents of the Prince de Condé and Wickham, but, fearing the consequences of their indiscretion, he had denounced the correspondence to the authorities in order to pre-empt his own arrest. Acting on Ferrand's information, police agents raided the Swiss domicile of a royalist agent named Charles Tinseau d'Amondans de Besançon, where they found stashed away five long bands of paper containing operational plans favouring the storming of Besançon's citadel and several of its forts. In a report to the Directory, the Minister of Police, Merlin de Douai, a thin, weedy man with a large mouth, pop eyes and a long, pointed nose, announced that the plans were very 'detailed and precise in execution' and formed part of a wider royalist movement that was to take place in six of the frontier *départements* of the Midi from Lyons to Hüninguen. The papers also contained propositions that were made to Besançon's constituent authorities and administrators for gaining possession of the citadel.[24]

To Pichegru, the whole affair must have appeared like a cautionary tale. He knew that he staked his own life and reputation at the mercy of individuals who could not be trusted to act with much discretion. Wickham himself never doubted Pichegru's good faith. But Craufurd began to have niggling doubts about the general's reliability. He thought that Pichegru's equivocal actions on the Rhine, as well as his reluctance to cooperate with Jourdan, could just as equally be attributed 'to jealously, to disgust or to disapprobation of the plan'.[25] Craufurd also harboured a well-founded distrust of Borel. In an interview, the colonel questioned the bookseller closely on his conversations with Pichegru. Borel's answers were less than satisfactory, leading Craufurd to doubt the man's sincerity. Wickham thus cross-examined Borel to compare his claims to Craufurd. The bookseller, he concluded, did not attach any importance to dates but his conversations with Pichegru were more or less accurate. Nevertheless, Wickham conceded that there were many aspects of the whole affair which 'seemed to him strange, contradictory and almost unaccountable'.[26] Craufurd, even so, was disinclined to repose unlimited confidence in the Swiss agent. He was, however, inclined to believe that Pichegru 'had not yet made up his mind as to the party that he would support but was endeavouring to gain the confidence of his army sufficiently to be able to dispose of it as he might think fit'.[27]

Despite the air of uncertainty, the secret negotiations continued. No longer requiring Borel's mediation, Pichegru corresponded directly with Wickham and the Prince de Condé, employing a musical code and a number of pseudonyms including 'Z' and 'Baptiste' in their long correspondence. He also maintained regular communications with Major-General Klinglin, who served in the Imperial army. Their letters were smuggled to and fro across the Rhine by the estate employees of Klinglin's niece, the Baronne de Reich, an adventuress whose property bordered the Rhine at Offenburg. Acting as a postmistress under the codename *Diogenes*, she also received intelligence reports hidden in pâtes de foie gras which were deciphered and forwarded to their destination. These extreme precautions were altogether necessary as the Directory had erected a rigorous system of surveillance across the Swiss frontier. As Reich confided to one agent, since the Franche-Comté affair, the frontiers were being guarded with 'an incredible exactitude'.[28]

In any event, Pichegru was fast becoming a lost cause. Despite his professions of good faith, it was increasingly evident that the Republic's esteemed general was unable to win his army over to the cause. It was alleged that he deliberately kept his men at close quarters in order to aggravate their discomfort and inspire their hatred of the government. Wickham suspected that he was playing a 'double game', but not from any cynical intention to deceive.[29] It was known that he was being watched closely by the Directory's commissaries and that even though they possessed no hard evidence of his treasonous correspondence with Wickham, they had solid grounds to suspect its existence. It was also certainly true that Pichegru was the subject of many unflattering rumours, including wild stories of his insobriety, which served to discredit him further in their eyes. But when the Directory finally decided to supersede him in February 1796, their decision was justified not on his unreliability, so they pretended, but on his inability to cooperate with Jourdan on military matters. And so it was that on 20 March General Charles Pichegru relinquished his command of the Army of the Rhine and Moselle and set off for Paris with a small but devoted band of followers.

***

In Paris, rumours abounded that Britain and France were engaged in secret peace talks. On the Calais–Paris road a group of Swiss tourists traveling in English carriages were mistaken for peace commissioners from Britain and were greeted with cries of, 'La Paix! La Paix!'[30] The war was deeply unpopular across most sections of the population, not least because of its ruinous effect on the economy. The Directory had inherited an enormous mess. The national treasury was empty, the *assignats* had been stripped of their value and peculation was rife. As the *Journal L'éclair* wrote in January 1796, 'There is but one opinion in France on this head: without a speedy peace, our finances can never be restored, we are threatened with a bankruptcy and this bankruptcy may perhaps become the tomb of the Republic.'[31] And so, when on 3 January the Directory issued an official declaration suggesting that peace might be restorable if certain conditions could be met, the hopes of France's citizens were momentarily raised.

The Directory's declaration came in response to a speech that Pitt had delivered in Parliament in December during which he inferred that the king was prepared 'to meet any disposition to negotiation on the part of the enemy, with an earnest desire to give it the fullest and speediest effect, and to conclude a treaty of general peace, whenever it can be effected on just and suitable terms for Himself and His allies'.[32] The king was in fact averse to opening peace negotiations with the Republic, but he reluctantly submitted to the Prime Minister's argument that not only was the country clamouring for peace but that a sufficiently stable government existed in France with which Britain could realistically treat.

Grenville, however, did not take the prospect of peace negotiations seriously, correctly believing that Britain could never acquiesce to the Directory's inflexible terms. He anticipated that they would include a return of all captured possessions in the Mediterranean and Indian Ocean as well as the acknowledgement of France's acquisition of Belgium as guaranteed by the new republican constitution instituted the year before. Yet, despite his reservations, Grenville was charged with sending out feelers for peace. He entrusted this commission to his friend William

Wickham, who received the official note to be transmitted to François Barthélemy, his opposite number at Basle, more than a month after Grenville had drafted it. The note was to be presented to the allies' representatives in Switzerland for their signature as well, but should they refuse then it would be handed to Barthélemy under Wickham's name alone. This way, the Directory could not be afforded the opportunity to use the note to divide the allies. The Austrians not only refused to sign it but also obstructed the lesser allies from doing so. As a result, the note was delivered to Barthélemy on 8 March with Wickham's name alone appended to it. The note asked for clarification on three essential points:

> Would France consent to sending plenipotentiaries to a congress to discuss the conditions of a general settlement?
> Would she consent to making known the basis upon which she would be prepared to negotiate?
> And has she any alternative proposal to make for arriving at a general pacification?[33]

Barthélemy was predisposed to discussing the terms of a general settlement but the instructions that he received from the Directory terminated any hopes that he may have privately harboured. The Directors were genuinely doubtful of Britain's sincerity, especially since the emissary was known to be Britain's 'most active' agent, who, according to one intelligence report dated 18 December 1795, was the centre of all 'intrigues, manoeuvres, emissaries and pamphlets'.[34] The Directory was reasonably well aware of Wickham's non-diplomatic activities and had even lodged an angry protest to the Helvetic body following the discovery of the conspiracy at Besançon. The English ministers had thus committed an error in making him the channel of communication with the Directory. On 26 March they issued their reply:

> The Directory ardently desires to procure for the French Republic a just, honorable, and solid peace. The step taken by Mr Wickham would have afforded to the Directory a real

satisfaction, if the declaration itself which that minister makes of his not having any order, any power to negotiate, did not give room to doubt of the sincerity of the pacific intentions of his court. In fact, if it was true that England began to know her real interests; that she wished to open again for herself the sources of abundance and prosperity; if she sought for peace with good faith. Would she propose a congress, of which the necessary result must be to render all negotiation endless'? or would she confine herself to the asking, in a vague matter, that the French government should point out any other way whatever, for attaining the same object, that of a general pacification? Is it that this step has had no other object than to obtain for the British government the favourable impression which always accompanies the first overtures for peace? May it not have been accompanied with the hope that they would produce no effect?[35]

The impertinence of the reply came as a surprise to Grenville. In his opinion, the Directory had blundered badly because the prolongation of the war could now be blamed on them. 'They have done their business coarsely and clumsily,' he told Wickham, 'and have in fact played our game for us better than we could have hoped.'[36] Wickham supposed that the publication of the diplomatic exchanges would increase the Directory's unpopularity. He also ascribed their rejection of Britain's overtures to the hopes which they entertained of concluding a separate peace with Austria.

For some time Wickham had suspected that Paris and Vienna were engaged in secret unilateral talks and that Pelin, the confidential secretary of the Austrian chancellor, Baron de Thugut, was the conduit. He had thus taken measures to intercept Pelin's letters and transmit copies of them to Grenville. Through these means he concluded that 'a sort of tampering' had been in progress throughout the winter. He also discovered that the Directory had dispatched to Vienna an intermediary by the name of the Marquis de Poterat, a disreputable figure, to deliver their proposals for a settlement in person. The Directory planned to blackmail Baron de Thugut into listening to their peace proposals. They possessed information on Thugut's past which could prove embarrassing and, depending on the temper of the emperor, lead to his ruin and permanent disgrace. It appeared that Thugut, a man of humble origin, had formerly been employed secretly by the *ancien régime* and had corresponded with the king's ministers. Upon learning of Poterat's mission, Thugut presented himself before the emperor and confessed the whole affair. He disclosed having receiving a stipend from the Court of France but insisted that he had never betrayed Austria's interest. His explanation appears to have satisfied the emperor for he later received Poterat without embarrassment and rejected the proposals without fear of the consequence. The Directory had hoped to seduce Austria from the British alliance by offering her Bavaria and territory at the expense of the Venetian Republic. Wickham had learnt about this transaction from one of his agents who had established relations with Poterat at Basle, where he had returned to await further instructions from his masters in Paris.

Despite the Directory's failure to detach Austria, the reality facing Wickham was that his 'Grand Plan' for regime change was collapsing; for as these negotiations were quietly proceeding, Napoleon's lightning advance into Italy was transforming the pace and direction of the war.[37]

3

THE ITALIAN TORRENT

When the twenty-six-year-old Napoleon Bonaparte submitted a bold plan to strike against Piedmont, the Commander of the Army of the Alps, General Scherer, presented it as 'the work of a madman' and suggested that it was only appropriate that the author of such a reckless initiative should be the same person entrusted with its execution.[1] The Directory thought so too, but for different reasons, and on 2 March 1796 appointed the young general to the command of the Army of Italy.

Quitting Paris ten days later, Napoleon dashed to the Italian front, leaving behind his new bride, Joséphine, the Vicomtesse de Beauharnais. He had come a long way following his violent suppression of the *vendémiaire* uprising. From relative obscurity, he had established himself practically overnight as a major figure in France. He was given command of the Army of the Interior, a powerful post which he used to police the capital, purge the army corps of royalists and close down the Jacobin headquarters at the Panthéon Club. He had also acquired great wealth, which he showed off with the purchase of a magnificent carriage and the hosting of extravagant *soirées* at his new official residence overlooking the Place Vendôme.

Just days after his arrival at his headquarters in Nice, Napoleon launched his assault into northern Italy. In a brilliant display of pyrotechnics that both dazzled and confounded the enemy, he marched his ragged troops with such extraordinary rapidity that by 14 April the Austrians were already retreating to Milan and the Piedmontese to Turin. The speed of his advance frightened King Victor Amadeus III, who on 23 April instructed the commander of the Piedmontese forces, the Austrian general Baron Michael von Colli, to sue for an armistice. In response, Napoleon advanced three columns into the towns of Cherasco, Fossano and Alba two days later, in turn preventing a junction between the Austrian and Piedmontese/Sardinian lines.[2]

On 27 April, at eleven o'clock at night, the Piedmontese delegation arrived at Napoleon's headquarters in Count Salmatori's palazzo in Cherasco, 130 kilometres south of Turin. Napoleon appeared dressed in his general's uniform. He wore high riding boots but not his sword, hat or scarf. His hair was not powdered and hung low over his forehead and down the sides of his face like the ears of a spaniel. He stiffly greeted the negotiators, General Sallier de la Tour and Colonel Joseph Henri Costa de Beauregard, and for the next two hours paced up and down the room, his hands clenched firmly behind his back, as was his habit, whilst Berthier, his Chief of Staff, conducted the negotiations. At one o'clock, after two hours of discussions, Napoleon pulled out his watch and, giving it a quick glance, intoned, 'Gentlemen, I warn you that a general attack has been ordered for two o'clock … It may happen that I will lose battles, but I shall never lose time through idle talk or sloth.' One hour later, having exhausted themselves in argument, the Piedmontese delegators signed the armistice on behalf of Sardinian king. In exchange for a suspension of hostilities, the French were granted occupation of the fortresses of Coni, Ceva, Tortona and Alessandria and direct passage through Piedmont. The campaign had lasted just ten days.[3]

On the same day that the armistice was signed, Willian Wickham received a note from the Prince de Condé requesting his immediate presence at Riegel, a small town in Breisgau in the Kaisersthul where the pretender to the throne, Louis XVIII, was expected to arrive that afternoon. Wickham was then at Freiburg, just fifteen miles away, conferring with Colonel Craufurd on future operations. Complying with the request, he immediately set off to the prince's camp, taking his Scottish adjutant along with him. The news of Napoleon's victories at Dego and Montenotte, and his subsequent advance upon Turin, had raised the alarm of the Venetian Senate which, fearing the effect that Louis' presence on Italian soil would have on the invading army, ordered his immediate expulsion from Verona where, under the assumed title of Comte de Lille, he had settled in exile two years earlier.[4]

On 21 April, at three o'clock in the morning, Louis XVIII stole away in a light *berline*, accompanied by his favourite, the Count d'Avaray, a colonel of the regiment de Boulonnais and master of wardrobe. They took the Bergamo St Gothard Pass whilst the Duc de la Vauguyon, who bore a striking resemblance to his royal master, took the road leading to the Tyrol in order to fool the republican agents and creditors hot on his trail. Criss-crossing Switzerland, he arrived at Riegel on the night of the 28th after a gruelling eight-day journey and, taking up residence at the house belonging to Prince Schwarzenburg, rejoined the émigré army, appearing in the iron-grey uniform of Condé's staff with a crown on the epaulettes and sword hanging by his side. He had hoped that by rejoining the regiments and visiting the outposts on the Rhine he would excite the enthusiasm of the troops, but these subjects had never overcome their distrust of his politics, which they never considered 'pure'.[5]

After inspecting the regiments, Louis was presented to the two English agents. He greeted them in the 'most distinguished and flattering manner' and asked that they convey his sincerest gratitude to King George III for the supposed generosity and munificence that he had displayed towards the émigrés.[6] For the next ten days the two remained at Freiburg, during which time they paid several visits to the royalist camp. Their time spent there permitted them to closely observe Louis XVIII and the persons dominating his council. The Pretender, Wickham was satisfied, possessed ability and judgement that far exceeded most of his courtiers and ministers. Nevertheless, he found it deeply unfortunate that Louis, whose misfortunes he heartily sympathised with, should be surrounded by men who were either deliberately intransigent or wilfully ignorant of the state of public opinion in France or both. Wickham was particularly irritated by the 'childish petulance' of the Count d'Avaray, who 'with not half the talents, learning, or good sense of the King, had the most absolute dominion over his mind'.[7]

Wickham hoped that Louis would disavow the revengeful intentions imputed to him by his followers. The infamous Comte d'Antraigues, for one, declared the rightful necessity of executing the surviving members of the Constituent Assembly and all the purchasers of the nationalised properties. The Comte de Ferrand was even more sanguinary and demanded that the counter-revolution be attended by 44,000 executions, i.e. one in every commune.[8] Moreover, Ferrand insisted that the men who had not emigrated should be sent to the gallows and the women whipped by the common hangman. Yet, although he did not speak of the revolutionaries with the same rancour, at least in public, Louis did little to restrain their intemperate behaviour or to assuage the fears of those who doubted his promises of clemency. Wickham was, nevertheless, astonished by the pathos of Louis' poverty. Despite possessing a council and preserving the formalities of Versailles, Britain's emissary saw how scanty the king's table was and how his few servants were so shabbily dressed. To ameliorate his condition, he provided a subsidy as authorised by Lord Grenville. He did not realise, however, that Louis was also secretly receiving funds from Spain, through the Prince de Poix and the Spanish ambassador in Venice, Don Simon de la Casas, as well as a subsidy from the ailing Russian Empress, Catherine the Great, who was alone in recognising Louis as a 'king without a kingdom'.[9]

In Paris, meanwhile, the political situation was not at all what Pichegru had anticipated. He fancied that the Directory would be deeply unpopular but was startled to discover that Napoleon's victories had raised the government in the public's estimation and that, as he put it, 'the scoundrels were blown out with pride'.[10] He had arrived hoping to embroil himself in the political scene but, presupposing that there were only two parties in contest, was bewildered to discover a multitude of factions all vying against each other, leaving it unclear who his friends or enemies were.[11]

Nevertheless, he tried to sound out a number of politicians, including the Minister of the Interior, Pierre Bénézech, whom he suspected was a royalist sympathiser. He reported back to Wickham that, whilst some of them seriously hoped to see the reestablishment of a monarchy in some form, they remained suspicious of England's intentions. The Directory, in any event, was conscious of his secret overtures, having placed him under twenty-four-hour surveillance. They also had good reason to believe that he was engaged in treasonous correspondence with Britain and Austria thanks to the information that they had been receiving from the French émigré, the Comte de Montgaillard, a 'Portuguese-looking Jew' who had originally recruited Borel on behalf of the Prince de Condé the year before.[12] Wickham, who was long convinced of the 'profound immorality and wickedness' of the man, suspected that Montgaillard had been working for the Directory since the failed *vendémiaire* uprising and had been feeding them piecemeal information as a means of making peace with the Republic.[13] The Directory therefore tried to remove him quietly from France by offering him the post of ambassador to the Court of Sweden. Pichegru, however, saw through the ruse and declined the offer. Sensing that trouble lay ahead, he left Paris in the same carriage that he arrived in and retired to the Abbey of Bellevaux near his birthplace, Arbois in the Franche-Comté where he lived in narrow circumstances to plan his next move.

It was not long, however, before he was accused of doing nothing. In his own defence, he wrote a long memoir dated 14 June which was smuggled to Lausanne and distributed amongst the émigrés in Switzerland. A précis of it was delivered to Wickham by the royalist leader, the Comte de Precy:

I have acted as the King intended, in perfect agreement with the English Ministry and the Austrian generals. I have been to see the King, and I am to see him again. He is to give me greater authority, submitting all the operations, all those employed, or who will be employed, to my command.

Up to the present the military operations have necessitated that I should not compromise our partisans; the Austrian army on the defensive on the Rhine and the success of the republican army in Italy require that we act with prudence. The moment of declaration will come; we can only wait for the right moment; I will be informed of it, and it is with the advice of those persons most concerned that I speak.

There will be money if sufficient support is forthcoming ... it is ready. And is at present being saved in all the places where it is judged necessary for our cause. I promise that we will be supported by this means, but I must arrange this with economy, not requiring too much from him (Wickham) who has the right to grant or to refuse.

I beg that our friends are supported; they must not feel beaten by this first reverse; tell them that it has been sworn to me that things will change; that the English court has asked that of Vienna to allow the King to remain with the Condé army and to join with London in recognising him ... Say also that I am the man of the interior, that no consideration will make me act against its interests, it is to the interior that I am totally devoted; that I ignore the clamour against my supposed inaction; that by this inaction I believe I have saved those faithful to God and the King.[14]

Pichegru knew that the Directory would learn of the promulgation but acted as if he didn't care. As Wickham told Lord Grenville, 'This extraordinary man still remains in our neighbourhood, caressed and fêted and almost adored by the inhabitants of Franche-Comté. He laughs at the Directory and says they are incapable of hurting him because they have not the courage.'[15]

Pichegru's popularity was so great that there was scarcely a home in the province which did not boast a picture of him displayed on its window. Encouraged by this, he decided to turn his celebrity to his political advantage, and from his residence at Arbois he wrote to Wickham and the Prince de Condé announcing his intention to hang up his sword and instead seek election to the Council of Five Hundred. It appears that he had discussed this project with the republican ambassador to the Swiss cantons, François de Barthélemy, beforehand; at a secret meeting held in Basle, they agreed to manipulate the March and May 1797 elections in order to bring a constitutional royalist majority which would see Pichegru assume the Presidency of the Council and Barthélemy achieve membership of the Directory.

Wickham greeted the news with much enthusiasm. Despite continued pressures from the émigrés he no longer favoured funding partial or isolated insurrections, believing that such counter-revolutionary violence generated 'more fright than fight' and served only to hurt the royalist cause.[16] He repeated the same to Lord Grenville, recommending that Britain only furnish the minimum funds necessary to maintain the spirit of disaffection without encouraging further uprisings. The Foreign Minister preferred to not see their plans suffer derangement but, trusting in his friend's judgement, authorised Wickham to conspire with Pichegru to topple the Directory not by force of arms but peacefully, through the ballot box.

The success of the plan depended on the formation of an alliance between moderates and pure royalists and for this unenviable task Wickham turned to Antoine Balthazar Joseph d'André, a former member of the Estates General who was said to be 'repulsively ugly but sagacious'.[17] Despite his confidence in d'André's abilities, Wickham was under no illusions about the difficulty of bringing these two intractable parties to the table, especially the émigrés, who would not relish the idea of conceding an inch of royal authority. However, as he told a fellow agent, he was not without hope: 'It has been peremptorily declared to me that the King would rather resign his Crown than come to an agreement with his People, the conclusion of which should be what they call a Permanent Representation. I have not abandoned hope of, if not bringing the others to think as I do, at least of making them act to a certain degrees as I should wish them.'[18] He would soon be disappointed.

* * *

Meanwhile, on the north-west coast of France, a new chapter in the secret war was dramatically unfolding.

4

PRISONERS

On 19 April 1796, the commissary at Le Havre sent a *communiqué* to Pléville, the Minister of Marine (the navy), notifying him of a sensational capture:

We have at length got into our hands that English firebrand and incendiary, Sir Sidney Smith, who burnt our ships at Toulon; the very same who also attempted, some time back, to set fire to the shipping and magazines at Havre. The man, in a word, who had solemnly sworn and promised to Pitt, that he would convert all our harbours and marine into a heap of ash. Having come to anchor during the night at the mouth of this harbour, on board the *Diamond*, which he commanded; he had scarce gone on board the privateer, the *Vengeur*, which he had taken after a smart fire, when a number of ships were sent out against him, which after a brisk engagement, obliged him to surrender, together with a number of officers of the English navy. There can be no doubt but that it was his intention to destroy everything here by fire; for a bundle of matches, like that which some months ago was discovered, was found placed under one of our frigates now on the stocks. We hereby informed you, that not having at Havre a proper place securely to confine him in, we have sent him off to Rouen under a strong guard, where he may wait the sentence which the national justice shall think fit to pronounce on his nefarious attempts.[1]

The Directory's commissary had good reason for the heavy-handed treatment of his prisoner. Since leaving Spithead two months earlier, Smith's squadron was widely known to be patrolling the river estuaries of northern France, intercepting neutral vessels and blocking up the ports.[2] Moreover, according to intelligence from double agents and intercepted correspondence, he was actively engaged in landing, and collecting, secret operatives along the Breton coast from his flagship, HMS *Diamond*.[3] In the Directory's view, therefore, Smith was not a conventional naval officer but a dangerous firebrand and spy who operated outside the accepted laws of eighteenth-century warfare.[4]

Smith's expertise on 'inshore operations' certainly qualified him well for what he called an occupation of 'a superior sort'.[5] He was born in Park Lane, Westminster, on 21 July 1764, the second son of John Smith of Midgham, Berkshire, a captain in the guards and gentleman usher to Queen Charlotte, the prudish wife of King George III. In June 1777, at the age of thirteen, he began his naval career on board the store-ship *Tortoise*, eventually seeing action in North America. At the restoration of peace he moved to France where he resided near Caen before travelling to Gibraltar and Morocco via Spain. On his own volition, he made observations on the dispositions of the Sultan's naval forces and bases, in anticipation of future hostilities, which he addressed to the secretary of the Admiralty. In 1788, a diplomatic rupture between Sweden and Russia led him to enter into the service of the former and in July 1790, in command of 100 Swedish light craft, he cleared the Bay of Viborg of the Russian fleet. On account of his distinguished performance he was awarded the Grand Cross of the Swedish Order of the Sword, one of the highest marks of honour conferred by the late King Gustavus. His services subsequently attracted the favourable notice of the British government, who accordingly dispatched him on a mission to survey the Black Sea region and gather intelligence on Russian and Turkish naval capabilities. It was there, at Constantinople, that he received news that Toulon had fallen into the hands of the allies; at his own expense he repaired to that naval port to offer assistance to Lord Hood, who entrusted him with the important commission of destroying as much of the French fleet as possible, a scheme that appealed to his daredevil nature. With a few small gunboats and a combined force of English and Spaniards he destroyed fourteen of the French ships, consisting of ten ships of the line, two frigates and two corvettes. A further twelve vessels were towed away. Equally important was that the immense mast-house and timber stocks were also set aflame. His feat – for which he received no remuneration, still being on half pay – was almost derailed by the pusillanimous Spanish, who injudiciously set the powder ships ablaze instead of scuttling them according to the orders given. In the ensuing carnage, a number of British seamen were killed and the town wantonly destroyed. As one commentator fittingly said, 'Toulon was hence doomed to suffer as much from the indiscretion of its friends, as from the violence of its enemies.'[6] The stage was now set for the Jacobins to administer their singular brand of punishment. Anyone suspected of loyalty to, or having had any affiliation with the hated English, was either butchered or tossed into the sea. 'Conspirators' were mercilessly disposed of by the infernal 'Marseillois weddings', a particularly cynical punishment in which husbands and wives, brothers and sisters, were tied back to back and cast from the quays into the harbour. Nevertheless, Smith was quite pleased with himself, having judged his role to have been executed most successfully. And although he was certainly immodest, he was not altogether unjustified for by all accounts he had dealt what one historian has described as 'the single most devastating blow to the French navy in the second half of the eighteenth century'.[7]

That evening, after having temporarily rested in a nearby hotel, Smith was conveyed to Rouen escorted by a detachment of gendarmes and one Monsieur Bauté, whom the prisoner found to be an 'attentive, gentlemanly man'.[8] He was accompanied by his 'secretary', John Wesley Wright, and a young buck-skinned lad who was dressed conspicuously as an English jockey. The latter was a Breton émigré by the name of Jacques Jean Marie

Francois Boudin de Tromelin, but to protect his identity it had been arranged that he would pass as Smith's servant and assume the character of a Canadian by the name of John Bromley.[9]

The next day the prisoners reached Rouen and were confined in Saint Lo prison. They stayed overnight before heading on to Paris escorted by two armed guards. Upon arrival in the capital, the prisoners breakfasted before being conveyed to the headquarters of General Hatry, the commander-in-chief of the army in Paris. A sixty-year-old veteran, he was puzzled what to do with the 'English monsters' and conferred with the French Minister of War, Claude Petiet. It was decided that a legion of dragoons would escort the prisoners to l'Abbaye prison where they would be temporarily incarcerated.[10]

Onwards the cavalcade rolled, passing through Paris' muddy, unpaved roads. Stopping outside a Gothic gateway built by Francis I, Smith asked one of the escorts where they were being taken.

'À l'Abbaye, monsieur.'

'Ah!' he exclaimed, and, alluding to the September massacres that had made the prison infamous, he added, '*C'est fameux, je crois, dans votre histoire, n'est ce pas?*'[11]

The cavalcade renewed its journey and, descending l'Avenue des Champs-Elysées, passing La Porte Sainte-Honoré, it stopped in front of the gloomy edifice with its pointed roof and four corbelled turrets. Clambering down from their carriage, the prisoners were escorted past a single file of armed sentinels manning the gates and, as soon as they entered the prison door, were presented to the keeper. Wright was singled out and separated from his two companions. He was escorted up a succession of spiral staircases and dark corridors until he reached his cell, whereupon the door was opened and he was thrust inside.

The interior of his cell was damp, malodorous and home only to a bed and a gendarme who stood *gardé à vue*. Unlike Tromelin, who remained at the side of his 'master', Wright was not allowed to communicate with anyone but was guarded and questioned, so he complained, with all the strictness and 'severity of the inquisition'. He was also subjected to petty indignities by the concierge, who refused to give an explanation for the separate treatment that he received. He was denied a razor and was eventually allocated a barber but under the precaution that a chef de battalion and a file of musketeers supervise the proceedings. His frustration spent, Wright addressed his grievances to Petiet, who granted him two hours' daily contact with Smith as well as the use of shaving implements.[12]

During his time alone, he wrote a long piece on the circumstances of their capture. The reason why Smith, a ship's captain, was commanding a cutting-out expedition was highly unusual, as was the presence of Tromelin, who was not only dressed for some purpose other than intercepting marauders but who was in the most peril if caught. It had also taken six and half hours before the *Vengeur* was boarded, which would have afforded the men sufficient time to make contact with the shore and engage in some clandestine operation.[13] Wright was only too aware that his cell would be searched and no doubt left an appropriate explanation for this reason.

The weeks passed without event. Then one day, the prisoners' hopes of liberation were raised. According to his own fanciful version, Smith awoke to find a mysterious figure eyeing him from one of the windows opposite his cell.[14] After they exchanged flirtatious smiles, the mystery lady dimmed her lights and across the back of the room he perceived a long sheet on which was projected a sequence of large letters spelling the words, '*Qui êtes vous?*' In order to reply, the commodore tore off a leaf from an old prayer book and with the soot from the chimney he drew the letter A, which he pressed up against the window. He then pointed to the top bar of the cell so as to represent A, the second bar representing B, etc., and through this painstakingly slow process he successfully devised an alphabetic telegraph from which he managed to inform her of his name and rank.[15]

When he awoke the following morning, Smith was greeted again by the sight of this female but this time she was joined by her younger daughters, both of whom were also smiling at him. The first action of the three muses, Thalia, Melpomene and Clio, as he fondly dubbed them, was to notify Tromelin's family of his imprisonment. The second was to source the funds necessary to finance the prisoners' liberation. At that time, the Sardinian ambassador to London, the Chevalier de Revel, was in Paris and so to procure the expenses necessary for his liberation, Smith instructed his deliverers to ask the former for money, knowing that, as a former ally at Toulon, he would oblige. The signal worked, for a week later the prison doctor slipped a rouleau of *Louis d'or* into the patient's hands whilst ostensibly taking his pulse.[16]

While this secret communication was carrying on, a second channel for procuring financial aid was opened by the Swedish ambassador, the Baron de Staël, who offered his government's assistance on account of Smith's former service to the Swedish crown. He had contacted Petiet and remonstrated on the Commodore's behalf. The ambassador also sent news to England that, despite certain protests being raised, Smith and Wright were not being subjected to the typical prisoner-of-war route, which, among other obligations, accorded them the right to parole and exchange. The British cabinet were already informed of the circumstances surrounding the prisoners' detainment, for on 7 May 1796 the *Morning Post* had reported that 'the Directory affirmed that as Sir Sidney was taken out of his uniform, he could not be considered as a prisoner of war, but as a Spy and therefore not to be exchanged'.[17]

Confronted with the impossibility of exchange, the muses continued to work at Smith's liberation. For weeks they had devised schemes that bore little chance of success, but just when they stumbled on a plausible project all hope of extrication was quashed. All of a sudden, and without prior notification, the Directory had issued an order for the prisoners to be immediately removed from l'Abbaye.

15th of *Messidor*, Year IV

In conformity with the letter of the Minister of the Interior, dated the 13th of this month, the keeper of the Temple Prison will receive the hereinafter named persons, coming from the Abbaye Prison.

Sir William Sidney, commander, Grand Cross of the military order of the Sword of Sweden, captain in the English service, commanding the squadron cruising in the Channel, native of London, thirty two years of age. Prisoner of war.

John Wesley Vright [*sic*] secretary to Commodore Sidney, and John Bromley, the Commodore's servant.[18]

Not far from the Bastille, in an ancient district which bears its name, stood the prison to which the prisoners were being transported under escort, three days after the order for their transfer was issued. Trundling down the rue des Fossés, they passed through the rue du Temple and pulled up in front of a large, heavy gate framed by columns and pilasters. At the signal of arrival, the porter, Monsieur Darque, an old beadle of the Comte d'Artois, opened the gate and after checking the transfer papers motioned them through. They rolled off and, traversing a grand court filled with lime trees, they were pointed to the very spot where Louis VI had mounted the carriage which drove him to the scaffold. Their carriage then glided between two sentry boxes, traversed La Cour de Fortin and drew up at the edge of the steps leading to the south wing of the palace. The prisoners, escorted by a detachment of guardsmen, jumped off and walked across the old residence of the Grand Prieur and paused in front of a twelve-metre-high wall constructed in 1792 by the architect Citizen Palloy. On either side of it were stationed two clerks who, equipped with different keys, fondled the two locks. The prisoners then walked into a grand enclosure and were immediately confronted by the enormous and sinister grand tower of the Temple, which stood fifty metres high and was flanked by four pointed capped roofs. As befitting his rank and situation, Smith was placed in the very best apartments on the second floor, previously occupied by the late king, whilst Wright was shown up to the fourth floor where the late queen, Marie Antoinette, had once been immured. The cell doors were then closed behind him and the bolts locked tight.[19]

Left alone, Wright proceeded to scan every part of the chamber to ascertain whether either the queen, her daughter or her sister-in-law the Princess Elizabeth had left behind them any memorial of their residence. After the strictest examination, he discovered two such indications. The first was an inscription, as he apprehended, in her handwriting and containing the following few words: '*La Tour du Temple est l'Enfer*'. Near it he discerned two marks, one above the other, which he imagined indicated the respective height of her two children. The second inscription had been pricked or delineated by Madame Royale, and like the daughter of Pandion indicated a poor child venting her woes to the walls of her prison:

> Marie Therese Charlotte est la plus malheureuse personne du monde. Elle ne peut pas recevoir des nouvelles de son pere, ni de sa mere, quoique elle l'est demandé milles fois.[20]

The following day, armed with a broomstick, Tromelin swiped clean Smith's apartment, the doorway of which had not been cleared since the departure of the king. It was a sparse room, arched and measuring approximately nine metres and occupying the entire floor. The commune had divided it into four small rooms, separated by thin partitions and consisting of a dining area, a soft yellow bedchamber fitted with a chimney, and a toilet cabinet forged from one of the turrets. The rooms were not the dreaded dungeons of imagination but resembled hotel lodgings of minimalist comfort where everything came with a price. Wright and Smith were separated, and though the official entry in the prison registers designated them as '*prisonniers de guerre*' they had been placed *au secret* in solitary confinement. They were also threatened with 'additional severity' if they fraternised with the guards during the hours of solitary exercise in the prison courtyard. Petiet wished to terminate this regime but was informed by Bénézech that the order emanated from the Directory. Indeed, the pentarchy were so preoccupied with ensuring that their prisoners were under the strictest tutelage that twelve days after their incarceration it ordered the concierge, Étienne Lasne, to pull out the iron footholds on all the towers and turrets because they represented a threat to the security of the prison.[21] The Directory's orders were, nevertheless, not entirely heeded, for Smith and Wright still managed to communicate outside the prison's walls through unapproved channels.

Only days into their confinement Smith had surreptitiously procured the sum of £960 through the Swiss bankers

Zererleder & Co. He also managed to secure a steady supply of *Louis d'or*, which he used to bribe his guardians to be permitted the unofficial company of Wright. The prisoners, of course, continued to remonstrate against the 'severity' of their confinement, all the while enjoying special privileges. No doubt they would have accustomed themselves to courses less appetising than those served on board the *Diamond* – salt junk, plum duff, sea pie, weevily biscuits and new rum – but after a couple of weeks' rations they were ministered a daily course of pea soup, a joint of Old England roast beef, two plates of lean beef, one and half pounds of white bread each and four bottles of wine. The concierge's wife, a middle-aged shrew, was soon to complain that her husband was paying for their dessert and emptying their home to provide Smith with all the amenities he needed, including a spit.[22] Indeed, the concierge and Smith appeared to enjoy each other's company and dined together on several occasions. Tromelin, too, was a favourite among the gaolers and turnkeys. His freckled face, voluminous red hair and execrable pronunciations in French all combined to great comic effect. It also became common knowledge that he frequented the concierge's private apartment, where he fraternised with the man's daughter, who took an evident liking to the 'Canadian' jockey.

Wright meanwhile remained in solitary confinement. Restricted from all formal communication with his friends, he found some solace in the correspondence which he exchanged with his young protégé Charles Beechcroft, who remained, with his other fellow captives, imprisoned in Rouen. Three months would pass without incident until one day news arrived that Mr Jackson, the ambassador from his Britannic Majesty, had just rolled into Paris. Wright immediately wrote to Jackson, entreating him to intercede on his behalf. He enclosed the letter and sent it via Petiet:

Sir,
Tower of the Temple, Paris, 8 October, 1796

The character of a British officer will be sufficient apology for this letter, and ample claim to the interest and protection of the British Ambassador.

I was captured on the 18th of last April, off the port of Havre, with a small detachment commanded by Sir Sidney Smith, from his Majesty's ship *Diamond*.

It will be needless to trouble you, Sir, with details of the action, as the principal circumstances of it have no doubt transpired through the medium of the English newspapers; but it may be necessary to say cursorily, that the conduct of all the officers, and seamen, received liberal praise from their captors, and was such as could furnish no reasonable pretence for a deviation from the usual treatment of prisoners of war.

I have to complain of a violation of the law of nations, in the persons of Sir Sidney Smith and myself, by an unexampled imprisonment, under the regime denominated Le Secret, implying solitary confinement, and privation of all society and communication.

I have endeavoured ineffectually, on several occasions, to provoke a declaration of the motive of this unusual rigour towards prisoners of war; the more unaccountable, as it even surpasses the severity exercised towards state prisoners, at present under this roof, who are permitted intercourse with each other, and their friends from without.

There is reason to fear, that this treatment may have influenced opinion, in a manner that will require individual justification of ourselves to the country, and to our friends; but there can be no doubt, that the bare recital of these circumstances to you, Sir, beget a more than common interest on this delicate subject, and produce a demand for my being exchanged, in a manner that shall efface evil impressions.

I have the honour to be, with great respect, Sir,

Your most obedient and most humble servant,

J. W. Wright.

H. E. Jackson, Esq. Ambassador from

H. B. Majesty, Paris.[23]

This letter was followed by a second to Petiet complaining that Lasne had refused to present copies of the orders under which his confinement *au secret* was imposed. The prison concierge had informed his prisoner that he believed it his duty to refuse sharing the orders. Sensing that on this occasion the concierge would not change his mind, Wright petitioned Petiet, who promptly ordered Lasne to acquiesce to this request. He presented his case to the ambassador again at this time, now adding that he had heard the term 'hostage' applied to them and that it had been hinted that their captivity would last until the end of the war. He also declared himself 'utterly ignorant of the motive for this unexampled detention, having in vain endeavoured to penetrate the mystery, and provoke a declaration on that subject'.[24]

Whilst awaiting a response, which appeared not to be forthcoming, Wright learned that his separation was expressly ordered by the Directory, to which there was no redress. Undeterred, Wright sent a letter to the Minister of War, and appealing to the latter's sense of correctness he claimed that his imprisonment regime, *'au secret'*, was foreign to the constitution of France, incompatible with the rights of man and contrary to the usages of war between their respective nations. He also stated that, besides acquitting himself of his duty to his king, his own conduct towards French prisoners of war previously under his care rendered it only equitable that he be offered the same treatment. Wright furthermore asked that he be granted an audience with the ambassador, which at the very least would enable him to arrange his affairs with his family.[25] It was to no end. Unbeknownst to him, the ambassador had been superseded by James Harris, 1st Earl of Malmesbury, who, it had transpired, had just arrived in town.

5

MALMESBURY MISSION

Having lost hope of a decisive military victory, Britain's prime minister, William Pitt, judged that it was time to put an end to the war. With the grudging consent of King George III, he charged James Harris, 1st Earl of Malmesbury, with renewing negotiations for a general settlement. On 17 October 1796, the aforementioned left the port of Dover to a chorus of three cheers from an audience of well-wishers. A contrary wind delayed sail for two days, and when he finally arrived in Calais it was discovered that his passport was stamped incorrectly, much to his irritation. The official delegation that met him professed themselves earnest in their desire for peace, and, dispensing with the new modes of address peculiar to the Revolution, greeted him with much civility and decorum. The delegation comprised the principal officers of the municipality of the town, the Commissary of the Executive Power, the Etat Major of the Garrison and the Director of Customs.[1]

After the usual formalities Malmesbury left for Paris, stopping over at Boulogne, Abbeville and Clermont en route. A group of women and children followed his carriage as it left Calais, and as he passed through the towns and village he was struck by the prevailing silence all around. He surmised that this stillness was borne not from a sense of repose but from the 'terror and perpetual fear' that gripped the population. The country did appear, nevertheless, in a state of good cultivation although he could not help but notice how some of the towns looked deserted, their houses shut and all signs of economy and industry gone. In some districts only the walls of the churches were left standing, defaced with slogans that defied the heresy of the revolutionaries – 'The French people recognise the supreme being and the immortality of the soul.'[2]

As Malmesbury continued on his journey he observed that it was only old men, women and children who pulled the horse-driven ploughs and that, contrary to his expectations, the streets were not filled with marching troops. Indeed, the further he travelled the fewer men there seemed to be. He concluded that the drop in the male population was the effect of war, leaving a ratio between women and men of approximately four to one. The locals he encountered on the journey nevertheless uttered warm words of encouragement and expressed themselves desirous of a return of peace. After a few days' journey he arrived in sight of Paris; passing the suburban towns on the way, he saw large characters sprawled on the entrance walls: 'Citizens, respect the properties and goods of others; they are the fruits and work of his industry.'[3]

On 23 October, Malmesbury arrived at his final destination. After a quiet night, he presented himself in the morning to Charles Delacroix, the fifty-five-year-old Minister of Foreign Affairs. Malmesbury was wearing His Majesty's uniform but with the tricolour cockade sensibly pinned to his chest. To his intimates his appearance resembled a *lion blanc* on account of his fine eyes and voluptuous mane of hair. The French minister, in turn, was reasonably well dressed, so far as the prevailing fashion permitted. He had a reputation for being coarse and repellent but he greeted the earl with the greatest civility, behaving in a manner which, though grave, was well bred. Delacroix spoke slowly, very little and without the vernacular of the Revolution. He also answered correctly and listened intently as Malmesbury presented the minister with his letter of instructions. The minister read his orders with care and then assured the earl that the Directory would raise no objection to its form and etiquette and that the negotiation could begin on a solid basis. Malmesbury in response expressed the king's earnest desire for the restoration of peace and was met by the following reply: 'I can also assure you, Milord, that I, and all those who compose the French government, sincerely desire a return of tranquillity to our unfortunate fatherland, which has suffered so much from its enemies, as much from outside as from within.' After a few exchanges, Malmesbury took his leave and was conducted to the door of the antechamber. The manner in which he was treated, he soon afterwards reported, was unexceptional and no different than the opening of most negotiations with which he had been charged. It was also too soon to comment on the likely progress of their discussions, especially since the minister had reserved almost every word for the approval of the Directory.[4]

That evening Malmesbury went for a leisurely promenade in the park, followed by a trip to the theatre where he watched the plays *Le Glorieux* and *Le Bourru bienfaisant*, seated in a very good box. He enjoyed mixing among Paris' fashionable circles and appeared to revel in the widespread attention that he attracted. Indeed, his fondness of the French would later meet the disapproval of Lord Grenville, who judged, rightly or wrongly, that it interfered perversely with the object of his mission. In any event, the following morning Malmesbury received notice that his diplomatic credentials had been accredited and, at half-past eleven in the morning, he was granted a second audience with the prickly foreign minister. Delacroix communicated his full powers, and after clarification of their respective titles, the ceremony of which was performed in the presence of their secretaries, they began proceedings. Malmesbury opened the conference by referring again to King George III's earnest desire for the restoration of peace in Europe, and then handed over a memorial drafted by Grenville specifying the proposed terms for a general settlement. Delacroix read it aloud and, again reserving the approbation of his superiors, added that it was 'too vague in its expressions'. He nevertheless assured Malmesbury that he would lay the memorial before the Directory but forewarned him that its object would be unlikely to lead to a restoration of peace when he could find so many objections to it after giving it only a cursory glance.[5]

Whilst the negotiations followed their course, Malmesbury busied himself with the second purpose of his visit in Paris, namely sending intelligence back to England on the situation and temper of the country. His regular dispatches disclosed general information on the composition of the Directory, the shifting balance between rival political factions, the state of finances, etc. On the last point, the general view was that they were in a parlous condition – that since the policy to circumscribe the circulation of *assignats* was introduced the amount of coin in the country only equated two-thirds of what she formerly contained, and consequently the government did not have at its disposal funds sufficient for the financing of another campaign. The distresses of the Directory, he reported, were severe, the desire for peace almost 'universal', and the general disregard of the people's yearnings might prove fatal to them. His perception of the Directory was that its existence largely depended on the duration of the war, but since the disposition of the people was resolutely in favour of peace, its leaders would look to find any pretext to break off the negotiation. It was for this reason, he explains, that the Directory had contrived to stymy the course of negotiations through prevarication. Malmesbury, then, recommended that if the negotiations did fail, which was most likely the case, it must be made clear to the peoples of Europe that the derailment of peace should not be attributed to the policy of the British government, which sought to achieve a settlement attendant to the interests of the other powers, but to the pugnacity of the Directory, who had accepted no terms for the restoration of peace consistent with these interests.[6]

A second point of contention concerned the confinement of Smith and Wright in the Temple. Prior to his departure for Paris, Malmesbury received the following note:

Downing Street, 14th October 1796

My Lord- I have his Majesty's commands to desire, that immediately on arrival at Paris, you should make inquiries respecting the situation and treatment of Captain Sir William Sidney Smith, who as it has been represented to His Majesty, has been confined in a manner highly injurious to him and utterly repugnant, both to the established maxims of war among civilised nations, particularly to the humane and generous treatment which the French officers, who have been made prisoners of war, having uniformly experienced in this country during the present war ... His Majesty's great reluctance to aggravate the calamities of war, but to make the strongest representations to the French Government and to obtain a detainment suitable to his rank and situation and to prevent the necessity of retaliation to which nothing but the indispensable obligation of protecting his officers from unmerited rigor and indignity could induce His Majesty to have recourse ...[7]

A month had passed since Malmesbury first sent the official note on this subject, and having failed to receive a reply he had sent a formal note to Delacroix making it explicitly clear that if Smith was not accorded prisoner-of-war status, including the right to parole, no French officer would be allowed a similar liberty. The Minister of Foreign Affairs informed Malmesbury that this matter was out of his jurisdiction and professed himself ignorant of the motives behind the Directory's prolongation of the prisoners' confinement. Malmesbury, in response, strongly prevailed upon him to obtain an answer to his note and warned again of the retaliatory measures that would be taken.[8]

Despite the tenor in which this threat was issued, he was not filled with much confidence in Delacroix's assurances and sent a dispatch to his superiors voicing his concern that, given the 'jealous and irritable complexion of this Government', any enforcement of the issue would only lead to the ill-treatment of all British prisoners without benefit for Smith. Lord Grenville was unmoved by such sentiments of caution and pressed upon Britain's envoy the necessity of following his original orders to the letter, and without delay, since the Directory could not withstand the 'clamour raised against them' if faced with actual retaliation.

Delacroix, however, continued to obfuscate, shifting responsibility to the Minister of Marine when in reality it had already been switched back to the Minister of the Interior. Indeed, before Malmesbury had confronted Delacroix he had made indirect applications to the former, as well as his subordinates, to procure Smith's release. The Minister of Marine was only helpful in that he acted as an intermediary through which Wright and Malmesbury could exchange letters. Malmesbury declared himself attentive to the Wright's situation and assured him that he would use every means within his power to procure him the 'indulgences he was so justly entitled to'. Wright, on his part, requested that the minister's endeavours also be extended to his young friend Charles Beechcroft, whom he had learned was exposed to a contagious fever which had had fatal consequences for a number of other patients in Rouen hospital. The hope was that his protégé would be permitted to be released on parole and returned to England where a French sailor of the same rank could be exchanged. Malmesbury also employed his confidant George Ellis with conducting back-channel negotiations, and though the latter tried to induce the French officers through bribery his efforts were unsuccessful.[9] The earl was somewhat dismayed with the Directory's truculence with regard to this situation, writing that they 'seem to me to completely misunderstand the Case of Smith: and serious as it is, to attach a much greater degree of political importance to it, than it deserves'.[10] It was actually Malmesbury who underestimated the propaganda value that Smith's imprisonment held, as well the bitter enmity that the Directory bore to his person.

Malmesbury's mission, in any case, was drawing to an end. The Directory's first major intercourse with England on the great issues of the day was evidently not serious and their suspicions of the real object of Malmesbury's mission added to the bad faith in which the discussions were held. They had received reports that Malmesbury had been secretly communicating with Smith and sending gold pieces to the partisans in Brittany. Malmesbury himself informed Lord Grenville of this, saying that the Directory were strongly swayed by the general opinion in Paris that he was there solely to gather intelligence on the internal state of the country and to foment discontent or at least 'encourage existing discontents'.[11] Grenville, who was sceptical of the peace initiative from the start, already knew what to expect, having been forewarned by William Wickham months earlier:

The Directory is expecting a negotiator from London. They consider this measure of the British Cabinet as perfidious and dangerous: perfidious as tending only to give them a pretext for the continuing the war, dangerous as giving permission to a man of talents and observation to come and examine the true situation of their affairs on the spot.[12]

So, with suspicion of his mission mounting, and the cause for peace lost, the Directory turned their attention to the two prisoners in the Temple whose attempts to subvert the Republic were of little doubt.

6

THE INTERROGATION

On 16 December 1796, two weeks before Lord Malmesbury was recalled to London, Wright was brought in front of the Juge de la Paix de la Place Vendôme where he was charged with an attempt to burn the town and port of Havre de Grace 'in concert with Sir Sidney Smith'. The judge then commenced the interrogation:[1]

'You are summoned to declare your name, first name, age, place of birth, etc. and to respond to the questions that are going to be asked of you.'

'I am not going to comply with your summons,' came the reply. 'I do not recognise any authority in France and any right to interrogate me. I am a prisoner of war. The officers, to whom I was rendered, are in possession of my name etc. In order to shorten the interrogatory which you are charged with subjecting me to, and to save you time, Monsieur le Juge de Paix, from a useless effort, I judge it proper to declare to you that I will not respond to any question which can have the slightest relation to the service of my King and my country: I will not refuse, however, to tell you, in a causal manner, about the facts that will clear all the calumnies that have been maliciously spread about our intentions and above all, about the reputation of my friend Sir Sidney Smith.'

'Your friend has already responded in a frank and satisfying manner,' the judge rejoined, and, presenting him with the evidence, added, 'You recognise his signature; here's his interrogation; he has signed it himself; besides the first question is nothing but pure form and the following cannot bring you any closer to liberty or to reunite you with your friend.'

'It has been nearly eight months since I was detained *au secret*, deprived of all communication with Sir Sidney,' returned Wright. 'I have not seen him since his interrogation; his answers consequently cannot influence mine. I am in front of my enemies. I must be wary of them; however, since the question is of little importance, and since I wish to challenge the suspicions which have obstructed our liberty for a long time, I accede to your question, but not pertaining to the affairs of service. My name is John Wesley Wright, born in Cork, Ireland, aged twenty-six, officer of the navy and secretary of Sir Sidney Smith.'

Wright's rank in the navy was just a cloak for his clandestine role as an intelligence officer. The circumstances of his early life are not well known but we can be sure that he moved with his family to the island of Minorca at a tender age on account of his father's occupation. There, he was taught by the 'best masters' in French (and music), the knowledge of which would acquire paramount importance throughout his years of service. At the age of eleven, upon the proposition of his father, he joined the navy and was placed as a volunteer on the HMS *Brilliant* where he began his education in nautical studies under the tutelage of Lieutenant-Colonel Campbell. Following the restoration of peace in the year 1783, again on the instigation of his father, he attended George Barker's academy in Wandsworth, London, and for the next two years prosecuted his former studies with the 'utmost faith and diligence'. On finding no prospect of advancement in the navy he suffered a career in commerce, taking a post in one of the leading counting houses in the city. Having won over the confidence of its patron, Wright was charged with an 'important commission' to St Petersburg, where he acquired an excellent proficiency of the Russian language and a thorough knowledge of the topography of the country and the customs of its people. The pursuit of this mercantile business, however, did not divest him of his 'martial inclination' and upon returning to England he chanced to bump into an old friend whom he had known during the Siege of Gibraltar and who notified him of a post on board HMS *Diamond* which had just been made available following the resignation of Sir William Sidney Smith's secretary. With the introduction to that distinguished naval officer successful, Wright assumed his new duties. The mutual attachment which they conceived for each other would ripen through their years of secret service together.[2]

Having obtained this small concession, the judge then proceeded. 'Were you present when the lugger the *Vengeur* was boarded, carried out by the boats attached to the English frigate, the *Diamond*, and commanded by Sir Sidney Smith in person?'

'Yes.'

'The sole intention of this enterprise, was it to carry off the said lugger?'

'Yes, to carry off or to destroy it.'

'Has Sir Sidney Sidney never been in disguise? Did he leave his frigate in uniform; and why did he abandon his command?'

It is notable that the judge did not directly accuse Wright of not wearing a uniform for, it will be recalled, it was precisely this charge that the English newspapers reported to have landed him in the Temple.

'Sir Sidney Smith has never been in disguise,' the prisoner made clear. 'He left his board in uniform as usual; and did not abandon his command; he was always in sight of his signals and had carried out his command by these means.'

The judge then turned to the main accusation lodged against the prisoners and asked, 'Did you not have the intention of burning the town and arsenal of Havre; and do you not have knowledge of a sulphur faggot that we found in one of your boats after your capture?'[3] The charges of incendiarism, formalised by the Acte of Accusation and signed by the director Paul Barras, were in reality a temporary measure that the Directory employed whilst its police searched for sufficient evidence to charge the two men with espionage, a crime punishable by death. Wright was no doubt aware of this and made sure not to acknowledge the premise of the question.

'You only need to have bombs,' he began, 'to burn Le Havre as the famous Admiral Rodney has well demonstrated in 1759 during the preparations for the descent on England. It is absurd to attribute to us the preference of personal risk to effectuate that what can be done without difficulty, with an inferior force than ours in every respect. Moreover, it is slanderous to accuse the same man of such project whose moderation Le Havre owes its existence for more than a year. My friend is among the most humane men that I know; the burning of a town was not in his intentions nor is reconcilable with the general orders of his squadron. It is reiterated to all commands of detachments approaching the enemy coast, to not fire on the inhabitants or persons unarmed. I do not think that I can cite a single example of a contravention of these orders. I do not know what was possibly found in the boats, not being present at the moment when one made a report of these objects. Besides, our naval regulations demand, logically, that every detachment has what it needs to burn or destroy what one cannot take away from the enemy.'

Making no comment, the judge continued.

'Was not your frigate attached to Sir John Warren's fleet, and under the orders of your friend, at the Quiberon affair?'

Smith's duties as a naval officer, it is true, put him under the official orders of Sir John Borlase Warren, Commander of the Channel fleet, but his secret service was not strictly directed by any formal branch of government – including the Alien Office, which administered foreign and domestic espionage – but derived from the implicit trust that his first cousin William Pitt and Lord Grenville vested in him. Wright, in any event, did not participate in the disastrous Quiberon expedition and answered to that effect.

'Did you not vomit the émigrés on our coasts; land arms for the rebels of Normandy and Brittany; did you not insult our coasts during the course of this war?'

'I do not really know what you mean by the word "vomit",' he replied caustically. 'The question seems to me to be ridiculous. Nor what you mean by "insulting our coasts". We have completed our duties in destroying your navy and your commerce, right under your batteries.'

'Do you not have knowledge of different transactions of arms and munitions made by your frigate for the rebels in Brittany and notably of the disembarking of barrels of powder and guns, carried out near the port of St Malo? Did you not land different arms and munitions in Jersey for the aim of depositing them on the coasts of France to the said rebels?'

Given its strategic proximity to the French mainland, Jersey had become a natural springboard for counter-revolutionary operations. Since the deposition of Louis XVI thousands of émigrés had sought refuge in the Channel Islands, where they were recruited, equipped with arms and transported by Smith to north-western France posing as supernumeraries on his muster. Whilst many of these nationalists professed their discomfiture at treating with the ancient and implacable enemy of France, they set aside their objections, without entirely allaying their suspicions, citing the advantages of a military alliance. As the interrogation demonstrated, the Directory was acquainted with their activities thanks to the intelligence that was supplied to them by republican agents planted in their midst.[4] Wright, in any event, continued to deny the competence of the French government in interrogating him on the facts of his service and the operations of his squadron. The judge, probably anticipating this, nevertheless continued with his line of questioning.

'Did not the frigate weigh in the bay of Cancale or near the Isles Chosée and did she not weigh anchor again in St Marcou, in the bay de la Hogue? Were you not yourself at St Marcou?'

'I have been everywhere where my squadron has been and especially at St Marcou: to the rest I refer to my previous responses.' In this instance, Wright had no need to dissimulate. Besides engaging in clandestine operations, Smith's squadron was also under Admiralty orders to protect the tiny island of Marcou and harass enemy positions on the French coast, both of which constituted conventional naval duties.

'Did you not write to the generals of the rebels in Normandy; and your friend, did he engage in a correspondence and relations with them? Do you know the generals of the Chouans? And your friend, does he not know them? Since he had correspondence with them ...'

The judge then picked up the letter in question and, pointing to Smith's signature, said incredulously, 'Here, take it; you recognise it, and above all his signature. And your one as well? Do you not know Louis Frotté, general in chief of the royalists of lower Normandy, and did you not address him by letter?'

'I do not know any of the generals of the Chouans,' Wright pretended, 'for that which regards my friend, I presume that he will have responded for himself; to the rest, I refer to my previous responses.'

'You are summoned to declare if the address on the envelope of this letter written to Louis Frotté himself by your friend promising to meet him on the shore and to succours in favour of the King and of the honnetes gens de la France. Is it not your signature? And if you do not have any knowledge of the said letter, how about this ciphered one? You are summoned to explain this last one, or to declare if the translation attached is correct. You are asked if you want to sign by your hand the letters and the envelope in question.'

Wright did, in fact, meet Louis de Frotté at his headquarters for the purpose of communicating Sir Sidney's desire to greet him on the beach of Cotentin; however, the Norman leader could not be enjoined to a meeting because of the inherent dangers in exposing himself.[5] Yet the idea that Wright would volunteer his signature to a document incriminating himself was an absurdity and was promptly presented as such.

'The summation is impertinent as it is ridiculous. I am not going to examine these letters and I am not going to sign anything.'

The interrogation thus ended as it began. Wright was escorted back to his cell where he was left alone to turn the episode over in his mind. He feared that it might be the preliminary to other, more challenging interrogations. But, as he later wrote, he resolved to protect 'the inviolability of Secret Service in which numbers of unfortunate men may be implicated'.[6]

Two weeks after the interrogation, the Directory received a report from Merlin de Douai, now Minister of Justice, in which he related the confessions of two French émigrés, Yves Cobert and Jean François Léde.[7] Douai had left his post at the Ministry of

Police, declaring himself incapable of sustaining an eighteen-hour work day. According to Paul Barras, the most powerful member of the Directory, Douai knew much about the niceties of law but next to nothing about war and the rights of those who wage it. It was he who, upon learning of Smith's capture, demanded that he be immediately executed, without due process, on the grounds of being a 'foreign revolutionary' or 'home corrupter'.[8] Douai was not without ability but his petty cruelties and vanities rendered him obnoxious to many of his contemporaries, and in deference to public opinion he would eventually be obliged to retire into private life.

In his report, Douai informed the Directory that the two émigrés had just been brought before the Minister of Police and upon being questioned had admitted to having treasonable ties with the English 'monsters'. The two prisoners, he makes clear, had served in the capacity of marines on board the frigate *la Republique* and, having quitted that vessel, had been brought to the Ile d'Aurigny, from where they proceeded via Guernsey to Portsmouth. From England, they were then conveyed on HMS *Diamond* to Champeaux, where they landed on 30 December 1795, at eleven o'clock in the evening with a packet addressed for Louis de Frotté, the leader of the Normandy rebels. Smith, they alleged, proposed to burn the frigates which were at the port of Havre and had furnished for this expedition artificial fuses which were designed to burn four hours without producing any fumes. He also had the intention of seizing the frigate *la Romaine* which was in the harbour of Cherbourg by means of launches.[9]

Despite the gravity of these confessions Smith wrote to the Directory complaining of the manner with which he was being treated. His letter elicited the fury of François Rewbell, one of its members. The Director, it was said, was oft to turn colour at the slightest annoyance and, though a former lawyer, was not the least sensible to any notions of justice, having considered liberty to be illusory and its establishment quite impossible. When the complaint was read out he brought forth the grossest declamations against Smith, saying that this 'infernal man' merited no consideration whatsoever and should have, quite legitimately, been hanged as an incendiary.[10] He added that the vivacity of the English ministry's solicitations for obtaining his liberty and exchange proved what interest England had invested in getting him back, thus making it their duty to keep him with the greatest precaution. Rewbell was not without reasoning but the vehemence of his views, recalling the language of Robespierre, aroused the objection of François Barthélemy, the duplicitous French Ambassador to the Helvetic Cantons, who argued that without doubt Smith had many talents but that if the British ministry put so much insistence on getting him back it was even less due to the importance that it attached to his service, since England possessed a large number of naval officers more skilful than he, and that 'by justice, decency and regard for the representations of his family' it would be more honourable to the Directory to return him to his country.[11] Barthélemy's supplications fell on deaf ears and so, as the New Year approached, Smith and Wright came no closer to being released through official channels. Their hopes, however, were soon to be raised with the unexpected arrival at the prison gates of three of Louis XVIII's most trusted agents.

7

BETRAYED

On the morning of 31 January 1797, the Abbé Brottier and Charles Honoré Berthelot La Villeheurnois, a former Master of Requests, trudged their way in the snow to the *l'école militaire* where they had arranged to meet Colonel Malo, the commander of the 21st Regiment of Dragoons. They were soon joined by the Chevalier Duverne de Presle, a former naval officer, who had arrived just a few hours earlier from London where he had successfully solicited additional funding for the Paris Agency, Louis XVIII's principal spy network in the capital.[1] At approximately eleven o'clock, Malo received the three conspirators with affected cordiality and led them to his private chambers to quietly confer on the subject of their propositions.

The agents had walked into a trap. After allowing his unsuspecting visitors to incriminate themselves, Malo caused them to be arrested by the handful of dragoons concealed in the room. Clapped in irons, the three men were handed over to the Bureau Central where they were interrogated by the local commissary, Citizen Limodin, and compelled to disclose the addresses of their respective lodgings.[2] The news of the arrests, however, spread quickly, giving time for the Chevalier Sandrié Despomelles, one of the founders of the Paris Agency, to destroy the most compromising documents filed away in their hidden archives whilst other pieces were hastily burned by Duverne de Presle's sister. The police, upon raiding the agents' office, were therefore only able to seize those documents which the conspirators had not contrived to destroy.[3]

Over the next few days the police swept the city, hauling scores of suspects away from their homes. The German-born royalist Baron de Poly was apprehended at his apartment at the Petites-Écuries after having been shadowed by police agents for a number of days.[4] In his cell he was subjected to a violent interrogation, during which he confessed to having been commissioned with enrolling 'likely young fellows' for the final *coup de main*.[5]

A few weeks later, the sensational trial of Presle, Brottier and Villeheurmois began. The three prisoners were arraigned before a Council of War convened at the Hôtel de Ville, where they were joined by thirteen other conspirators. Outside, the streets were lined with crowds of Parisians eagerly waiting to catch a glimpse of the king's notorious emissaries. During the proceedings, Colonel Malo testified that the conspirators had planned to storm the centres of the government/military complex, overthrow the Directory, disperse the legislature and purge the Jacobins. The documents seized by the police were also presented as evidence which included a list of names of potential ministers for a new royalist cabinet.[6]

The defence challenged the military tribunal's jurisdiction on the grounds that the agents had not been taken in arms and that the charges of conspiracy could only be heard in the civil courts. Despite the attempts of several deputies in the councils to second their defence, the Directory was nevertheless determined that the agents be tried before a military tribunal as they had attempted to suborn officers of the army. To this the agents countered by arguing that, though they were emissaries of the Louis XVIII, they had only been charged with propagating royalist ideas, not employing force in favour of a restoration.[7]

Alone in the cells, the prisoners reflected on their terrible predicament. Faced with the prospect of being dragged blindfolded to the plain of Grenelle, Duverne de Presle's fortitude broke and on 1 March, whilst the competency of the military court was being deliberated upon, he wrote a twenty-three-page declaration on the existence of the 'English conspiracy', expounding at great length on the machinations of the royalist agency and the web of correspondences that linked together Louis XVIII's exiled court with Paris, the insurgent zones in the west, the Swiss cantons where Wickham was operating and the British government. He also denounced the names, residences and resources of each of his accomplices. Presle followed with a second declaration, made exactly one week later, in which he detailed the lengths taken to corrupt the various organs of state as well as promising to provide a list of the names of the 184 deputies who had pledged their fealty to Louis XVIII.[8]

Presle did not consider his confessions to be treacherous but just a means of purchasing his life. His behaviour was hardly honourable, but he could scarcely be chastised for betraying his king, especially under thumbscrew, when the Prince de Carency, the unprincipled son of Louis XVIII's own prime minister, had also been disclosing the secrets of the Paris agency and the royal council to the Directory.[9] His motives, it appears, were not greed or jealousy but a desire to derail the possibility of a constitutional settlement. Wickham had always seen Carency for what he was, a rake and a mountebank, and had instructed his subalterns not to admit him into the secrets of their correspondence. But, being a gifted impersonator, the handsome prince had managed to pass himself off as a messenger in the British service, intercepting letters addressed to the Prince de Condé and Colonel Charles Craufurd as well as extorting money from Jean Frédéric Perregaux, Wickham's Swiss banker. He also managed to dissipate the suspicions of the Paris agent, the Abbé Brottier, who lodged him in his own apartment. It was not long, however, before Carency and his father, the Duc de Vauguyon, were exposed. On 1 March, the same day that Presle made his first confession, Louis XVIII convened his council at his tiny court at Blankenburg attended by Vauguyon, the ducs de Villequier and de Guiche, the Marquis de Jaucourt, the Baron de Flaschlanden and the Comte Francois d'Escars. All of a sudden, his favourite, the Comte d'Avaray, made a dramatic entrance, waving in his hand a batch of letters compromising the two. Vauguyon was immediately expelled from the court and warned never to return. His humiliation was complete when on the following day, under the authority of Louis XVIII himself, a bulletin was sent to the gazettes of Europe publicising the incident. The king, though saddened, had for a long time conceived the gravest suspicions of La Vauguyon's fidelity, but even after withdrawing his confidence in him he was still unable to agree with his council on the motives for the betrayal.[10]

The trial, meanwhile, continued unaffected. Having objected to the competency of the tribunal, the defendants appealed to the Court of Cassation, which, having heard the evidence on 22 March, found that the military tribunal was exceeding its jurisdiction. The Directory intervened at this point and set aside the judgement by forbidding the Minister of Justice to transfer the trial to the highest court of the land. After more than a month of hearings, the military court countered the Directory's flagrant attempt to subvert judicial procedure and independence by acquitting fourteen of the defendants.[11] The three agents were condemned to death but, by unanimous vote, Brottier and Presle's sentences were commuted to ten years' imprisonment and Villeheurnois' to just one. As it turned out, in saving his own head Duverne de Presle had saved those of his fellow agents too since the tribunal could not level unequal penalties on conspirators found to be equally guilty.[12]

Whilst this drama unfolded, William Wickham was confronted with the fallout from the affair. Among the other mischiefs produced by the arrests he lamented to Lord Grenville the 'almost total privation' of his correspondence with Paris.[13] His top agents had dispersed in the face of the police hunt, with d'André quitting the capital and Louis Bayard retreating safely across the frontier to Switzerland. He also inveighed heavily against the imprudence of the agents for allowing 'false brethren' into the 'fraternity', suggesting to Britain's Foreign Minister that all they could do now was to 'leave them to themselves and get out of the scrape as cheaply as possible'.[13] He had considered tendering his resignation, such was his exasperation at their recklessness, prompting the Prince de Condé to send him a desperate letter, couched in the most flattering terms, entreating him to stay the course: 'There is only you who can bring to a happy end this important affair on which depends the safety of Europe, and of which you hold all the threads in your hand.'[14]

Wickham, in any event, swallowed his displeasure and turned his attention to monitoring the progress of the electoral campaign. For this, he relied on reports that his crafty agent Louis Bayard, now back in the interior, collected from local members of the Institut Philanthropique, a sort of secret Masonic society that canvassed the country for royalist support. Despite encouraging reports from Bayard, Wickham feared the prejudicial effects that the arrest of the Paris agents and the subsequent revelations at their public trial would have on the electoral outcome. He need not have worried. As the results soon showed, the Directorial candidatures actually benefited little from the proceedings. Of the 216 ex-members of the Convention who sought re-election, only eleven were returned. The Directory was now confronted by a hostile majority in both assemblies. At the same time, just as planned, Barthélemy was elected to the Directory whilst Pichegru assumed the presidency of the Council of Five Hundred.

The elections, in fact, resolved little. The royalists remained a minority in the councils, accounting for perhaps 200 of 750 members, of which there were 'scarcely ten persons who were attached to the present King'.[15] They also enjoyed no influence in the upper house. Significantly, d'André failed to get elected himself, thus depriving the new assemblies of a powerful personality who could exert influence on the legislative proceedings.[16] Yet, as Wickham had predicted, Barthélemy's appointment succeeded in producing a serious schism in the Directory. Barthélemy vehemently opposed the Directory's war policies and, ranging himself with Lazare Carnot, the celebrated 'Organizer of Victory', came to support the cause of the pacific majority in the assembly. The two Directors were now pitched against the warmongers, Louis Marie La Révellière-Lépeaux and François Rewbell, with Paul Barras hesitating as to which side to take. The latter initially appeared disposed to the party of peace but towards the end of June, whilst he secretly engaged in negotiations with the Court of Blankenburg, he switched allegiances and allied himself with the opposition, taking the other two by surprise. The Triumvirate, as the three Directors would become known, were now geared up for a showdown.

In London, the cabinet was also divided. With the country exhausted by the war, Pitt wanted peace at almost any price, arguing that a respite was essential for the country to regain her strength. He was, however, opposed by a number of ministers, including Lord Grenville who threatened to resign his cabinet post. Despite his inferior position, Britain's Foreign Minister regarded himself as Pitt's equal and often spoke to him with 'brutal frankness'. He was not as naturally brilliant as his haughty and priggish first cousin but he was still formidable, a practical man of domineering temperament, both inflexible and unyielding, and although his 'nose was not turned up at all mankind' like Pitt's he still remained both imperious and indispensable.[17]

Grenville saw no reason to subject the country to a needless humiliation by submitting peace proposals that would invariably be rejected. But again, Pitt's will prevailed. With the king's permission, a note was subsequently sent to Paris declaring that the British government was once more desirous of discussing the conditions of a general settlement. The Directory responded to the overture with good grace this time, and on 30 June Lord Malmesbury set out to meet the French plenipotentiaries at Lille, accompanied by George Ellis and Henry Wesley, as Secretary of Legation. He arrived in Calais on 3 July and was conveyed to Lille, where he installed himself in the Maison de l'Intendance, an elegant hotel on the rue Royale. He felt more optimistic this time. The French legation was represented by Étienne François Le Tourneur, the ex-Director who, by lot, had relinquished his seat in the pentarchy six weeks earlier. Small in stature and extremely conceited, he nevertheless contended that the continuation of war was fiscally irresponsible and that if negotiations were sensibly conducted the Directory would not be able to withstand the general clamour for peace. Malmesbury reported that, although all diplomatic forms and ceremonies were strictly observed, the discussions were performed in much better spirit and transparency than previously.[18] The British government, in its desire to reach a settlement, had instructed him to offer no objections to France's retention of all her conquests in Europe and was even open to considering a demand, presented by the French delegation, for a restitution of the ships taken and destroyed at Toulon.[19] The talks began to stumble, however, when the French plenipotentiaries, not satisfied with England's acquiescence to the massive extension of France's natural borders, also demanded that she return the Cape and Ceylon to the Dutch and Trinidad to Spain.

In Lille, Malmesbury kept abreast of the turbulent events in the capital. The reports were not very reassuring. According to the intelligence communicated to him, Pichegru was adopting a 'waiting' policy and was even trying to effectuate a compromise between the Directory and the assembly. It was true that as President of the Council of Five Hundred General Pichegru exhibited few qualities required of a parliamentary leader.[20] He appeared only occasionally in the assembly, intervened rarely in the debates and otherwise employed his time attending the meetings of the military committee. His continued aloofness during the political deadlock even sparked growing criticism in the councils. The deputies sought to pass a bill to reorganise the National Guard, which had been practically disbanded following the *vendémiaire* uprising. Under his superintendence it could have been a formidable military body allied to them, but, despite speaking of its urgent necessity, he essentially remained noncommittal, preferring to bide more time and see how events evolved. And so, as Pichegru dithered, Barras prepared to strike the first blow.

The Director was, by his very indolence and profligacy, ill-suited for routine government business, but in moments of national emergency he displayed a rare resolve and audacity suitable for the occasion. The constitution contained no provision which enabled Barras to dissolve its members or prorogue the sessions and so, ever sensible to stark political realities, he proposed to break the political deadlock by force of arms. On 1 July 1797, following secret talks with Barras, Lazare Hoche, the young commander of the Army of the Sambre and Meuse, sent his troops marching on Paris within twelve leagues of where the legislature held its sittings; this was in breach of the constitution of year III. In gratitude for this service, Hoche was appointed Minister of War in a cabinet reshuffle which saw five other key ministerial positions being filled by creatures of the Triumvirate. Explanations for these manoeuvres were angrily demanded in the assembly. The deputies were, however, unimpressed by the Directory's feeble assurances that the troops had been detached from the Rhine to join a planned expeditionary force to Ireland and considered arraigning the Triumvirate.[21]

At first Carnot hinted that he would support the impeachment of his colleagues, claiming that he had no prior knowledge of Barras' arrangement with Hoche. He thought better, however, and withdrew at the critical moment. The crisis only subsided when Hoche arrived in Paris to discover that not all the members of the Directory had agreed to his deployment. Angered by the revelation, he ordered his troops to withdraw to Brest, but not before resigning his ministerial post.

The Triumvirate and the councils now agreed to an uneasy truce. Barras, of course, had no intention of honouring the accord and, whilst still secretly negotiating with the exiled court at Blankenburg, he turned again for support to the same general who had rendered him such timely service on 13 *vendémiaire*: the great Napoleon Bonaparte.

8

LE COMTE D'ANTRAIGUES' PAPERS

During the autumn of 1796, there appeared in Venice a strange, hunch-backed figure with a pallid complexion, dark gimlet eyes, bristly, pitch-black eyebrows, a long nose and a chin that looked like 'the toe of a boot'.[1] He arrived in search of employment. After having lodged himself in a comfortable villa and presented his credentials to the Minister Plenipotentiary of the French Republic, Monsieur Lallemant, he paid a visit to the arch-royalist the Comte d'Antraigues, who was residing there under diplomatic cover with the Russian legation. This hunch-backed man, the Comte de Montgaillard, had written to d'Antraigues in March the year before from Rheinfelden, near Basle, claiming to be serving Louis XVIII with 'pen and pocket', and had requested 12,000 *livres* from the count as well as 24,000 *livres* from Francis Drake, the British Minister Plenipotentiary to the Republic of Genoa and the Court of Milan, for the purposes of bribing Napoleon to desert to the royalists. D'Antraigues' sardonic reaction was that the sums proposed were too little for Napoleon and too much for him.[2] On 4 December, the two men met again. By then, D'Antraigues' suspicions were confirmed; knowing that Montgaillard was a double agent in the pay of the Directory, he carefully kept a record of their conversation, as was his habit in any event.[3]

D'Antraigues could scarcely have looked more different from this impossible rascal. He was forty-three and tall, with a high forehead and prominent eyes. His manners were insinuating. He listened indifferently as Montgaillard boasted of having subverted officers under Napoleon's command, of entering into treasonous correspondence with the general himself and of having devised the scheme to corrupt Pichegru. Committing the details of their conversation to memory, d'Antraigues took prudent steps to dissociate himself from Montgaillard, much to the latter's bitter resentment. He was, in any case, already a marked man on account of Duverne de Presle's confessions to the Directory. Besides being a known royalist agent, the count was also suspected of having stirred up a public protest on 17 April 1797, an Easter Monday, which saw the inhabitants of Verona rise up against the French garrison and kill 400 soldiers, including the wounded laying in hospital.[4] And so, when Barras found out that he possessed evidence purporting to expose Pichegru's treason, orders were immediately issued to capture him and his papers.[5]

The Comte d'Antraigues was still residing in Venice when French troops entered the town in May 1797. He could have fled earlier but chose to remain in the protection of the Russian legation, believing it to be the safest option. On the 16th he set off in the company of the Russian minister, but before he did so he deposited the bulk of his papers at the Austrian legation and kept with him only three small trunks containing documents of varying import. They had not reached very far on their journey when their carriages were stopped in Trieste at bayonet point. The entourage was then conducted to the French military headquarters, where the commandant of that town, General Jean Baptiste Bernadotte, was waiting with orders of arrest. Pointing his finger at d'Antraigues, the general barked at Mordinov, the Russian Minister:[6]

'I order you, Sir to declare to me the name of that person!'

'I believe I should be failing in the dignity of my Court if I were to hide the name of a person attached to my mission on the express orders of my sovereign,' he replied. 'That is M. the Comte de Launai d'Antraigues. On his behalf I request the consideration which human rights ensure for all members of a public mission.'

'But this cannot apply to the Comte d'Antraigues who is said to be the ambassador of Louis XVIII, our enemy. Consequently I must inform you that he is under arrest. If it were he who was in the position of strength, he would have had us all shot. Now that we are in control here, we use the same right!'

'Since you yourself claim that might is right,' the Russian minister rejoined, 'I can only repeat my protest at the disgraceful procedure being employed with regard to myself. If you detain M. d'Antraigues, you insult the Sovereign who has deigned to place him in my care. The passport issued by the French minister specifies no exception among the staff attached to my legation, and I shall have to send a courier to His Majesty the Emperor to inform him of what is happening to me.'

'You had better know then that with respect to the arrest of M. d'Antraigues I am acting under express orders from my government. As for you, I have arranged suitable accommodation for you and your company at the inn. You may stay, or continue your journey, as you wish.'

Whilst the count strenuously protested against this treatment, his Alsatian wife, the famous singer Madame Saint Huberty, busied herself destroying the contents of two of the portfolios. She thought that the third only contained documents of literary interest, and when she realised the importance of her omission it was too late as the captors had already seized the trunks. Once these were searched, d'Antraigues and his family were escorted in separate carriages to Napoleon's headquarters in Mombello near Milan, but to add to their humiliation they were made to bear the cost of their transportation in advance.

Things were not going so brilliantly for young Napoleon. His Italian campaign was rousing loud criticism at home, his wife was in the arms of her lover and the application of leeches was not helping to reduce his haemorrhoids. Given his preoccupations, he was pained to suffer further embarrassment by having his name associated with a general suspected of treason. So, knowing that d'Antraigues possessed documents to this effect, Napoleon took the irregular step of breaking the seals of d'Antraigues' briefcase. His faithful secretary, Louis de Bourrienne, then made an inventory of the contents, listing the last item, *My Conversation with M Le Comte de Montgaillard, 4 December 1796 at six in the evening until midnight*.[7] It was, he correctly judged, a delicious piece of evidence to destroy Pichegru's reputation. And he needed it. His position, following the recent electoral gains for the royalists, was less than secure back in France. A number of deputies in the assemblies were critical of his unsanctioned expansionist policy in Italy, and the Directory, whose general preference was for security on the left bank of the Rhine above the creation of new satellite republics in the north of Italy, was divided on the issue.[8] Napoleon was, however, aware that the memorandum contained embarrassing information relating to his flirtation with the royalists. He therefore needed to invoke d'Antraigues' help to doctor the document as any suppressions of his name would most certainly be detectable.

Then, at 3 a.m. on 1 June 1797, the count was summoned to the presence of Napoleon at his headquarters in the summer residence of the Crivelli family, old friends of the Serbellonis. He was escorted into the interrogation room and motioned to sit down by a small table that the Chief of General Headquarters, Major General Berthier, had laden with papers. Napoleon was already there, pacing up and down, his head slightly leaning forward, his hands clasped behind his back. He was, the count perceived, incapable of keeping still for a moment. D'Antraigues also saw something cruel in his mouth and noticed how his eyes, grey and expressive, had the unsettling effect of piercing every object that they so happened to land upon.[9] Indeed, it was said by the great novelist Alexandre Dumas that no one image of him exists that is a perfect representation, and though many artists have vied with one another to paint or sculpt his features they have never managed to capture his 'extraordinary essence'.[10] The interview began with d'Antraigues enquiring about his confiscated passport.

'Bah! Passports!' the diminutive figure cried. 'Why do people rely on passports? I've had my eye on you for a month, and I let you have a passport only to be all the more sure of catching you.'

The count responded that this undiplomatic conduct was unheard of in Russia.

'It will be known there,' Napoleon assured him, and then in his offhand way added, 'The Emperor can take this event as he pleases, that doesn't concern me.' Fixing his eyes on the count, he continued. 'If I had been in Trieste, his minister would have been arrested, his effects and paper seized, and I'd have sent him off by himself to report the matter. You are my prisoner, and I do not intend to release you.'

He then paused, and, shifting tone, said, 'Now let us speak about another matter. You are too intelligent not to realise that the cause you have been defending is lost and that the sovereigns of Europe will not exist ten years from now. I wanted to talk frankly with you. At first I gave orders that you should be driven to Paris so that the Directory could extract the required information from you ...'

'I have no information to give you,' d'Antraigues replied. 'Even if I had, you can be sure I should not be so weak as to divulge any of it.'

Napoleon dismissed this. 'You're just in a bad mood. Listen, you're not in Paris; all this is simply between ourselves ... What do you want to achieve in Europe? You can see what will happen. People are tired of fighting for idiots, and soldiers too are fed up with fighting for milksops. The Revolution must take its course in Europe ... What will happen to you then? There is only one country for you: France. You simply must go back there, and be of service to France. You can do this. A new faction is forming, which doesn't want Louis XVIII any more than I do; they know and despise him. But they want to cast us once more into the agonies of a new revolution – you know their plans and so do I. I want to liquidate them. You must help us to do this, then you will be pleased with us ...'

It was evident to d'Antraigues that the general, although only twenty-seven at that time, had the unconquerable desire to be master of France, and that through France he would presume to control the destiny of Europe. All his endeavours were just a means to this end.[11]

Napoleon picked up some of the documents that were lying on the table and, laying them before d'Antraigues, said, 'Look, sign these papers. I advise you to do it.'

The papers consisted of copied extracts of letters that were exchanged between himself, Pichegru, the Prince de Condé and

Baron Flachslanden, one of Louis XVIII's counsellors. D'Antraigues pretended that he didn't recognise them and despite the offers that were made – including permission to return to France, the restitution of his property and even a diplomatic appointment at the Court of Vienna with an allowance of 100,000 écus – he refused to incriminate himself by acceding to the demand. Napoleon, nevertheless, persisted. 'Ah yes, you will accept, Monsieur, for here is my final proposal; if you do not accept, I swear I shall have you shot, I shall put you on trial before my War Council for attempting to incite my army to disaffection.'

'Monsieur that is absurd', the count remonstrated. 'I don't know anyone in your army, I have never written a single word with that crime in mind. You do not have the slightest proof.'

'Proof!' Napoleon burst out. 'Proof! If we need proof, we shall make it!'

After the interview, d'Antraigues was transferred from his dungeon to an elegant apartment in the castle of Milan, where he was allowed an unusual degree of latitude. At midnight on 7 June, he was brought in front of Adjutant General Couthard and interrogated again. Couthard began by asking whether he received back all his papers, to which d'Antraigues replied that some literary scripts and a letter from Jean-Jacques Rousseau were gone.

'Is that all?' asked Couthard. 'A certain conversation with Monsieur le Comte de Montgaillard is missing. Do you admit that document was in the briefcase?'

'No. But let me see it, then I'll examine it and I might recognise it.'

'How could you recognise it if, as you say, it was never in the briefcase?'

'Because in Venice, in 1796, I saw an adventurer who said he was the Comte de Montgaillard. As I have never seen him before, I could not possibly be sure who he was, particularly as he showed me passports under the name of Roger de Roucherm to go to the Tyrol and to Leghorn, and another made out to Don Iago-Henriquez-Francesco d'Almontro, of Barcelona, professor at Salamanca, for travel in Italy, authorised, he claimed by General Bonaparte, so that he could go and see him. This man wanted to extort money from him, including a sum of 36,000 *livres* for unlikely and unbelievable schemes. It is possible that I kept some note or other of what he said to me and to my secretary, and letters or memoranda he sent me. If that is so, I should be very glad to see such notes, to recognise them in their totality, because if Monsieur Buonaparte has read them, his curiosity must indeed to aroused by them, since he was the object of the Comte de Montgaillard's journey. Show me those notes, then I won't refuse to sign them; indeed, I wish to do so.'

'Monsieur, you are saying things that are irrelevant to what I am asking … Will you admit that a notebook, containing your conversations with Montgaillard, is written in your hand?'

'No, I shall never acknowledge such a document without seeing, reading and signing every page, noting the condition of every page. That is only right and fair. No one is ever asked to sign an acknowledgement of a document inculpating himself, without being shown the document.'

'This document does not inculpate you at all. I have read it and can assure you about that.'

'It does if it is like the one Monsieur Buonaparte presented to me to sign on 1 June, at 3 o'clock in the morning. I refused to sign it because its content is completely false and has clearly been written by a hand other than mine. I have never seen, known of even read any letter from Pichegru, Moreau, Desaix or Carnot.'

'I am not talking about any of that. Be quiet, reply clearly and unequivocally. Will you, yes or no, acknowledge and sign to the effect that a document found in your briefcase, about your conversations with Monsieur Le Comte de Montgaillard, is written in your hand?'

'No, I do not acknowledge it. I declare it to be false, and will not acknowledge anything without seeing it first.'

'Well. That's an end of the matter. I have nothing more to say to you and you will live to regret this.'

D'Antraigues did live to regret it, but for different reasons. In just two months, his reputation would be devastated and the confidence which Louis XVIII reposed in him permanently withdrawn. He would be suspected of purchasing his freedom by betraying Pichegru's negotiations, and though he would protest his innocence, claiming that he was the unwitting victim of Napoleon's artifice, it was too improbable to the king and his ministers that a man schooled in the art of intrigue could have been duped so easily. Indeed, he would also have trouble explaining why, after his interrogation, he was treated so leniently and incarcerated in a facility that enabled him to so effortlessly make his escape a month later. Moreover, how was he to explain why Napoleon himself, after having denounced him as the 'very soul and agent in Venice of all the conspiracies being concocted against France', would also appeal to the Directory on his behalf by asserting that he could not be tried under the law relating to the émigrés as he was not involved in any armed coup?[12] The only likely explanation for these series of mysteries was that the count had modified certain passages of the conversation in exchange for his liberty. For in its original form the transcription of the conversation between Montgaillard and d'Antraigues covered thirty-three pages, but only sixteen survived, of which the version transmitted by Napoleon to Barras only implicated Pichegru but extricated himself and his Italian army. More than that, the transcription of their conversation was about to be published and posted on every wall for all of Paris to read.

9

BANISHED

On the morning of 5 September 1797, Lord Malmesbury received news of a 'great commotion' that had taken place in Paris the day before. The information received was sketchy, having been pieced together from a number of imperfect accounts, but it was reported that sixty-two members of the Council of Five Hundred had been sentenced without trial to deportation to Guyana where they faced certain death from disease. Two of the Directors, Barthélemy and Carnot, were among the number forcibly removed from their seats of power. The whole affair, he reported to his superiors in Whitehall, rested on a 'vague accusation of a royalist-sponsored conspiracy', and what was even more troubling was that the people of Paris, either from 'apathy or astonishment', did not show any inclination to move in their favour.[1] During the night, several detachments commanded by General Pierre-François Augureau, a tall, 'swaggering ruffian', had silently entered the city from neighbouring towns and, after taking possession of the bridges crossing the Seine, had seized the quays and drew cordons around the Hôtel de Ville and the Tuileries.[2] After sounding the alarm gun from the Pont Neuf, Augureau's troops breached the iron gates and wheeled the supporting pieces of artillery up to the hall of the Councils of Elders.

The Directory defended its actions in the name of self-preservation but the real intention was not, as Lord Malmesbury observed, to preserve the present form of government but to alter some of its laws and abrogate others, in order to arm the executive with greater powers and give full reign to its 'despotic' character.[3] Having disposed of the deputies, it demanded the exclusion from public functions of relatives of émigrés, the re-establishment of all revolutionary laws pertaining to the policing of religious worship, the muzzling of the press and the suspension and dismemberment of the National Guard. It also invited the legislature to enforce Article 359 of the constitution, authorising random house-to-house searches to find hidden émigrés, subversives and anyone who was not in possession of a passport.[4] None of these enactments were necessarily sanguinary but they did invest the Directory with the power of a revolutionary character.

That same day, proclamations were posted on the walls over the city, canvassing public support for the coup and threatening anyone who supported the restoration of the monarchy with trial by military commission. The Directory also printed the Comte d'Antraigues' conversation with Montgaillard, Duverne de Presle's confessions and a selection of the letters that had hastened the Paris agent Pierre Lemaître to the guillotine two years before. Despite the stunning revelations, the coup appears to have made little impression on public opinion except to excite the Parisians' resentment of England and divest Pichegru of all public sympathy:

> The Executive Directory is about to lay before the nation the authentic documents which it has collected concerning the manoeuvres of the royalists. You will shudder with horror, Citizens, at the plots entered into against the safety of everyone of you, against your property; against your dearest rights; against your modest sacred possessions; and you may calculate the extent of the calamities from which in future you alone can be preserved by the maintenance of the constitution …[5]

Among the individuals reading the placards was the very man whose name and physical description was scrawled all across them: the bookseller of Neuchâtel, Louis Fauche-Borel. That evening, he wandered through the deserted streets listening out for the sound of the heavy, rhythmic tread of Augureau's hussars patrolling the city. He had been staying at the Hôtel du Nord in the rue de Richelieu under the pseudonym Frédéric Borelly, but, knowing that the Directorial police were searching the city for him and other wanted agents, including Louis Bayard and Dandré, he decided to head for Montrouge to the home of Monsieur Mercier, the author of the *Tableau de Paris*. He hoped that the memory of their former business relations might predispose the latter to offer him shelter or perhaps procure him a means of escape. When he arrived at the barriers of the city, however, he found them shut. The police were trying to stop the émigrés from fleeing the capital. Learning that the severest punishment would be meted out to those who tried to slip through without permission, he retraced his steps back to the centre.[6]

Walking through the neighbourhoods Borel encountered gangs armed with sabres glazed in rags shouting violent, patriotic chants. He managed to avoid molestation, having disguised himself in a blue frock coat resembling the one worn by the National Guard. He continued to brave the streets until he arrived at the *Cour des Fontaines* where he bumped into Monsieur Guth, a clerk who worked at the Panckouke publishing house and who was associated with a journal that was formerly edited by friends of the king. Guth gave him shelter until nightfall arrived, whereupon Fauche headed to the residence of David Monnier, a provincial lawyer and partisan of Rousseau whom he hoped would facilitate his escape from the city. Making his way in the dark, he crossed the bridges into Faubourg Saint Germain until he eventually reached the rue Saint Dominique, just before the Hôtel de Luynes. Monnier greeted Fauche with warm protestations of friendship and then ushered him into a handsome room upholstered in yellow satin. He declared himself au fait with the bookseller's predicament, telling him that if he heard any strange noises coming from outside he should hide in the secret compartment in the wall which he demonstrated by pulling on a cord. Closing the door, Borel removed his coat and boots and on placing his head on the fluffed pillows he fell soundly asleep.[7]

Having restored calm to the capital, the Directory proceeded to deal with their political prisoners. At midnight on 22 September, the same day that Merlin de Douai and François de Neufchâteau were elected to the Directory in replacement of the deposed Barthélemy and Carnot, Pichegru and fifteen of his fellow exiles, including the Paris agents Brottier and Villeheurnois were taken unexpectedly from their cells and, under the pouring rain, manhandled into three chariots waiting for them. In the prison courtyard, a crowd of soldiers had gathered to hoot and jeer at them. In protest, they demanded to see the orders of deportation issued by the Directory, but Pierre Sotin, the new Minister of Police, just sneered at them: 'It is of very little consequence, gentlemen, to show you the orders; for when we come to these extremities, it is the same thing whether we commit ourselves a little more or a little less.' Just as the horses were whipped into a gallop, the Adjutant General Hochereau quipped, 'Messieurs, I wish you *bon voyage*.'[8]

The armed cavalcade then set off, shadowed by a hundred horse chasseurs. It slowly crisscrossed the width of Paris in appalling weather conditions until it reached the Barrière d'Enfer, which led onto the Orlèans road. Through the breast-high, iron-barred windows the prisoners caught a final glare of the fire-pots blazing round the Odéon théâtre and the lights of the Luxembourg Palace glowing in the distance. At two o'clock in the afternoon, after a tedious, jolting journey lasting twelve hours, the prisoners arrived at Arpajon, a sleepy village eight leagues from Paris. The commandant, a petty little man named Dutertre, led them to a dirty old prison where they laid to rest on filthy straw. The fatigue of the journey and mephitic smell of the dungeon took a physical toll, compelling one of the deputies to plead to Dutertre, 'Let me be shot immediately and spare me the horrors of dying by inches.'[9]

The following day, they passed through the little town of Étampes in the department of the Seine and Oise where they were made to halt in the public square and be exposed to the pillory of its inhabitants. They were insulted and pelted with mud for three hours before they set out for Augerville, four distant leagues from Orlèans. There they passed the night in a convent formerly belonging to the Ursuline nuns. They were not guarded by their escort but by the gendarmerie, whose commanding officer discharged his duty 'in a polite and gentlemanly manner'. At Blois, they were less fortunate. Their chariots were violently assailed by an assemblage of watermen: 'There they are,' they cried in ignorance. 'There are the miscreants who killed the king! There are his assassins! They have loaded us with taxes; they eat our bread, and are the cause of the war!'[10]

After a few days, the prisoners finally arrived at the port of Rochefort where a vessel was waiting to transport them on the long voyage to Cayenne. On the banks of the Charente, the dock workers, soldiers of the garrison and sailors ran to the waterside and bade them a final farewell. 'Down with the tyrants!' they exclaimed. 'Make them drink out of the large cup.'[11]

Having banished its opponents, the Directory now sent Britain's peace emissaries packing. Believing that Pitt was using the negotiations to distract them from the events in Paris, the Directory replaced their negotiators with a more aggressive and virulently Anglophobic delegation. The talks soon turned sour, and by 19 September they had completely broken down. The Directory attributed blame for the breakdown on Pitt's government and published a pamphlet in their state newspaper, the *Rédacteur*, titled *Lettre de Lord Malmesbury, oubliée à Lille* (1797), in which it unleashed a long epistle full of sarcasms against Britain's peace emissary, his Prime Minister and his Machiavellian 'system' of government.[12]

The Directory thereupon proceeded to dispose of Wickham. On 7 October 1797, the same day that the pamphlet was published, the contemptible French commissary Citizen Mengaud arrived in Berne and delivered a note from the Directory to the government peremptorily insisting upon the Englishman's prompt departure from the cantons:

> The Executive Directory, convinced that the mission of Wickham to the Helvetic Cantons has no reference whatever to the respective interests of England and Switzerland; and that his sole object is to excite and encourage plots against the internal and external security of the French Republic, charge the Citizen Mengaud to invite and require the government of the Canton of Berne, and also the other Helvetic Cantons, if necessary, to give directions for Wickham's immediate withdrawal from the territories of Switzerland.[13]

Mengaud's note also warned of the dire consequences that would befall the Swiss should they fail to comply. The threat of military action worried the head of the government of Berne, L'Avoyer Nicolas Frédéric de Steigner, so much so that he enjoined Wickham to leave the canton immediately. At first Wickham refused to accede to the Swiss request, declaring that he would only withdraw his mission if the British government recalled him. He argued that his sudden and unsanctioned departure would only give credence to the Directory's accusations.[14] Yet he was also aware that the French had in their possession correspondence proving, without doubt, that his diplomatic mission was nothing more than a cloak for espionage. As pressure on the Helvetic body continued to mount, de Steigneur's importunities became increasingly more strident. And so, without awaiting instructions from the Foreign Office, Wickham declared his intention of leaving that country without further fuss.

To prevent embarrassment to his government, Wickham announced that he would pay a visit to his adjutant, Colonel Craufurd, who was making a miraculous recovery at Frankfurt after having a fragment of his skull blown off during the Battle of Amberg. As he explained to Lord Grenville, he was most anxious that the Directory was not furnished with a pretext for inflicting 'injury and outrage upon a peaceful and happy nation' on account of his continued presence there.[15] He consequently desired to return to England with the staff of his legation, but just as he had finished arranging his affairs he fell ill. It was not until 7 November that he and Eleanor, his wife, left Switzerland, their place of residence for the past three years.

10

ROGUE AGENT

Returning to England, William Wickham assumed the position of Under Secretary of State at the Home Office and immersed himself in the affairs of Ireland and the United Irishmen. Before withdrawing from the cantons he took precautionary measures to ensure that the 'channels of intercourse' with the royalists remained open.[1] To oversee the correspondence he left behind as chargé d'affaires his imperious thirty-year-old assistant James Talbot, in whose 'industry and discretion' he had complete faith.[2] Talbot had accompanied Lord Malmesbury as a lowly clerk on his unsuccessful peace mission to Paris the preceding year and was tasked with obtaining 'low-grade' information on future diplomatic contacts. Though a novice, he nevertheless proved himself conversant with the methods of intelligence gathering and the ways of the royalists.[3] At the beginning of the following year he was attached to the legation at Berne to replace Charles Flint, who was recalled to England and appointed the new Superintendent of Aliens. His position in Switzerland demanded the possession of 'a considerable degree of circumspection and caution' owing to both the presence of swarming secret agents in the employ of the Directory and to the perfidious nature of many of the emigrants who were 'not suspected of want of attachment to their Sovereign'.[4] As Wickham warned in his instructions, he was to trust no one, 'for there is no spy so good as a double one'.[5]

On 18 November 1797, ten days after Wickham left Berne, Talbot drafted a private letter to Lord Grenville in cipher, with a plan to once and for all rid France of the Directory. He claimed that the majority of the population were resentful of the prevailing system of government and, in their desire for a return to prosperity, favoured the restoration of the Bourbons. The problem, however, was that although the members of the legislative councils were almost universally opposed to the Directory, they were paralysed by division and possessed neither the constancy nor the fortitude to act. The solution, Talbot proposed, was that they find 'a sufficient number of resolute men who ... should make themselves masters of the Five Directors and perhaps some of the Ministers, particularly the Minister of Police'.[6] He believed 'that upon the contingency of the Directory being put to death, the majority of those bodies [the councils] would decree ... a change in the form of Government'.[7] Talbot seems to have entertained second thoughts about sending such an injudicious and intemperate proposal to Grenville, especially so soon after his appointment. In any event, he received no response from the Foreign Minister, and so, shelving the idea for the moment, spent the following two months in Berne devoting his waking hours to uncovering the domestic and military plans of the Directory.

In January, however, Britain's diplomatic mission in Switzerland came to an end. In accordance with Grenville's instructions, Talbot returned to England, arriving in London on 24 January 1798. He was debriefed two days later by Wickham at the Alien Office. Then, on Sunday 4 February, he had a long interview with Grenville in which they discussed, *inter alia*, rigging the forthcoming French elections.[8] Talbot was instructed to provide pecuniary assistance to a group of proscribed deputies who had taken refuge across the French borders so that they might keep their clandestine lines of communication with the interior open. His mission, however, took on new urgency when, that same month, French troops marched into Switzerland before war had even been declared.

It was the opinion of the cabinet that the French advance should be repelled, and with England's king in agreement Talbot was ordered to repair at once to the Swiss border and provide urgent assistance to the government of Berne. He reached Ulm on 2 March, having briefly rested at Cuxhaven in Lower Saxony along the way. Travelling under the pseudonym James Tindal, he was accompanied by his younger brother Robert, who acted as his secretary and courier. They had arrived too late. From Ulm, they learned that the Swiss cantons had already been radicalised from within, that the Berne government had fallen and that the French army were being welcomed into the lowland regions by the Swiss Jacobins.[9]

A couple of days later, Talbot held a meeting with the leaders of Louis XVIII's newly formed royalist agency at the Abbey de Salmansweiler in Ulm in Swabia, chief among whom were Wickham's trusted agent Balthazar d'André and the arch-royalist the Comte de Precy. Their news was not much better. They reported that the proposed plan to influence May's elections was rendered void with the passing of the law of 12 *Pluviôse* an VI (31 January 1798), which gave the outgoing legislature in Paris the power to arrogate to themselves the right to examine the credentials of incoming deputies.[10] With his instructions now in tatters, Talbot and the king's agents refocused their energies on an altogether more daring scheme.

In March, d'André sent a confidential despatch to Louis XVIII and his council at Mittau, disclosing the existence of a secret plan to assassinate the Directory at Paris: 'I believe it my duty to inform you that, independent of the *travail* we act in together, I am actively involved with another project of which I speak little, because secrecy alone can bring it to fruition. This is the project of assassinating the Directory. I have asked all the Presidents de l'Institut [Philanthropique] for some *hommes de main*; if a sufficient number is found I will return to France to endeavour to strike the grand coup.'[11]

Talbot agreed to furnish the conspirators with the necessary funds. He displayed considerable political naivety here in believing the royalists' exaggerated accounts of domestic support within France. He had conferred at Augsburg with a royalist emissary from Paris who had assured him that the Directorial regime was utterly discredited and that 'the moment was favourable for restoring the ancient order of things'. This was only half true.

Despite the Directory's evident unpopularity and widespread unrest, public opinion still did not favour the pure royalists; nor did it long for a return of the *ancien régime*. Nevertheless, Talbot was so convinced of the practicality of this schemes that he placed £25,000 at the immediate disposal of Royer-Collard, one of Louis XVIII's councillors, whom he had met in November.[12] In his estimation, Royer-Collard was 'the person on whose judgement and opinion we have the greatest reliance, an active man, under 40, thoroughly acquainted with the Revolution and the persons engaged in it'.[13]

The first step of the plan was to subvert the system of government by manipulating the legislature. The second was to appoint a 'select band of intrepid men' to deliver the *coup de main*. Once armed, they would assemble on the outskirts of Paris but only pass the city gates twenty-four hours before the appointed time. They would then invade the Luxembourg Palace, and should they succeed in 'making away with the Directory', the tocsin would be sounded to assemble the sections and Louis XVIII would be proclaimed king. Meanwhile, couriers would be dispatched throughout the *départements* to announce the abolishment of the Conventions and to vest the government with a commission of four men (including Royer-Collard) until the arrival of Louis XVIII on French soil.[14]

Talbot wrote to Lord Grenville trying to convince him of the viability of the plan. However, the Foreign Minister was less enthusiastic and spared no time in expressing his disapproval. In his despatch dated 25 January he wrote:

> I do not mean to attribute any blame to you. But I cannot disguise from you that the Plan which appears to have been in contemplation of certain persons at Paris (which if I understand rightly ...) means nothing else than a personal attempt against the lives of the persons comprising the Directory, would by no means meet with any countenance here, but must altogether ... be regretted as a Measure which H.M. entirely disapproves as being wholly abhorrent from the Sentiments of Honour and honesty, which, whatever the

Conduct and Character of the Enemy, become the Character of a Civilised Nation. You are distinctly to put an end to the Operations of which such an attempt was to make apart, into your own hands.[15]

Grenville followed with a second despatch on 15 March ordering Talbot to terminate the negotiations with the conspirators and to hand over the whole of his mission to Lieutenant-Colonel Robert Craufurd – the future commander of the famous Light Brigade, who would be sent out now that war had erupted – and put it on a military footing. Talbot was also made aware that he had never been vested with authority to dispose of such large sums and it was only to avoid the government being discredited that his drafts would be honoured. For the future, Grenville concluded, Talbot was to disassociate himself from the agents of the king.

For the royalists there were few immediate consequences arising from the entire episode. However, a dangerous precedent had been set. As their situation grew increasingly desperate, the idea had taken root among France's most extreme royalists that political assassination was a legitimate means to promote their fledging cause.[16] And as shall soon be shown, it was to be resurrected with disastrous consequences.

II

A SIMPLE PLAN

The arrest and confinement of the Paris agents in the Temple prompted the commander of the royalist units to the west of Paris, the redoubtable Comte de Rochecotte, to make plans to effect the liberation of Sir Sidney and Wright. For this mission, he selected three trusted Chouans who had marched under the leadership of Louis de Frotté, the Norman leader, whom Wright had met at his headquarters in Brittany just days before his capture. The lives of these three men were as adventurous as they were improbable, and, being accustomed to attempt impossible feats, they accepted the commission to which they were entrusted.[1]

Foremost among the three was Count Louis-Edmond Phélippeaux, the inspirational leader of the 'War of the Little Vendée', named after an insurrection which he had instigated in the country around Sancèrre.[2] Like many of his compatriots, Phélippeaux fled France following the upheavals in 1792 and enlisted in the Prince de Condé's émigré corps on the frontier of the Rhine. Wickham had selected from Condé's corps a band of ten worthy chevaliers to be instruments in an intelligence network linking his office with the west of the country.[3] Phélippeaux, who was ranked lieutenant-general, was chosen among these intrepid men, and on leaving the army he crossed the frontier and began his career as an agent in the service of England. His adventures were many, his fortunes varied, but the one constant was his pluck and courage in the face of the gravest dangers.

Following the outbreak of the 'War of the Little Vendée' Phélippeaux was arrested and brought in front of the town's magistrates. With the accomplishment of a skilled actor, he managed to bewilder them so much with his deceptions and facial transformations that they began to doubt that the man in front of them was the same one they had accused of inciting so much trouble. A trial was nonetheless scheduled, and, fearing that it would shed light on his true identity, he resolved to escape. He pulled this off with a well-tempered file and some bedsheets knotted together.[4] Phélippeaux had roamed across La Vendée with Wright and had introduced Mme Tromelin to his young friend Hyde de Neuville, who was living in Paris with a price on his head. Neuville, otherwise called Charles Loiseau, descended from the Earl of Clarendon and would later achieve notoriety for draping a large black flag on the belfry of the Madeline church, the burial place of Louis XVI, on the anniversary of his execution.[5]

To extract funds from the British government, the Chouans agreed to include the English prisoners in their escape plan. They immediately set to work. Neuville found a house to let close to the prison and upon inspecting the place ascertained that the cellar touched the adjacent prison wall. The liberators then set about digging a twelve-foot-long subterranean passage big enough for a man to squeeze through. They proceeded to pick away with the greatest precaution, but just as they thought their plan had worked, the last stone accidentally fell out and rolled into the garden of the Temple. A sentinel noticed and raised the alarm. When the commissaries of the Central Bureau examined the apartment they found only a few pieces of furniture, some trunks filled with logs of wood and hay and a handful of hats with tricolour cockades.[6]

The Directory was nevertheless convinced of Smith and Wright's complicity in the escape plan and ordered that they be subjected to closer observation. They also ordered the separation of Tromelin from his 'master' and on 8 July 1797 sent a small detachment of gendarmes to the prison, accompanied by Brigadier Dulmatera, bearing the following decree:

> John Bromley, servant of Sir Sidney Smith, should be removed from the Temple, to be conducted from brigade to brigade, to the port of Dunkirk, and from there across into England.[7]

Once his affairs were packed, Tromelin was removed from his cell. As he bade farewell to everyone, Sir Sidney handed him a certificate of recommendation before emptying his purse into his hands. Tromelin then embraced the concierge's weeping daughter for the last time and, under the protection of the gendarmes, was escorted from the prison and all the way to the port. He embarked on 22 July, and two days later arrived in England. After a couple of weeks had passed, he sailed back to Normandy where his wife was waiting for him. His real identity as a French émigré was never once discovered.[8]

Wright, meanwhile, continued to remonstrate against the 'rigours' of his confinement. He penned a letter to the Minister of Marine and Colonies in Paris requesting that his rights as a prisoner of war be restored immediately. He also addressed his correspondence to Henry Swinburne, Britain's commissary for prisoners of war. The Directory told Swinburne that they would agree to the exchange of Smith on the condition that the British government render up 4,000 prisoners of war to be accounted for at the conclusion of peace. Swinburne thereupon notified Smith of the negotiations, informing him that he would first need to seek the approval of the British cabinet as he had only been empowered to agree to the exchange of 1,000 French prisoners.[9] It did not strike him as obvious that the cabinet could never realistically agree to such a provision and that it was obviously a deliberate ploy on the part of the Directory to assign blame to the British government for the inevitable breakdown of negotiations. Swinburne nevertheless declared himself delighted with the news, thinking it an honourable exchange. He also boasted upon his recall that he had left his successor, Captain James Cotes, nothing to do, having 'cleared all French prisons' and having effected Smith and Wright's exchange. In private, he found the whole affair to be an embarrassment and beneath his dignity. He complained that Smith was consorting with sordid types, having visited the three muses in the rue de la Corderie and found 'an old hag rocking a child and the two women undressed, unpainted and filthy looking'.[10]

By this time, Wright and Smith were officially allowed each other's company during the day but under the close supervision of Citizen Boniface, a former policeman and lowly patriot who had replaced Lasne as the new concierge of the Temple. The new 'broom' appeared, on all accounts, to be particularly suited to his new position and immediately set about executing his command to the satisfaction of his superiors. He was, however, not insensible to his prisoners' situation and agreed to personally hand a letter by Smith to Napoleon, who had just arrived in Paris on 5 December fresh from his victories in Italy. Having wrung the Low Countries, the Rhineland and the Adriatic islands in exchange for Venice, the general was in triumphant spirits but nevertheless refused to receive Boniface at his house in rue Chantereine, now renamed the rue de la Victoire in his honour.[11] Not so easily deterred, Smith wrote him another letter, but this time pencilled it on the wooden shutter of his cell window, wistfully hoping that his little prophecy may one day reach Napoleon's personal attention:

> Fortune's wheels make strange revolutions, it must be confessed; but for the term Revolution to be applicable, the turn of the wheel should be complete. You are to-day as high as you can be. Very well. I envy not your good fortune, for mine is better still. I am as low in the career of ambition as a man can well descend; so that, let this capricious dame, fortune, turn her wheel ever so little, I must necessarily mount, for the same reason that you must descend.[12]

Wright, in the meantime, continued to lodge complaints to the Minister of the Interior about every privation, including the insufficient provision of bread and the denial of warm baths, despite the last being certified by the prison doctor. But by now it was evident that he had exhausted all hope of appeal and, entering into the final stages of the struggle, he addressed himself to the British Commissary, Captain

Coates, this time professing a resignation to his lot and expressing his gratitude to his guardian, Citizen Boniface, for having tried his best to alleviate the unpleasantness of his confinement.[13] It was all part of a deception. Wright had not abandoned hope of liberation. In fact, he and Smith, with the backing of the British secret service, were planning to stage a prison break.

The mastermind behind the plan was Richard Cadman Etches, a British-sponsored agent whose ability to slip in and out of the Temple without detection may have been the inspiration behind Baroness Oczy's *The Scarlet Pimpernel* (the other is Wickham's favourite agent, Louis Bayard).[14] Etches, a Dane by birth, was formerly the Commissary General of Marine from Ostend to Copenhagen and was Smith's opposite number during the war between Russia and Sweden. In 1796, the year Smith and Wright were imprisoned, he was living in London in Bryanston Street, just off Portman Square. There he offered his spy services to Earl Spencer, the First Lord of the Admiralty, and journeyed to Paris, whence he communicated to his masters in England the purpose of the large naval and military preparations which had so long been kept secret. Being an accredited purchaser of prize vessels, he was easily able to spy on all the French ports and then transmit the information to England's head of naval intelligence, Evan Nepean, via the blockading fleets upon his return home. During his visits to Paris he had occasion to spot Smith and Wright, but, not daring to accost them openly, he obtained an order for fifty *louis* from the banking house Messieurs Herries & Co. and conveyed it to Smith with a message concealed in an orange, informing Smith of who he was and asking how his designs could most surely be effected. In reply, Smith related Madame Boniface's taste for fine possessions and suggested that his escape could best be promoted by the purchase of a silver coffee set. Etches returned to England, where he applied to the Transport Board for an advance of funds. He was, however, rejected on the grounds that every effort had been made to secure the prisoner's release. Seeing no possibility of appeal, he therefore petitioned Nepean, who assured him that if he raised the funds himself they would later be repaid by the government. And so Etches travelled back to Paris and confidentially engaged Mr Keith, a Scottish associate at Messieurs Herries & Co., to manage the funds. With money in his pocket he bought Madame Boniface a lovely coffee set, and in return Smith was permitted to visit the theatre at night, the occasion of which he turned to good account.[15]

The health of the Minister of Marine, Georges de Pléville, had been ailing for some time, and on 12 April 1798, having long failed to show any ardour in the prosecution of his duties, he submitted his letter of resignation after an otherwise successful career. He was a bent old man with one wooden leg, 'forever fawning, yet adept at flattery', boorish and with that 'coarseness tolerated in sailors'.[16] But before being succeeded by Admiral Bruix, he wrote to the Minister of Police warning him of a plot that he had caught wind of:

> I have just received private information, my dear colleague, that Captain Sidney Smith, imprisoned at the Temple, will escape in ten days, and that he is being allowed the privilege of going out to sup in town because he was seen yesterday in the evening in a house in the Rue Honoré at the corner of the Rue Richelieu. I must request you to order that an officer should be set to guard him, and another to watch the gaoler and prevent him from granting leave of absence until I have been able to obtain more ample and more certain information respecting this prisoner and his secretary.[17]

The dinner party that Sir Sidney had attended took place at a small restaurant at the corner of the rue de la Loi run by an Irish lady known as Madame Seguin. It was usually patronised by several seafaring men. Among the guests that night were a Mr Driskett, who had just arrived from Baltimore; an Anglo-American shipmaster and Quaker named Captain Brennan; the banker's associate Mr Keith; and an English teacher named Mr Thompson, who appears to have been a police spy in the pay of the Central Bureau. The next day, the conspirators left Paris. Driskett and Brennan rushed to Le Havre and Boulogne respectively, where they boarded packets destined for England. They arrived just before orders had arrived from the Minister of

Marine to search all neutral vessels in the Channel ports. Etches was informed by a 'lady in the secret' that he had been denounced and hastened to Calais in disguise, not taking a single article of luggage. All the arrangements had been made.

On 24 April 1798, at about nine o'clock in the evening, a large fiacre pulled up before the gates of the Grand Prieur, and two officers, sporting epaulettes, plumes in their hats and large swords by their sides, clambered down and rang the bell.[18] A guard appeared and, seeing before him a staff officer and a captain of Voltigeurs, summoned the concierge. After a few minutes, the head guard returned with Boniface, who was holding the *livre d'ecrou* in his hands. The order read:

Paris, the 5th of Floreal, Year VI
of the Republic, one and indivisible
3rd Division
Bureau of Prisoners of war.

The Minister of Marine and the Colonies to Citizen Boniface, head gaoler of the Temple.

The Executive Directory having ordered, by its decree of the 28th of *Ventose*, sent herewith, that all English Prisoners of war, without distinction of rank, should be collected into one prison, I charge you, Citizen, Etienne Armand Auger, Commodore Sir Sidney Smith and Wright, prisoners of war, to be transferred to the general prison of the Department of Seine et Marne at Fontainebleau.

You are enjoined, citizen, to observe the greatest secrecy in the execution of the present order, of which I have informed the Minister of Police, in order to prevent any attempt to rescue the prisoners whilst on their journey.

The Minister of Marine and Colonies
Pléville-Lepeley[19]

The officer also handed Boniface a copy of the decree of 23 *Ventôse* (23 March) signed by Merlin de Douai declaring that until the

British government behaved towards the prisoners of the Republic in a manner analogous to that which had always been observed between the policed nations, all English prisoners of war, without distinction of rank, were to be regrouped, incarcerated and treated the same. Smith and Wright were provisionally excluded from this measure but were able, on submission of request, to be displaced. Having been informed of the decree, Boniface handed the documents to the clerk and ordered that they be faithfully copied in the prison register. Smith, during this time, was immersed in reading *Gil Blas*, a picaresque novel written by Alain René Lesage. His friend and physician, a Dr Blane, had recommended a number of books to keep him occupied, including the historical writings of Vertot and Sully, the travels of young Anacharsis, Algarotti's letters and the scientific works of Lavoisier, Fourcroy and Chaptal.[20] Wright and Smith were ordered to collect their belongings and prepare for transfer. With the release book signed, the two men were escorted outside the prison gates and into the fiacre, which was then parked on the rue Saint-Antoine.

The fiacre sped off, but just as it turned the first corner it skewed into a fruit stand, breaking a wheel and knocking over a small child. A woman screamed, a crowd collected and a small commotion was raised. The prisoners and their companions instantly jumped off and, shuffling through the crowd, darted off amid cries of 'Assassins! Stop! Take them to the police station.' Running through the warren of Paris' dark and narrow streets, they made their way towards a hiding place which was located at no. 903 rue de l'Université, on the opposite side of the Seine. The following day, disguised as French seamen, Smith, Wright and Count Phélippeaux set off to Rouen via Nanterre. Near Le Havre, they found a small boat in a creek which led to the mouth of the harbour. Once the tide was right and the night had fallen, they boarded the craft and rowed out to sea in the direction of Sir Richard John Strachan's squadron, which they had earlier spotted from the heights about the town. At three o'clock the next morning, they perceived the *Argo* frigate in the distance. Signalling with a white handkerchief, they were observed and taken on board.[21] The captain of the frigate, Captain Bowen, accordingly sailed for Portsmouth and on Saturday evening, 5 May 1798, after two years' captivity, Wright and Smith landed on English soil.

Immediately upon his arrival in London, Etches sent a despatch to Lord Nepean communicating his arrangements for the prisoners' escape. On the following Saturday, he received a letter in cipher from John Keith, his friend, which had been transmitted via the dispatches of a French minister to Mr Otto, the commissioner for French prisoners in London. Otto affixed his official seal to it, and sent it to Etches through a confidential servant. The latter then took it personally to the Admiralty, where, with nobody aware the fugitives had been codenamed as different varieties of meat, it was mistaken for an irrelevant document that related to navy provisions. Etches deciphered it, and announced before his superiors at Whitehall that the escaped prisoners would arrive within twenty-four hours. The announcement proved accurate, for the following day Smith and Wright were on their journey to London. On the outskirts of the metropolis they were fêted by the locals, who removed the wheels from their cart and dragged the two heroes through the streets in triumph.

The following day, Smith and Wright dined with close friends at Wimbledon. As they would soon have occasion to do very often, they recounted their adventures, adding fanciful details with each recital. That same evening, while staying at Camelford House, Etches learned that they would be staying at the Prince of Wales Hotel on Conduit Street and on the Monday morning he stopped by. The instant Smith saw him he lifted him in his arms and carried him from one end of the room to the other, depositing him on a table and embracing him affectionately, exclaiming several times, in the presence of the other gentlemen there, 'Here is my deliverer!'[22]

Back in Paris, the mood was not quite so ebullient. On 25 April, the day after Smith and Wright were removed from the Temple, Boniface communicated to the Central Bureau and the Minister of Police the circumstances of their transfer in one of his daily reports. He submitted a copy of the order signed by the Minister of Marine and also relayed the same to the military authorities and the police commissariat. So unexceptional was the prisoners' supposed transfer that a weekly inspection of the prison and its books by the Central

Bureau on the very same day saw the documents registered without remark.[23] A week passed without event and then, without notice, Boniface was summoned before the new Minister of Police, Pierre Sotin, to answer for what he was then informed was the prisoners' escape. Sotin had applied to the Central Bureau for information on the affair. In turn, it requested the same from Pléville, the outgoing Minister of Marine. The plan, it turned out, was simple enough. Before he left for the peace negotiations in Lille the sickly minister had appended his signature to some blank note papers with official heading just in case they should be needed during his absence. Right after his departure, these very same papers went missing from his office. No one presumed to suggest that the minister was the perpetrator, and indeed the theft would soon be attributed to Antoine Viscovitch, an international agent, but nevertheless the Minister of Marine was compelled to tender his resignation immediately. The second to lose his post was the Minister of Police, who had to suffer the embarrassment of reading how his officers were being ridiculed in a sell-out play at the Astley's Theatre titled *The Lucky Escape, or the Return to the Native Country.* The search for Madame Seguin and her friends led to no arrests except that of the Swiss banker Monsieur Perregaux, whose daughter had just wedded Mormont, Napoleon's aide-de-camp. Viscovitch was escorted to the border pursuant to a deportation order from the Directory. The Comte de Rochecotte, who had sponsored the first prison break attempt, was not so fortunate and was executed, having gone heroically to his death without disclosing his real name or those of his friends. He had survived for three months in Paris living under the alias Rozette, but was denounced by an accomplice named Richard.[24] The Directory sentenced Boniface to six months' incarceration in the same prison he once warded over; though no evidence was furnished against him, the leniency with which he treated the prisoners prior to their escape was sufficient grounds for his demission.

Convinced that Rochecotte's execution could have been delayed if the police had been bribed on time, Smith turned his attention to the prisoners who had been deported to Guyana. He communicated his unease to his superiors in Whitehall and even recommended that Louis Fauche-Borel be charged with effectuating their release, having formerly enjoyed Pichegru's confidence and being one of the few interested men supposedly capable of performing it. He awaited the necessary orders to be given for a ship to be devoted to this service and added that Wright will readily sacrifice all other objects to this end and take a trip across the western ocean at a moment's warning.[25]

The government, however, had already set the wheels in motion. After learning of the deputies' deportation to Guyana, they commissioned the Marquis de Tilly-Blaru, a French émigré, to break them out as he not only possessed real estate in the West Indies as a privateer but also had permission to visit the penal colony. On the day of the escape, he gifted the guards a fine case of Bordeaux wine while the prisoners escaped on a boat that was waiting for them in the inlet below the fort. They were shortly thereafter picked up by a British frigate further up the coast and brought to England, where they were interviewed by the king's ministers.[26]

During the summer, Wright enjoyed the freedom of London's social scene before he returned secretly to the French interior to re-engage the royalists. He was spotted at the Adelphi club where he met Frederick Reynolds, the renowned British dramatist, and talked about the dangers they had faced. Wright struck Reynolds as that class of 'hearty sailors who were as pleasant to their friends on shore as they were disagreeable to their enemies at sea'. As for Smith, among his many acquirements was his professed love of dramatic literature. Smith told Reynolds that during an early period of his life he had resolved to try his success on the stage – a frivolous boast, no doubt.[27]

After enjoying an audience with the king, Smith applied for a brief leave of absence, during which he renewed his acquaintances with the émigrés in England. Upon his way to Smitham he was paid a visit by Louis XVIII's agent, the Prince de la Tremoille, who wanted to know the disposition of the British government towards the exiled king's pretensions and also to establish, in concert with the royalists and malcontents in the French interior, measures against the common enemy. The prince was about to leave for Mittau and expressed himself anxious to please Louis XVIII and to cooperate with his partisans in France, who were unable to undertake anything in his favour till George III could also give him some positive assurance on the subject. The prince proposed to Smith that either he or Wright accompany him to France as their appearance might serve as evidence of the British government's goodwill. Smith countered that he and Wright were otherwise employed and could not undertake such a journey without receiving orders from their government. Smith nevertheless promised to relay Tremoille's concerns to the British cabinet and to underline the importance of a rapprochement between George III and the royalists.[28]

Weeks later, Smith journeyed to Portsmouth where he watched as his new flagship, *Le Tigre*, came out of the dock. He then made arrangements with the Admiralty to inspect her equipment and summoned his officers to the port. He and Wright were shortly to set sail for the Orient.

12

DESERT TRICKS

When Napoleon landed in Egypt with the sworn intention of threatening England's East Indian possessions, the cabinet accordingly dispatched Sir Sidney Smith to Constantinople where his brother, Spencer, was accredited to the Ottoman Porte as chargé d'affaires. By an 'Instrument of Full Powers' dated 3 October, the two brothers were appointed Joint Ministers Plenipotentiary and charged with signing a treaty of defence alliance with Turkey, the terms of which Spencer had been negotiating throughout autumn that year.[1] The decision to confer Sir Sidney with a ministerial character angered the two admirals in the Mediterranean, Lord St Vincent and Horatio Nelson. Nelson was so irritated by Smith's diplomatic appointment that he threatened to resign his post and return to England with his friends, the Hamiltons. He was, however, ordered to temper his petulant behaviour and resume his command by St Vincent, the acerbic commander-in-chief, who was no less astonished at Sir Sidney's apparent ascendancy over His Majesty's ministers.[2]

On 29 October 1798, *Le Tigre*, of eighty-four guns, set sail from Portsmouth. After a few days she entered the Dardanelles, but owing to contrary winds was forced to anchor at Rodosto, twenty leagues from Constantinople. With the winds permitting, *Le Tigre* renewed course and, passing Stamboul, entered the magnificent Golden Horn, docking on 2 January 1799.[3] That day, Smith's brother Spencer came to dine on board, accompanied by his wife, the charming daughter of Baron Herbert, the Austrian minister there. He announced the rupture of diplomatic relations between France and the Porte, the incarceration in the Seven Towers of Citizen Ruffin, the republican chargé d'affaires, and the conclusion of a treaty of alliance between Russia and Turkey. Three days later, the brothers Smith held a conference with the Reis Effendi, Ibrahim Bey, the Porte's foreign minister, on board *Le Tigre*. On behalf of George III, Sir Sidney presented the grand seignior with a perfect model of the *Royal George* as well as twelve brass three-pounders.[4]

Smith thereupon took up residence at the beautiful palace of Bailes, where the ambassadors of the Venetian Republic formerly stayed. The Ottoman Court received him with great distinction and accepted his credentials as a 'Naval Minister of his Britannic Majesty to the Ottoman Porte', a status that had no precedence but which, as *The Times* reported, 'related to the intimate connexion of the political system and power of Turkey with those of Great Britain'.[5] It was agreed that in future operations Smith would have supreme direction of all the naval forces of the Porte, whilst organisation of its land forces would be handed to General Köhler, an American of German extraction with 'penurious' habits.[6]

Days later, Smith and a number of his officers were admitted to a private audience with the grand seignior. They signed a defence alliance in which the Sultan accepted British protection and agreed to declare war on France. In semi-secret clauses, he also acknowledged the royalists' special status as part of the British expeditionary force. Wright became the diplomatic emissary between Sir Sidney, the Grand Vizier and the Paschas while John Keith, who abetted his escape from the Temple, was sent to Napoleon with secret proposals. As Smith told Lord Grenville, 'One does not catch flies with vinegar – therefore I offer them honey; and it is not to Buonaparte alone that I offer this *pont d'or* but by other channels indirectly to all individuals of his army.'[7]

Smith was convinced that Napoleon had privately accepted the principle of a Bourbon restoration and would implement the change in government if he returned to France unmolested. However, as he reminded France's general, his safe passage depended 'entirely on the British squadron cruising off Alexandria, and that, according to agreement with the Porte', his passports alone 'were valid with them and the Barbary powers, for British prisoners of war'.[8]

Napoleon, however, was not going to leave Egypt without a fight. By December 1798 French forces had subjugated much of Upper and Lower Egypt, massacring their inhabitants by the thousands. They then marched eastwards and, crossing the Sinai desert, captured Gaza, Ramleh and Jaffa successively before setting their sights on Acre, a fortress town in the classical Holy Land.

Smith was already well informed of Napoleon's intentions thanks to the successful interception of letters and infiltration of his army. On 19 February, he left Constantinople and sailed to Rhodes on *Le Tigre* in order to concert operations with Hussan Bey, the venerable Ottoman governor of that island, whom he described as 'my very old friend'.[9] Smith also recruited a mercenary force composed of Balkan troops, Albanians and Bosnians. En route, he fell in with HMS *Swiftsure* which was transporting to that island Joseph Beauchamp, the French consul-general of Muskat in Arabia. Beauchamp, a seasoned diplomat and distinguished astronomer, was sailing to Constantinople with orders to open secret negotiations with the Porte. His vessel, however, was intercepted and taken in disguise by a Turkish frigate, the *Okap*. Smith then sailed to Alexandria and, after having captured the *Mariamme*, a French gun vessel, he arrived on 3 March looking less like a British naval officer and more like a Turk with his curly black locks trimmed short 'à la Titus', high-bridged nose and enormous mustache.[10] He immediately relieved Captain Troubridge, the senior officer commanding the blockade, and dispatched Wright to Acre, attended by an interpreter of the English legation at Constantinople, to concert measures for the defence of that fortress with its notorious governor, Hadshi Ahmad Pasha al-Jazzār, a Bosnian by birth, otherwise fittingly known as 'the Butcher'.

Before setting off to Acre, Wright had landed Smith's own barge a short distance from Alexandria, 'not openly as a British naval officer but bearded, moustachioed and shawled à la Turque for the express purpose of obtaining valuable information'.[11] Just as he stepped on shore he warned the boat's crew, 'Men, beware of your words! I am going to serve my King and country, if, by the help of God, I can.' Then, turning to his commander, he exclaimed, 'Sir Sidney, do not forget the boat's crew.'[12] Watching his friend disappear into the night, Smith then rowed back to *Le Tigre* and after a few days chartered course to Acre.

On the evening of 15 March 1799, *Le Tigre* rounded the headland of Mount Carmel and entered the Bay of Acre. Once docked, Captain Miller from the *Thesus* and Colonel Phélippeaux came on board to report on the state of the city's defences. They had found the bastions and limestone walls on the landward side to be in a dilapidated state and virtually undefended except for a few cannon pointed towards the sea. With Jazzār's consent, Phélippeaux, a skilled engineer, set to work. Approximately 4,000 Turks, Syrians, Kurds, Albanians, Bosnians and Africans were immediately dragooned to reinforce the city's walls, to mount guns and stockpile ammunition. Smith meanwhile landed additional pieces of artillery, gunpowder, cannonballs and provisions for Acre's 15,000 inhabitants. He also put ashore 800 marines and seamen from two ships of the line and mounted on the ramparts a number of his ship's guns. He then posted pickets beyond the crenulated walls, lit fires and hung lanterns on the ramparts to illuminate the approaches at night and dispatched scouts to look out for Napoleon's approaching army.[13]

On the night of 17 March, the enemy's advanced guard was spotted at the foot of Mount Carmel by *Le Tigre's* guard boats. Reaching the city walls, the French forces bivouacked out of range of the guns and at nightfall began digging zigzag trenches, camouflaged behind straw bales. Then, just before dawn on 28 March, the artillery barrage began. Their objective was to breach the walls so that they could be scaled. They were instantly answered by punishing heavy fire from the fortress as well as from the British and Turkish ships anchored offshore. Forty French gunners fell and all but seven of their guns were rendered inoperable. Nevertheless, the French had forced a breach.[14]

A week later, on 6 April, Smith learned that the French troops were employed in mining the tower on the north-east side of the town wall. To thwart the operation, a party of British seamen and marines made a sally before daylight to gain possession of the mine, while Turkish troops assaulted both sides of the French trenches. The seamen pioneers were commanded by Wright, who, having been delayed *en passant* at Cyprus, had missed the beginning of the siege, much to his chagrin. Despite receiving two balls to the upper part of his right arm and a sabre thrust, he sprang the mine with the pikemen and, pulling down the supports, effected its destruction. His strength, however, was much reduced; being unable to climb out of the enemy's trenches, he fell to the ground.[15]

When it was reported that his friend had actually been killed, Smith's grief was so intense that he immediately summoned Colonel Douglas of the Royal Marines to his tent and asked him to retrieve Wright's corpse. The colonel turned to one of his men, a burly, red-haired Irish marine named James Close, and, pointing to the mass of carnage that lay in the ditch below, said, 'Close, dare you go there, and bring us the body of poor Wright?'[16] Obeying, Close stumbled over the morass of limbless bodies in search of his comrade. Despite being exposed to heavy musket fire, he managed to spot Wright lying wounded, not dead, and safely carry him away. The rescue complete, Close conveyed him to the hospital. Wright was then transported on the *Alliance* to a British camp in Beirut where he was left to coalesce, supposedly not far from the spot where Jonas was thought to have been thrown up from the whale's mouth.

In Beirut, Wright received regular reports from Smith on the progress of the siege. He was slowly recovering from his injuries, but the sweltering heat was having an effect on his 'weak nerves'. He was also deprived of use of his right arm due to musket shot. Yet, as he told Smith, he 'would willingly lose all the limbs' in order to 'conquer the iniquitous scoundrels' they were fighting. He was every day more convinced that theirs was the 'cause of all hope, the cause of all virtue, and humanity' and he hoped to be back 'in the smoke' as he could no longer bear the separation from his comrades-in-arms.[17] He learned that Napoleon had made several desperate attempts to carry the town after having levelled the north-east wall and made a lodgement in the north-east tower. Smith also told his close friend how his men had reverted to their 'old Chouan practices' by disseminating fake letters, one of which purported to be penned by Napoleon to the Directory in Paris alerting them of his army's distress. Napoleon was so infuriated by the success of this *ruse de guerre* that he reportedly tore the letter up in a paroxysm of rage.[18]

Smith also threw proclamations over the ramparts to stir up the republican soldiers who, he correctly judged, had lost the will to fight. One proclamation pretended to be issued from the Sublime Porte and bore its official imprimatur. It was addressed to 'the generals, officers and soldiers of the French army which has arrived in Egypt' and censured the Directory for its violation of the rights of man and for dispatching an army to Egypt in violation of the laws of war.[19] The proclamation also warned of the imminent arrival of 'innumerable armies and immense fleet' poised to strike and offered:

> Those amongst you, of whatever rank, who wish to escape from this danger which threatens you, must, without the least delay, indicate your intentions to the commanders of the land and sea forces of the allied powers who give safe guarantee that they will have them shipped wherever they desire to go, and will issue them with passports so that they will have free passage and need have nothing to fear from the allied fleets or any other battleships they encounter on their way.[20]

On 20 May, Wright learned that his friend Colonel Phélippeaux had perished from a fever brought on by want of rest and exposure to the sun. Before expiring he had been taken on board the HMS *Thesus*, but no ailment or medical treatment could save him from his affliction. That same day, Napoleon gave the order to retreat. For two months the opposing armies had been within a stone's throw of each other. The French had made no less than eleven desperate sallies to carry the fortress by assault and each time at a heavy cost. Furnished with shoes and water gourds, they began their gruelling retreat back across the Sinai desert, laying waste to the settlements en route. On 24 May the first columns arrived at Jaffa, where they camped for four days. It was there that Napoleon controversially administered laudanum, an opiate solution, to his feverish and plague-ridden soldiers. From there they continued to march southwards, reaching Gaza on 29 May and crossing the Sinai, passing El-Arish and Katia before entering Cairo on 14 June.

With his army reduced to half its original strength, his troops blinded by the sun and lacking basic provisions to cope with the intense desert conditions, Napoleon knew the game was up and on 17 August wrote to the Grand Vizier, commander of the Turkish army, proffering the terms of a general settlement.[21] He did not wait for the Vizier's reply and instead dispatched Lieutenant Descorches under flag of truce to parley with Sir Sidney on board *Le Tigre*. During the course of discussion, Smith was surprised to discover that Napoleon's camp had not received any news about the political and military situation in Europe for a number of months. Smelling an opportunity to cause mischief, he presented Descorches with two recent newspapers, the *Gazette de Francfort* and *Courrier Français de Londres*, dated 6 and 10 June, featuring articles about the reversal of France's fortunes.[22] They reported on the formation of the Second Coalition by Austria, Britain and Russia, the retreat of the French army across the Rhine, the British blockade of Malta, the Austrian invasion of French-occupied Italy, the defeat of republican forces at Mantua and their subsequent retreat to Genoa. The newspapers also reported how the French Atlantic fleet under Admiral Bruix, consisting of twenty-two battleships and eighteen frigates, was bottled up at Toulon under a British blockade, how La Vendée had erupted once again in fratricidal war and how the Jacobins were resurgent in the interior.[23]

In light of this information, Smith correctly predicted that Napoleon would abandon his Army of the Orient. He knew, from an intercepted letter, that the Directory wanted the general to return forthwith to France so that the Republic could concentrate its forces. He also had received intelligence from Wright in Alexandria that Admiral Honoré Joseph Antoine Ganteaume had two frigates waiting to leave at a moment's notice. Consequently, Smith granted Napoleon tacit permission to abscond on the condition that he return to France and take command of the Army of Italy. In exchange, Smith agreed that the British squadron would abandon its blockade of Alexandria.

With his dream of an oriental empire fading away, Napoleon resolved to leave Egypt. On 17 August, he received a despatch from Admiral Ganteaume in Alexandria notifying him that Smith had temporarily lifted the blockade. There was no time to spare. Quitting Cairo at night, he darted off in his carriage accompanied by five of his best generals, Berthier, Murat, Lannes, Marmont and Andréossy, as well as several aides and the court artist, Vivant Denon. They set off for Boulac and boarded a rivercraft at three in the morning, sailing down the Nile before transferring to horseback. On the afternoon of 23 August they reached the sea a few miles east of Alexandria, where they were greeted on the beach by Admiral Ganteaume and General Jacques Menou. At sunset, they were picked up by some sloops and transported to the frigates *La Muiron* and *La Carrère*, then riding at anchor offshore. On board, the generals scanned the horizon nervously for British ships. Napoleon, however, acted as if he had not a care in the world. Twice they caught sight of British ships off the North African coast, but by good fortune they managed to escape detection. In appalling weather, they reached Corsica on 30 September where Napoleon spent a few nights at his old home with his mother Letizia. Sailing thence, the ship ran into a severe gale and, after a forty-seven-day passage, they arrived off the coast of France. In the distance, the sails of British ships could be discerned through the shifting mist. The British took no action, supposing that they belonged to the Royal Navy, and let them through unmolested.[24] And so it was that on 9 October 1799 Napoleon landed at Fréjus, not far from Cannes, where, notwithstanding the disastrous failure of his expedition, he was acclaimed as a conquering hero.

13

GEORGES

With the popularity of the Directory at its nadir, speculation was rife that summer as to what form the government replacing it would take. So, when the news reached the royalists that Napoleon, after three weeks of political machinations, had seized power on 18 *Brumaire* (9 November 1799) they greeted it with great approbation, having deceived themselves into believing that France's 'saviour' would restore the Bourbons to their rightful seat and prevent the country from descending further into civil war. Napoleon was even reputed to have signed a *Pacte de Lyon* which agreed to the rendition of the throne to Louis XVIII in exchange for his appointment as lieutenant-general of the king's armies.[1] Louis thus waited idly by for Napoleon to communicate his intentions and finally, on 20 February 1800, after a 'transitional' period of four months, during which time Napoleon and Josephine had moved into the Tuileries, he belatedly wrote to the general recalling him to his engagement: 'Men such as you never inspire apprehension or uncertainty. You have accepted an eminent position and I know your opinion of it.' Having received no reply, he wrote a second letter, this time with added desperation. '... No, the conqueror of Italy and of Egypt cannot prefer an unfounded reputation to one of glory, you are wasting time, we can assure peace for France; I say we because I have need of Bonaparte for that, and he cannot do it without me. General, glory awaits you and I am patient to give peace to my people.'[2] Again, no reply. Instead, Napoleon turned his attention to the pacification of western France. He had been able to overthrow the Directory without much public opposition because of the overwhelming desire in the country for strong leadership and the termination of the war. However, until the royalists had been fully disarmed he could not claim to have realised either, at least not without inviting public ridicule.

On 27 December 1799, Napoleon summoned Hyde de Neuville to the Luxembourg Palace at ten o'clock at night for an interview in order to convince the young royalist leader to bring the partisans to his side. Neuville was so surprised by the diminutive figure before him that he first mistook Napoleon for a servant. The general walked across the room without taking any notice of Neuville and then, leaning his back against the chimney piece, raised his head and looked at the young royalist with such an expressive, penetrating glance that the other lost all assurance of himself. By Neuville's estimation, Napoleon had suddenly grown taller by 'a hundred cubits'.[3] The First Consul received him coldly but nevertheless tried to ingratiate himself to the royalist leader by pronouncing his admiration for the Vendéans who had served their cause 'nobly' but who now had little alternative but to render their arms to the newly installed government. The Consulate, he added, was resolved to make concessions at any costs but it must be understood that, though the Bourbons had honoured France in their resistance, the times demand that they now stand on the side of glory. Neuville listened respectfully to Napoleon's perambulations but when asked what he required to bring civil war to an end, he replied proudly, 'Two things, Louis XVIII to reign by right and Bonaparte to cover France with glory.'[4] The First Consul smiled without spreading his lips, but then added that if the Bourbons, whom he vowed never to restore, did not reconcile themselves peacefully to the Consulate, he would burn their 'towns and villages'. Following the interview, Napoleon issued a proclamation to the people wherein he granted amnesty to the rebels, cancelled the lists of proscriptions against the émigrés and restored liberty of worship on the proviso that they lay down their arms:

The authors of these troubles are the senseless partisans of two men who have neither done honour to their rank by virtue, nor to their misfortunes by exploits. Despised by the foreigner, whose hatred they have aroused, without inspiring his sympathy, they are, nevertheless, traitors, sold to England and tools of their fury ... To such men, the government owes neither consideration, nor a declaration of its principles; but there are citizens dear to their country who have been led astray by their artifices: it is to these citizens, that enlightenment and truth are due.[5]

Though these words were intended to cloak the extent of his concessions, it only served to remind the Vendéan leaders, even those among them who were tired of war, of Napoleon's bad faith and to make them reject at once terms that expounded such calumnies against Louis XVI's two younger brothers. Napoleon therefore issued a second proclamation in which he abandoned the promise of concessions in the former, espousing the most ferocious measures: 'Let me soon hear that the lives of the rebel leaders are ended! Be inexorable towards the brigands!'[6] Under his orders, Napoleon's minions put to the sword the same persons whom he disingenuously declared to so admire. Among the royalists executed was a friend of Neuville's, an eighteen-year-old officer named Toustain who served in the army of Maine and Anjou. The handsome officer was accused of travelling to Paris for the object of purchasing arms and munitions of war and, finding a few white cockades in his place of rest, was condemned by a Council of War and shot on the plain of Grenelle, eliciting murmurs of sympathy and indignation from the gathered crowd.[7] The royalists were incensed and promised to continue the struggle for God and king in honour of their fallen comrade. From the Channel to the Mediterranean, the Atlantic to the Rhine, disparate groups of Chouans staged attacks on various government posts. In response, Napoleon hastily dispatched reinforcements to General Guillaume Marie Anne Brune with orders to begin active operations. It took a fortnight to compel the insurgents' surrender. Crushed beneath the weight of enemy numbers, the Breton leaders Georges Cadoudal and Count de Ghaisnes de Bourmont tendered their submission. Louis de Frotté continued to resist in Normandy, but by the middle of February 1800 he was forced to temporarily lay down his arms and enter into negotiations with the Consulate. He and his officers were granted safe passage to meet and confer with General Guidal at his headquarters in Alençon, but hours after their arrival they were seized by twelve grenadiers at their inn, made prisoners and carted off to Paris. On their journey they stopped at Verneuil, and on orders of Joseph Fouché, the notorious Minister of Police, were brought before a court martial, condemned to death and shot just a few hours later.

Despite his 'invincible repugnance' at the promise of peace with the Napoleonic regime and the indignation that he felt at the perfidious execution of Louis de Frotté, a deed that brought the Vendéan war to an ignoble end, Georges Cadoudal kept his word of honour and travelled to Paris to parley with France's new ruler and conclude a treaty of peace. He knew what to expect from the good faith of Napoleon, as evidenced by Frotté's death, but the idea of appearing to retreat from danger decided him. And so, on 19 February 1800, the day before the First Consul and his wife, Josephine, were transported by a large coterie into the Tuileries Palace, Georges Cadoudal, among the last of the rebel leaders, had an interview with his nemesis. He was dressed like a rich Morbihan peasant, in Breton suspenders, large grey gaiters nearly touching his knees, a white quilted vest, a sabre hanging at his side and a soft felt hat sporting a white cockade, the edges of which, like his collar and lapels, were trimmed with a gold stripe. The burly Chouan was not the rude, untutored boor his enemies had hitherto regarded him as but was born a wealthy miller's son in the village of Kerléano, situated in the parish of Brech, Lower Brittany, and was the recipient of a stern and complete education at the college of Vannes.[8] He admitted having been first intoxicated by the revolutionary ideals but when the cherished symbol of his faith had been trampled upon Georges heart revolted, and crossing the Vilaine with a band of determined men he joined the Vendéan army. And though he would suffer many failures, his commitment to a cause so sacred to his heart would never falter.

The meeting lasted in excess of two hours, during which time he listened as Napoleon tried to attach the obstinate Chouan to his rising fortunes. He offered him a choice between the rank of general of division in the army of Italy and a pension of 100,000 francs, but on the condition that he refrain from mingling in France's politics. Georges, barely concealing his contempt, refused to be conquered, to the growing fury of his opponent who, having exhausted his eloquence, was exasperated by the Chouan's iron will. The two men thus parted with renewed hatred for each other, and upon leaving the Tuileries, Georges, gritting his perfectly white teeth after having repressed his anger for so long, held out his tense arms and exclaimed, 'How I should have liked to crush him with these strong arms!'[9] He was, it is true, physically powerful, with broad shoulders and a bulging corpulence. His head was also remarkable for its prodigious thickness, and so perfectly round was it that it earned him the fond nickname General 'Rond-Tête'.[10] He had very short, light chestnut hair, rather dense and curly at the front. His eyes were grey and of unequal size and his nose looked squashed but enlarged at the tip. With a friend, La Carrière, he and Neuville soon left from Boulogne for England, after having received intelligence from Louis Duperou, the new head of the royalists' surveillance organisation, the 'counter police', that the Central Bureau of Police had just announced a fresh conspiracy to restore the monarchy, and that renewed denunciations had been made against them with warrants about to be issued for their arrest.[11] They were delayed by bad weather and also by Georges' insistence that he attend midnight Mass. That night, as dark clouds rolled across the sky, they braved the stormy passage in a boat that, though of sturdy design, was almost swallowed up by the heavy sea.

Before leaving Paris, Hyde entrusted the Abbé Goddard, an elderly defrocked priest, with the disposal of the papers relating to the 'English Committee', the poorly named clandestine royalist agency of which he was a leading member. Having passed the cipher to one agent, Goddard was instructed to deliver the correspondence on Duperou's counter-police to another agent at Livry and destroy the rest. Goddard, however, took it upon himself to hawk some of the royalist propaganda tracts, such as the 'witty' *Les Adieux de Bonaparte*, instead of restricting their distribution through safe channels.[12] His 'extreme frivolity' would cost the organisation dear. He was spotted by a police spy handing two copies of the pamphlet in public to a well-known royalist and was followed. On 3 May the police staged a raid at the agency's headquarters, at the home of one Madame Mercier, and found two or three parcels of pamphlets and correspondence. A commission of four Councillors of State was appointed to examine the discovered papers once they were deciphered. The seizure then led to the arrests of Hyde de Neuville's wife and brother and the Chevalier de Coigny, the king's intermediary.

The arrest of the head of the 'counter-police', Louis Duperou, soon followed. He knew nothing of these unhappy events, having already left for London in order to coordinate his activities with his chief British contact, Charles Flint at the Alien Office. Duperou owed his employment to William Huskisson, formerly the Superintendent of Aliens, whom he had supposedly met by chance at a café in London a year earlier and whom he reputedly impressed by his perfect command of five languages and service to General Francisco de Miranda, the legendary Venezuelan revolutionary.[13] Miranda gave his permission for the German-born Duperou to be covertly employed by the British government. So, issued with an Alien Office passport and a forged French one, he installed himself in France's capital with the intention of procuring intelligence within the interior. He had formerly held a minor bureaucratic post at the Ministry of Foreign Affairs which gave him access to government officials but his most important commission was to reorganise the 'counter-police', which had been disrupted following 18 *Fructidor*, in order to thwart the operations of the real police.[14] He used his connections to recruit moles to penetrate the secrets of the Central Bureau's headquarters, at 11–13 Quai Voltaire (today Malaquais). Among other artifices, the 'counter-police' produced daily bulletins which were sent to Napoleon in order to deceive him as to the apparent state of disaffection in France.

In London, Duperou and Charles Flint discussed plans for the French interior which were subsequently formalised in a memorandum drafted at the Alien Office. The plan envisaged a multi-pronged attack beginning with the seizure of Calais by 2,000–3,000 men assembled at Dover. At the same time, a small expeditionary force would take the Isle d'Houat off the coast of Brittany and set up communications with the royalists in the west. Once secured, a Russian army of 25,000 troops would invade northern France whilst additional men and munitions were landed along the coast.[15]

Unfortunately, Duperou was betrayed by the failings of his own intelligence gathering. Upon landing in Calais he was seized by Citizen Mengaud, the commissary of police at the Pas de Calais who was awaiting his expected arrival with a detachment of gendarmes. Duperou had tried to pass himself off as *Pierre Geoffre* but the gendarmes were not deceived by his Prussian passport or fabrications, being in possession of a full physical description of him.[16] He was arrested on 23 May, and despite managing to escape two days later he was recaptured on 13 June. During this interlude he had continued to correspond with Charles Flint and Henry Stow, an agent from the Alien Office at Dover who had procured him a passport from the Prussian ambassador, Baron Jacobi-Kloest in London. The copies of his letters were seized, deciphered, edited and, together with the correspondence found at one Madame Seigner's home, published on Napoleon's orders under the title *Conspiration Anglaise* (*English Conspiracy*) in order to give the discovery of the plot the widest possible publicity. In total, 164 individuals were implicated and prosecuted.[17]

* * *

Exactly one week after Duperou's capture, uncertain news reached Paris of a highly contested battle that had been fought in the small village of Marengo in Piedmont. It was not until the following morning, during a reception of the diplomatic corps held at the Tuileries Palace, that official confirmation arrived from two French couriers that Napoleon had scored an important victory and that the Austrians were in full retreat. Admitted into the private antechambers of the Consuls, the most prominent ministers and officials were treated to a highly coloured account of the day's proceedings. Despite the acclamations, Napoleon, thinking the battle was lost, had actually conceded defeat to the Austrians and made preparations to flee.[18] His plans were disrupted once he received news of General Desaix's arrival with reinforcements and General François Kellerman's powerful cavalry charge. The battle, in either event, proved to be a turning point in Napoleon's military career. Ten days after having acceded to an armistice, he was back in Paris to a triumphant reception. He had, as a matter of fact, returned in discretion, being not altogether assured of his position. Despite his successes that summer, he knew that discontent ran high among many of his generals and that, with his back turned, they had intrigued to dislodge him from power.[19]

This, at least, was the intelligence which the king's agents in France were propagating. Wickham reported how he had received a letter from a friend in Paris who described the feeling of '*une sorte de terreur*' that prevailed in the capital. Accordingly, Lord Grenville instructed him to hurry General Charles Pichegru back to London 'with the least notice and observation possible.'[20] It was hoped that Pichegru could convert the generals' dissatisfaction into action, having enjoyed their confidence and friendship in days gone by. However, although he travelled with great haste to London, he did not reach the capital before the end of June by which time Napoleon's victory at Marengo had dramatically, and negatively, changed the situation.

The Battle of Marengo dealt a 'devastating personal blow' to Wickham.[21] With the destruction of General Melas' army, all hopes of sponsoring an insurrection had ended. He became despondent and twice tendered his resignation as Under Secretary of State at the Home Office to the Duke of Portland. He retreated to an abbey in Munster, where for almost three months he withdrew from the world. He was not, however, deprived of all luxury. As he confided, 'Obscure as this corner is, it is not without its comforts and its pleasures, among which I mention an ice house in this sun season – then the best Hungarian wine – delicious fish, and more delicious figs – and a theatre where we have heard Haydn's *Creation* performed by a band of above forty musicians, not to mention a large and well furnished observatory with all the best modern instruments and an excellent and extensive library.' He ruminated about joining a Benedictine monastery and taking up residence in Upper Austria, which he found to be 'one of the most delightful and habitable countries' he had ever visited.[22] The Duke of Portland reassured him that, despite the failure of his enterprises, his position at the Home Office was secure and that his actions had met the satisfaction of England's ministers as well as the approbation of the king himself. Nevertheless, Wickham was entirely disillusioned with the Austrians and particularly the pusillanimity of Baron Thugut, whose actions had reduced the fighting capability of the Imperial army to the point where it had squandered all former advantages. He had good reason to complain, having expended £666,666 per month on the Austrians and all to no avail. The time had thus come to take more drastic measures.[23]

Since Napoleon's triumphant return from Marengo, the secret police had reported the proliferation of amateur attempts on his life. They included one attempt to 'catapult missiles' into his moving carriage on the road to his retreat at Malmaision and a second to accost him during a forest hunt. Despite Napoleon's complaints, Fouché insisted that the Ministry of Police, which he superintended since the end of August 1799, could not be held accountable for either these acts, especially as every *attentat* had been followed by the arrest or execution of one or all of its perpetrators. This was not an empty boast. He had, in fact, created a *bureau particulier* (or special branch) within the Haute Police to uncover all plots and conspiracies hatched within the interior, appointing as its departmental head (or *Chef de la Sûreté*) his secretary, a thirty-something defrocked priest named Pierre Marie Desmarest. This was in keeping with his basic adage that 'the first pledge for the safety of any government whatever is a vigilant police'.[24]

Desmarest, a former Jacobin, was the son of a breeches maker from Fontainebleau, of small stature but 'quite rotund'. He was a skilful administrator, both intelligent and cautious. He had a wide range of interests including botany, phrenology, esotericism and astrology.[25] As head of the secret police he excelled in the examination of prisoners, deceiving them by his geniality before serving them to the judges 'beautifully cooked'.[26] One contemporary described him as an 'orderly and upright' person, possessing that gravity and discretion that are 'the mark of the honest man'. Fouché considered him to be 'a supple and sly man'.[27] Others were less admiring and denounced his cynicism and brutality. He was accused of sending his benefactor to the scaffold and causing his own brother, whose poverty was an affront to his affluence, to be transported to Cayenne where he subsequently perished. He also lorded violently over his wife and child and kept a mistress under the same roof.

Despite the Consulate's attempts to repress knowledge of these incidents, reports of them made their way to Louis XVIII at Mittau. By now, there was no doubt that Napoleon would never support a Bourbon restoration. For on 7 September 1800 the First Consul finally replied to Louis XVIII's letters of the previous December and February, extinguishing all hope:

> I have received your letter, Monsieur. I thank you for the honest things you tell me. You must not wish to return to France, it could only be over 500,000 dead bodies. Sacrifice your interest to the peace and prosperity of France, history wills you to account for it. I am not insensible to the misfortunes of your family; I will contribute with pleasure to the pleasures and tranquillity of your retirement.[28]

Even if he did not endorse assassination, the king probably took small pleasure in the government's concern about public disinterest in Napoleon's fate. With ten reported assassination attempts by December that year, one would sooner or later succeed.[29]

And one very almost did.

14

THE RUE NIÇAISE BOMB

Monsieur Durand had come to Paris to claim his father's confiscated estate in the *département* Côte-du-Nord and had chanced to find a room to rent on the rue Neuve-Saint-Roch, at the corner of the rue Moineaux, owned by Citizen Leclerc, a pastry cook. Durand was thirty-two but apparently looked beyond his years. He reached only five feet two inches and was of slender build, with a very long and thin face, a high forehead, an eagle's nose and a dimpled chin. Judging by his brilliant white teeth, he had no need for the dentist's brush. He was also very well groomed. His boots were immaculately polished, his blue trousers never creased and his hat, with its mother-of-pearl buckle, was impeccably clean.[1] Durand's real name was Picot de Limoelan, and along with Robinault de Saint-Réjant, an old officer of the marines, and a young subaltern named Carbon, otherwise known as 'Little Francis', he had come to Paris for the sole object of assassinating Napoleon Bonaparte.

The conspirators had originally planned to shoot Napoleon at short range, but upon discovering that their target only travelled in a closed carriage, surrounded by an armed escort with drawn sabres, they had to conceive of another method; and so it was decided that what could not be achieved by bullets could be by gunpowder. In mid-December, Carbon purchased a little black mare barely bigger than a pony and a light, two-wheeled cart, approximately five feet long, from a seed merchant in the rue

Meslée named Monsieur Lambel. He paid 200 francs and when asked his profession, Carbon, who prior to this engagement made a living as a highwayman, returned that he was a hawker and that he needed the cart to transport the linen that he sold in the marketplace.[2]

Once the money had exchanged hands, he pulled the cart to a stable that he had already hired at no. 19 rue Paradis and placed an iron-bound cask upright in the cart and fixed a large tarpaulin on top. On Christmas Eve 1800, Carbon and de Limoelan arrived at the stable dressed as carters. They harnessed the horse to the cart and, leading it by the bridle, led it to the Porte Saint Denis whereupon they removed the cask and transported it to the domicile of Citoyenne Vallon, a laundress who resided at the rue Saint Martin. They were joined by Saint-Réjant, and together the three men, with great effort, poured gunpowder into the cask and lifted it onto a hand-barrow, dragging it to the cart outside. Down the rue Neuve-Egalité they led the horse, pulling its heavy burden, and on the way they would bend down, pick up flints and pebbles and toss them into the cart. On reaching the Place des Victoires Carbon parted, leaving the other two to convey the cart to the Place du Carrousel, the public square situated in front of the splendid Palace of the Tuileries. A few paces from the Carrousel stood the old Hôtel Longueville, where they parked the cart against the opposite wall and, lifting the tarpaulin off, placed a slow match, with one end in the cask and the other dangling under the cart's cover. At half-past seven, Limoelan bade his partner good luck and walked to the corner of the Carrousel, where he was to look out for Napoleon's cavalcade. Saint-Réjant, meanwhile, swung the mare around so that the cart was stationed far enough across the street to encroach on traffic. Just as the moment was at hand, he happened to encounter a young thirteen- or fourteen-year-old girl named Pensol, whose mother sold rolls in the rue du Bac, walking past and offered her twelve *sous* if she would hold the horse by the bridle for a few seconds. They would be the last of her life.[3]

Napoleon had planned to hear Haydn's magnificent oratorio of the *Creation* at the Opera, but on the first night of its performance it happened that he was running late. Upon climbing into his carriage, he ordered the coachman to drive furiously. With a sharp tug on the reigns, the horses charged off. He was accompanied by Lannes, Bessières and Alexandre Berthier, three future marshals of France, and guarded by two grenadiers on horseback. Just as the escort emerged from the Tuileries courtyard, Limoelan, who was posted near its entrance and was entrusted with the task of signalling Napoleon's approach, momentarily froze. It is not quite certain whether he was seized by a pang of conscience, but in any case, his partner, Saint-Réjant, was caught unawares by the speed at which the grenadiers' horses were galloping. He had calculated that it would take six or seven seconds for the fuse to burn, which was time enough to escape the explosion, but in fact it took longer than this, so the coach driver, who was cursing at the obstruction on the road, succeeded in pushing past. A moment later the carriage was rocked by an explosion. The grenadiers felt themselves lifted off their saddles. Ten seconds later, the coachman, having turned into the rue St Honoré, pulled the horses to a standstill and climbed down from his cabin, checking behind to see that no one was injured. By singular chance, only Mademoiselle Beauharnais had received a slight injury to her right hand. Lannes alighted to survey the scene. Napoleon, so the legend goes, just shrugged; turning to the coachman, he cried, 'Drive to the opera!'[4]

At the moment of the explosion, Joseph Fouché and his subordinate Pierre François Réal were entering the opera. Upon hearing what happened, they darted off on foot, each taking a different route, to the spot where the explosion reportedly took place. Police agents were already at the scene, scouring for evidence. The rue Niçaise was filled with ruins. Glass was shattered everywhere. Beams, tiles, windowsills and fragments of stone and brick were tossed all over the perimeter. Twisted, mangled corpses lay strewn about. Naked souls walked in a daze, their clothes stripped from their bodies. Pensol lay in the gutter, her arms slung on either side of the road. Two days later, her grief-stricken mother recuperated her charred remains.[5] The cart had disappeared. The horse's carcass lay in flames amid the ruins, its limbs so violently torn asunder that only a single leg could be recognised. Réal, observing a hoof and fragments of the cart, motioned a sentinel to be placed on guard so that all the blacksmiths and cartwrights could be summoned to examine the evidence. And so, in one of history's first example of forensic investigation, the hunt for the authors of the 'infernal machine' began.[6]

No sooner had news of the affair spread through Paris that the grand salon on the ground floor of the Tuileries was brimming with a crowd of functionaries waiting to pay homage to France's ruler, who had just returned from the opera. 'This is the work of the Jacobins; they have attempted my life!' he exclaimed. 'There are neither nobles, priests, nor Chouans in this affair! ... I know what I am about, and they need not think to impose on me ... It is scarce three months since my life was attempted by Céracci, Aréna, Topino-Lebrun, and Démerville. They all belong to one gang!'[7] The last was a reference to the attempt by a gang of vengeful Corsicans who were found armed with daggers waiting for Napoleon outside the Opera a month earlier. Fouché hazarded to point out that no evidence could be produced against the Jacobins and that before they be accused it would be right to ascertain their guilt. This naturally was not what the First Consul wanted to hear from his Minister of Police, and he reproached him violently on this point. Fouché, great actor that he was, kept inflexibly calm, his countenance betraying no emotion, whilst Napoleon raged on.

A Council of State was convoked the following day. It proposed reinstating the revolutionary tribunals, the notorious instruments of death which despatched countless victims to the guillotine during the Reign of Terror. Napoleon, however, was unsatisfied with the measure and demanded immediate retribution. He complained, 'The tribunals you talk of would be too slow in action. More drastic vengeance is needed, something as rapid as gunfire. *Blood must flow!* As many culprits must be shot as there were victims.' He was seconded by Antoine Claire Thirabeau, one of the council's members, who added, 'It is no longer a question of judging according to existing laws or according to laws that have yet to be passed, but of deporting and shooting as a measure of public safety.'[8] Fouché accordingly submitted a report to his master more concordant with his prejudices. An exemplary punishment was served but not to the real authors of the crime. Two individuals, having the misfortune of formerly possessing a barrel of powder, of which they could not render a satisfactory account, were expiated for the crime and forfeited their lives on 31 January 1801. Of course, no specific charges were brought against them but it was presumed from their past conduct that only they could have been the infernal machine's contrivers. The first was a pyro-technician with Jacobin sympathies named Alexandre Joachim Chevalier. He was credited with the invention of *oeufs rouge*, or *oeufs incendiaires*, a type of hand grenade that exploded like a Molotov cocktail.[9] He was arrested on 7 November along with his accomplice Pierre Vecyer, who had betrayed him. A primitive 'multi-firing gun' was seized at their warehouse. In their plan to assassinate Napoleon they included the use of fireworks to frighten the horses and iron spikes laid in the streets in order to bar mounted troops rushing to his assistance.

The police directed their investigation against other political undesirables and unearthed evidence which was specious at best. Nevertheless, it had the intended ramifications for the remaining Jacobin factions. Possessing no authority to exact punishment, the government took recourse to what has been called 'an extraordinary act of high police', and by a *senatus consultum* the guardians of France's constitution gave by decree what the government could not otherwise have enforced by law. The most violent measures were proposed against the Jacobins. Forty were banished to the Seychelles, an altogether different experience from what tourists enjoy today.[10] A list of proscribed names was jumbled together, among which was a man long dead and a second who had quitted France four years before. The senate's obsequiousness in the face of government pressure alarmed many observers as to the precedence that this act would have. Fouché nevertheless drafted the list of the 130 proscribed names, and although he submitted it dutifully to Napoleon he remained undeceived as to the real authors of the crime.

In fact, Fouché knew more than he let on. On 16 November, just over a month before the attack, he had received a note informing him that a royalist priest, the Abbé Ratel, a former member of the

Paris Agency known otherwise as *Le Moine*, had arranged for a 'large sum of money' to be handed to the Chouan leader General Bourmont, who was then in Paris. The courier was François Carbon, who, as it turned out, was the servant of Achille Bijet, a known close confidant of Georges Cadoudal. Together with the forensic evidence from the scene and eyewitness statements, Fouché turned the focus of his investigations on the Chouans.[11]

Following the attack, Carbon had taken refuge in a convent where he remained for three weeks. He passed the time assisting the nuns and attending all the services. His boredom, however, got the better of him; unable to cope with the claustrophobic surroundings, he ventured outside. It was to his ruin. He was instantly recognised, probably on account of his diminutive size (he only reached five feet one inch) and the scar above his left eye, and followed by a police agent who, on 18 January 1801, knocked at the door of the convent with an order for his arrest.[12]

Ten days later, a soldier patrol happened to cross Saint-Réjant in the rue du Jour. For nearly a week he had been wandering the city streets, too afraid to enter a stranger's house. Punishment was certain, and on 20 April 1801 the two men went to their deaths. Picot de Limoelan was never found. At the time of their trial he had sought refuge in the deserted vaults of the church of Saint-Laurent, and remained there for four months under the protection of his cousin the Abbé Joseph Picot de Clos Rivierea and a former nun, Mademoiselle de Cice. It was not until May that he felt safe to leave its walls and, quitting Paris, he set off for his beloved homeland, Brittany. It is not certain what became of him. Some believed that he retired to America, where, having adopted his uncle's name, he posed as a priest.[13]

Georges still remained at large. The Chouan had, so it was claimed, burst into a violent fit of anger upon hearing of the failed assassination attempt: 'I could wager that this is some hare-brained doing of that blockhead Saint-Réjant. He, no doubt, wished to be able to come and boast to us that he, by his unaided hand, had rid us of Bonaparte. He has damaged all my plans. Besides, we are not yet in a condition to act.'[14] The evidence against him was limited to two letters, one obscured by unidentifiable handwriting, the other penned by Saint Réjant but bearing neither the name nor address of the person to whom it was addressed. However, to the authorities it was evident that he was the mastermind, given his position of leadership and close ties to the perpetrators. A reward of 24,000 francs was therefore offered to anyone who delivered him 'dead or alive'.[15] His movements were eventually tracked to England where, not without good reason, the government of William Pitt was suspected of having sponsored the attack.

In England, Georges had been received by the government with great distinction, despite having long been regarded with suspicion, and along with a letter of felicitations received from Louis XVIII at Mittau, he received the *Cordon Rouge* and other honours conferred upon him by the former's younger brother, the Comte d'Artois. He was introduced to London's polite society where he assumed the airs of a gentleman, modelling his comportment upon that of the British ministers with whom he was placed in contact. Although he self-consciously moderated his manners, it was said that he harboured a love of refinement and that upon arriving in London that April he booked himself into Grillon's on Brook street, the most fashionable hotel of the day.[16] It was also related that he wrapped himself in fine linen and had even refused to be seen in Piccadilly with one of his followers whom he complained was not attired to his fussy standards. However, it was not long before Georges grew tired of his life of inaction; unable to master his impatience any longer, he set sail for Brittany in September, supposedly with £20,000 of Britain's money tucked away in his purse. He had been keen to rejoin the Chouans in the insurgent provinces and busy his time with forming new plans for insurrection. His intuition, however, told him that the theatre for *chouannerie* should be transferred from the west to Paris and that it was there, in the political capital, where the *coup essentiel* against Napoleon should be struck.

England's ministers perfectly understood the meaning of this and similar expressions. On 13 August, the staunch Minister of War, Windham William, noted in his diary that Napoleon would 'be cut off before two months are over, though professes not to know specifically of such intention, seems to think that the course of proceeding legitimate and has thrown out the idea to Pitt, as he had done before to me. Not necessary to say that no countenance was given to it.'[17] Then, on 16 September, Windham recorded a conversation with General Charles Pichegru in which the Frenchman 'talked of the design to cut off Bonaparte by assassination and of the general instability of the government to which latter opinion I felt inclined to assent. On the other hand, having before expressed my opinion I did not now say anything.'[18]

Windham may not have countenanced the idea of assassination, so he claimed, but he did lobby the incoming ministry of Lord Henry Addington, 1st Viscount Sidmouth, for Georges' safe repatriation back to England. Addington, the former Speaker of the House, had assumed office on 14 March 1801 following Pitt and Grenville's resignation over the divisive question of Catholic emancipation. The matter, however, required some delicacy. At this time, preliminary peace discussions had begun between Lord Hawkesbury, who now held the seals of the Foreign Office, and Louis-Guillaume Otto, a civil servant at the French Foreign Ministry. The initiatives had come at a time of great disaffection in Britain, during which a movement favouring the restoration of peace was gathering momentum. It was strengthened by the Treaty of Lunéville, which had been signed on 9 February 1801 between France and the Holy Roman Empire following General Victor Moreau's crushing defeat of the second allied coalition at Hohenlinden two months earlier. The terms were personally humiliating for Francis II, who was forced to cede his title of Holy Roman Emperor.

Although hostilities between England and France had not been suspended, great care had to be taken not to irritate Napoleon. However as Windham, one of the retiring ministers, argued, it was Britain's moral duty to take immediate measures to save Georges owing to the services he had rendered. In a private letter to Lord Hawkesbury, he urged that Georges' life was 'in the most imminent danger every moment that he stayed in France'.[19] Moreover, once the war came to an end, nothing could be done to extricate him. Hawkesbury agreed. Noel Prigent, a royalist agent, was accordingly dispatched to Brittany to arrange for the safe repatriation of Georges and approximately fifty other Chouans who were in British pay or whose former activities made it expedient that they escape from France before the conclusion of peace. Most of them were smuggled back to Jersey. Addington's ministry considered sending them to Canada. Georges himself was safely conveyed back to London, where he arrived at the end of March 1801. The British authorities, however, were anxious that his presence in England not be made known to France, so he was deliberately kept away from the capital and installed first in Dunstable and then in St Albans, north of London.

Georges still visited the great metropolis and eventually lodged in Down Street, Piccadilly. During his time, he passed by the name of Masson and benefited from a weekly allowance of £8 from his hosts.[20] He also maintained a correspondence with his Chouans in the Channel Islands whilst trying to embroil the British government in his violent schemes. The months in exile otherwise passed without event, but then, in October that year, an announcement was made to the public that the preliminaries of a peace accord between Britain and France had, after protracted negotiation, been reached.

15

THE AMIENS INTERLUDE

Shortly before eight o'clock, on the morning of 10 November 1801, the thirty-seven-year-old Sir Sidney Smith arrived at Whitehall on horseback attired in Turkish dress with a turban, robe and shawl. A girdle was wrapped around his waist with a brace of pistols. He had landed in Portsmouth the day before having endured a long and stormy passage, during which he dined on stewed rats, as was his unusual predilection. To his mortification, however, he discovered that the news of Britain's final victory in Egypt had arrived a fortnight earlier from another ship carrying duplicate despatches. He was also piqued to discover that his rival, Lord Horatio Nelson, was glorified by his countrymen, despite his own fair claim to having removed the French threat from the Levant. He was, nevertheless, received as a hero in his own right. At Guildhall he received a magnificent sword from the Corporation of London and was presented with the Freedom of the City. In his acceptance speech he represented the sword as the most honourable reward which could have been conferred on him. In peace it would stand as 'his proudest ornament', and in war he would draw it 'in defence of his country and for the protection of the city of London'. Then, accompanied by the Lord Mayor and several of the Aldermen, Smith retired into the Painted Room, where he placed a handsome donation in gold into the poor box before leaving amid the rapturous applause of an immense concourse of people assembled outside.[1]

The same day that Smith rode triumphantly into London, Britain's new minister plenipotentiary, Francis James Jackson, set out on his diplomatic mission to Paris. He was appointed to the post in place of Antony Merry, the British envoy, who had been instructed to accompany the elderly Marquis Cornwallis, the former Governor General of India and Ireland, to the town of Amiens in order to conduct negotiations for a general pacification now that the preliminary peace agreement had been ratified.

The news of Jackson's diplomatic mission generated enormous excitement in London. Before leaving, he was invited to a dinner soirée at the residence of Louis-Guillaume Otto, the French chargé d'affaires, to celebrate the cause of peace. On the table the Union Jack and Tricolour flags were balanced on the centre plateau symbolising Britain and France's pretended union of interests. The evening was attended by a number of distinguished guests including a 'great *célébrité*', the famous chevalier Mademoiselle d'Éon, who, for nearly forty years, served the French service masquerading as a man. Besides receiving well-wishes Jackson was beset by scores of émigrés entreating him to pass on parcels to their friends and relatives in France. At the Foreign Office boxes and packages had piled up 'without end' directed to his care as well as innumerable commissions for the purchase of French silk, lace and cambric.[2]

On 22 November, Jackson dined at Talleyrand's residence on the Place de la Concorde, attended by France's chief ministers as well as Generals Moreau, Berthier and Massena. He was seated next to Napoleon's brother, and head of the French delegation at Amiens, Joseph Bonaparte, who accorded him great civility and attention. The following day, Jackson and his younger brother, George, observed the First Consul for the first time at a parade that was staged in the courtyard of the Tuileries palace. It was, in their estimation, an unrivalled display of the 'pomp and circumstance of war'.[3] Amassed in the courtyard were cavalry, infantry and artillery as well as numbers of field officers, generals and commanders of different ranks, all wearing splendid uniforms embroidered in gold and silver. George Jackson noticed how even the upper parts of the boots had tracings or inlays of gold. The proceedings began with the Consular Guard carrying the French colours to the audience chamber where Napoleon waited. He then mounted a white charger with rich trappings. Like many foreign observers, Jackson was struck by the appearance of the First Consul. The caricatures in the English newspapers depicted him as a 'miserable pigmy: hollow eyed, yellow skinned, lantern jawed, lank hair and a disproportionately large nose'. But, as he confided in his diary, he was surprised to find in Napoleon's countenance and bearing a 'mastermind', a man 'born to rule'.[4]

The following weeks passed without great event. Then, on 12 December, Jackson heard rumours circulating of a conspiracy that was afloat to overthrow the Consulate. It was reported that inflammatory handbills were being openly distributed and that the government was subject to harsh criticism in public. The Haute Police were vigilantly scouring the streets for the supposed conspirators but it was believed that Fouché had deliberately magnified the danger in order to claim credit for its suppression. It was nevertheless apparent that Parisian society was 'rife with intrigue, plots and counterplots'.[5] Not a day passed without George Jackson being reminded of the necessity for caution and circumspection in his every word and deed. Fouché had, in Jackson's estimation, established a system of espionage that equalled the one notoriously practised by Jean-Charles Pierre Lenoir, the twelfth Lieutenant-Général de Police de Paris under the *ancien régime*. It was believed that there did not exist a single family in the capital considered 'worthy of notice' who did not employ one or more servants in Fouché's pay. Naturally, given the prevailing climate of suspicion, the Jacksons supposed that any servant or maid that waited on them was also employed by the Minister of Police. Fouché, it was commonly believed, was acquainted with the private transactions of every individual, including the First Consul, who was disturbed to find himself the object of his minister's observation. The omnipresence of moles was self-defeating, so Jackson supposed, as it inevitably put people on their guard. He also found it amusing that whilst Fouché contrived to find out what others were doing and saying, an 'unexpected person' had discovered that he was conspiring with an 'officer of high standing' to overthrow Napoleon and install a new form of government.[6] As it turned out, the officer in question was Jean Victor Moreau, the victor of Hohenlinden.

Ever since the peace of Lunéville, signed on 9 February 1801, General Moreau had been living in retirement in the hamlet of Gros Bois, which he had purchased from the ex-Director Paul Barras, then exiled to Brussels by Napoleon. He affected to remain aloof from the business of government, preferring the quiet retreat of the country where he could rest on his laurels and leave the management of his affairs to others. But his indifference to its seductive power, like his ambivalence to ceremonial honours, was probably an affectation, for he had imprudently attempted, at the prompting of his friends, to lecture the First Consul on the art of politics and the business of administration soon after his return from the army to Paris. He had failed to influence the younger Napoleon, who received him in a most frigid manner. Napoleon's animus towards Moreau, so Jackson supposed, was perhaps actuated by professional jealously as well as resentment of the high estimation in which he was regarded in public.

In private, Moreau confided to Jackson that, unless the monarchy was established in the form of Louis XVIII, he would take no part in any *coup d'état*. He professed not to be a royalist in the traditional sense but that he was nevertheless convinced that the restoration of the 'rightful Dynasty' was absolutely essential for the fulfilment of peace and prosperity in France. He also claimed that he had no desire to abrogate exclusive power to himself, that he coveted no reward other than the honorary title of 'High Constable of France' and that his sole object was to protect the monarchy at the moment of its restoration. As he told Jackson, 'the effort to establish success in this enterprise would be short although perhaps violent, that it would require the sum of a million and a half livres'.[7]

Surprisingly, Jackson also met Fouché. He suspected that the minister of police would not consent to any plan as it clashed too much with his own principles and personal ambitions. He also surmised that the only point on which the two men were fully agreed was that Bonaparte should be removed from office. Yet he was doubtful that the affair amounted to anything more than empty talk as he could not conceive how such wholly disparate characters could possibly be in league together. Fouché, Jackson judged, was 'coarse-minded, vulgar, and brutal'. He also found him physically 'repulsive', with his small, hooded grey eyes and thin lips. The Minister of Police was certainly a man with few principles. A habitual liar with a bloodstained past, he had gained notoriety for superintending the massacres at Lyons, so it was said, on horseback with a pair of human ears dangling from the side of his hat. Nevertheless, he remains a remarkable historical figure, 'the peer of Philip II, Tiberius or Cesare Borgia', an unrivalled master of duplicity and manipulation.[8]

Moreau could scarcely have been more different. He was handsome, witty and in possession of a naturalness and simplicity of manners that women, at least, found attractive. He had a dark complexion, a full, round face, a strong nose, sensual lips and a well-formed chin. Though unassuming, his eyes sparkled when he spoke freely of subjects that interested him. His conversations were mostly one-sided, as he rarely entered into a dialogue of any length. He was otherwise an accomplished soldier, efficient and knowledgeable but not endowed with any brilliant qualities or political discernment.

Then, on 26 March 1802, a courier arrived from Amiens bringing news that the peace treaty was about to be signed. He had made the journey in just nine and a half hours, having galloped at a tremendous pace. Immediately upon his arrival he presented Maurice Talleyrand with a preliminary copy of the treaty. Having scanned its contents, the inimitable Minister of Foreign Affairs quickly brought it to the attention of Napoleon, who was then engaged in the Council of State. Interrupting the proceedings, Talleyrand read it out aloud to the assembled members, adding that there were no secret provisions. The effect was instant rapture. At approximately five o'clock that afternoon, a round of cannon fire was discharged announcing to Parisians the glad tidings of peace. Celebrations broke out in the streets. In the theatres, plays were interrupted as messengers burst onto the stage announcing the news to an ecstatic audience.

The Treaty of Amiens was signed the following day. Despite the public acclamations, not everyone was happy with the prospect of peace. Behind the scenes, Napoleon was violently denounced not only by extremists on both sides of the political spectrum but also by dissident generals who were jealous and unemployed now that France was no longer at war.[9] To neutralise the pretended threat, Napoleon chose to disperse them. He accredited General Massena to the Porte of Constantinople and reassigned General Bernadotte, along with his friend and chief of staff General Edouard François Simon, to the command of the Army of the West in Brittany and La Vendée. The second two were charged with printing and distributing thousands of anti-government pamphlets branding Napoleon a 'tyrant' and calling the army to arms. Napoleon also ensured that the commanders of the consular guard were frequently rotated so that they did not spend enough time together to concert any political or military action against him. The commander of the Consular Guard, General Jean Lannes, was dismissed from his post, placed under arrest and exiled far beyond the perimeter of Paris.

The police was next to be purged. In July, Fouché was denounced by his rival Jean Baptiste Dossonville. He was accused of having protected a number of 'anarchists' in the aftermath of the 3 *nivôse* bomb attack and, more insidiously, of plotting 'to deliver the First Consul to the villains who imprudently dare to demand his head'.[10] Whether Napoleon gave the charges much credence is unclear, but in any event he was determined to strip Fouché of the powers which he exercised as Minister of Police. However, he thought it was advisable not to arbitrarily dismiss Fouché from his post, certain of the minister's skill and craft, and so used the general amnesty which was granted to the émigré population as a pretext for abolishing his office altogether. Napoleon had originally opposed the idea of recalling France's exiles, believing that their sudden return could provoke disorder and spell danger. He eventually came around to the idea, and on 26 April, by a *senatus consultum*, the amnesty became law. Only the princes of the House of Bourbon, the deputies declared outlaws and the leaders of the rebel bands were excluded from its general provisions.

Although the returning émigrés were 'swaddled' by police surveillance, Napoleon declared in public that the Ministry of Police was no longer necessary for conducting such operations. In September that year, he therefore decreed that Fouché's ministerial duties were to be incorporated into the post of Grand-Juge and Minister for Justice and reassigned to Claude Ambroise Régnier, a former deputy of the National Assembly in 1789 and President of the Conseil des Anciens under the Directory, disparagingly known as the *Gros Juge*.[11] Régnier was terribly ill-suited to his new post and, as Fouché predicted, would soon reveal his weakness by fumbling the management of the counterespionage machine that Fouché had so effectively handled since inheriting it from the Directory. Among Régnier's first measures was to drastically reduce the secret police funds that were earmarked for recruiting spies and to dismiss a number of Fouché's most able agents. Fouché appears to have accepted his demission without complaint. Doubtless he felt confident that circumstances would necessitate his reinstatement before long. In the meantime, assuming an air of perfect affability, he remained on excellent terms with Napoleon. His position, though diminished, was nevertheless 'preserved' through the appointment of his Belgian subordinate Pierre François Réal as Director General of the Haute Police. Réal was aptly described as the 'complete policeman from head to foot'.[12] He possessed regular features, dissolute blue eyes and a transparent gaze that produced a charming effect. To others, however, he had the head of a tiger-cat, his impression hard to erase from the memory of those who regarded it. Nevertheless, he was a man of great wit and joviality but was equally shrewd and disposed to cross-examine prisoners in a harsh and ironical tone that some found improper.[13]

Overseas, however, the country that Napoleon was transforming into a personal dictatorship that summer had once again become an object of great curiosity. Almost every day, a stream of post-chaises rattled up the road from Calais, conveying excursionists eager to visit the renowned capital. They included the great poet William Wordsworth, the engineer James Watt and the future Prime Minister Lord Aberdeen. Also among those individuals who crossed the Channel at this time was a shabbily dressed, jowly, heavy-drinking British politician with drayman's shoulders: the wily Whig leader of the opposition, Charles James Fox.[14] Fox had arrived in Paris that August, the same month that Napoleon had been proclaimed

Consul for life by a *Senatus Consulte*, to conduct research at the *Archives Nationales* into seventeenth-century Jacobean history for a book that he was writing. He was accompanied by his wife, who shared his curiosity in seeing the city that was renowned for being the 'centre for everything interesting and elegant'.[15] Fox was recognised often in the street and greeted by passers-by who believed that he was an intimate friend of France, as indicated by the nationalist newspapers. His evident discomfiture at this reception was witnessed one night during the performance of *Phèdre* at the Theatre Français where, sitting crimson-faced in the spectator's box, he received a standing ovation from the audience.

Fox first met Napoleon at a reception held in the Salle des Ambassadeurs at the Tuileries Palace. The First Consul was dressed plainly in his embroidered consular coat. His hair was un-powdered and his general comportment appeared to Fox's secretary devoid of all haughtiness. As Napoleon greeted the diplomats and other dignitaries in attendance, his eyes darted at different objects as if his mind was elsewhere. He appeared a little flurried until reaching the distinguished English politician, whereupon he cheerfully exclaimed:

Ah! Mr Fox! I have heard with pleasure of your arrival. I have desired in you the orator and friend of this country, who, in contantly raising his voice for peace, consulted that country's best interests, those of Europe and of the human race. The two great nations of Europe required peace; they have nothing to fear; they ought to undertand and value one another. In you, Mr Fox, I see with much satisfaction, that great statesman who recommended peace because there was no just object for war; who saw Europe desolated to no purpose and who struggled for its relief.[16]

Fox stood silent and only ventured a brief reply when Napoleon asked him about his impressions of Paris so far. He later recounted to English friends that he judged Napoleon to be 'easy and desirous of peace without effort'. He also observed how Napoleon exerted his superiority by sometimes posing questions without waiting for the answers before proposing further ones and that he smiled with his mouth but not his eyes. Fox was invited to a number of interviews with the First Consul which he found perfectly cordial. But then, on the evening of 23 September 1802, at a dinner soirée held at the Tuileries, Napoleon accused the British government of having orchestrated the rue Niçaise bomb attack, directing his particular vehemence to the person of William Windham, the former Secretary of War. He opened the conversation musing on a number of diverse subjects including interracial marriage and polygamy in the Indies. His mood quickly changed, and to Fox's dismay he began accusing Britain's former Prime Minister, William Pitt, of having plotted to assassinate him. He judged Windham's talents to be 'mediocre and that he was an unfeeling, unprincipled man'.[17] Fox at once sprung to Windham's defence but Napoleon cut him short, countering, 'It is easy for you who know public debate. But for me, I detest him and that Pitt who together have attempted my life.' He pretended that he would have 'forgiven open enemies in the Cabinet or the field but not cowardly attempts to destroy him, such as ... setting on foot the infernal machine'.[18]

Fox assured Napoleon that he was deceived and that Pitt and Windham, like all Englishmen, would 'shrink with horror' from the practice of covert assassination. Dismissing this, Napoleon darted back, 'You do not know Pitt,' to which Fox rejoined, 'Yes, I do know him and well enough to believe him incapable of such as action. I would risk my head in that belief.' Evidently disturbed by Fox's defiant reply, Napoleon thereupon turned his back and skulked away in silence.[19]

* * *

Exactly one week later, on 1 October 1802, the inhabitants of Verdun were roused from their beds by the crack of artillery fire. The sound emanated from the neighbouring town of Orbe, in Switzerland, which had been taken by storm by the Swiss counter-revolutionary Colonel Pillichody. The town, however, was quickly surrounded by Swiss revolutionary government troops, and within twenty-four hours he escaped to Jura under the cover of fog. The revolt gave Napoleon the pretext to occupy the country. On his orders, General Ney crossed the frontier at the head of 30,000 troops.

Upon hearing of the French deployment, Lord Castlereagh wrote a 'Memorandum for Consideration' for Lord Addington in which he suggested that Britain should uphold its obligations and continue to recruit and finance mercenary regiments whilst at the same time issuing a remonstrance to the government of France. As he asserted, 'The steps already taken pledge us to continue to give her pecuniary aid, so long as she considers resistance preferable to subservience.'[20] He observed that a French invasion constituted a violation of the Treaty of Amiens and in turn justified Britain's retention of her conquests that had yet been transferred to France, in particular the island of Malta. The Prime Minister heeded his advice, much to the fury of Napoleon, who would no sooner vent his displeasure at the new British ambassador to the Court of St Cloud.

16

THE INSULT

On 10 November 1802, at three o'clock in the afternoon, Charles Lord Whitworth, Ambassador Extraordinary and Plenipotentiary to the French Republic, landed in Calais after a pleasant sea passage lasting four and a half hours. As he set foot on the gangway, a resounding cheer erupted from the immense crowd of spectators. Everywhere, on church steeples and public buildings, tricolour flags flapped furiously in the wind. Upon arrival at his inn, he found nothing was wanting. He was greeted, in accordance with the strictest protocol, by the constituted authorities, consisting of the mayor, the commissary-general Margaud, the *Juge de Paix* and other notables. Afterwards, he had an audience with General Barbasaude, the head of the officers of the garrison, followed by the *poissardes*, who presented him with a sumptuous tray of seafood.[1]

After dinner, the town mayor invited Lord Whitworth and his prissy wife, the Duchess of Dorset, to attend the theatre in order, so the former related, that the public might behold in person, what had so long and ardently been denied them, a British Ambassador in France. For a quarter of an hour the orchestra played 'God Save the King' while the whole house, following their example of playing it in the English tradition, stood and applauded throughout. The next morning, they left for Paris. The journey took longer than expected because of the 'indifferent' state of the roads and because a number of horses from each post had been transferred to the service of Napoleon, who was at the same hour travelling back to the capital with his usual celerity. Whitworth found the country through Picardy to be in a high state of cultivation but, compared to his earlier impressions, it seemed that the peasantry had fallen on much harder times. They were escorted by a detachment of dragoons as far as Boulogne where they were greeted by the officers of the garrison, and the roar of artillery fire being discharged from the ramparts. Onwards their carriage rolled, stopping only occasionally, until they reached St Denis where they found, according to the old custom, the *poissardes* of Paris waiting for them. Through the city gates they went, and on the evening of 14 November Lord Whitworth's carriage stopped in front of the Hôtel Caraman on the rue St Dominique in the exclusive Faubourg St Germain, now the official residence of the British Embassy, where he immediately relieved Jackson, the temporary chargé d'affaires.[2]

When the final terms of the Treaty of Amiens were announced on 27 March 1802 they instantly appeared to a great body of the English population as contrary to their country's best interests, and that the restoration of peace, though so ardently desired, had come at too high a price. The terms were far from favourable. French hegemony in Europe was effectively recognised. Britain furthermore had to abandon all her wartime overseas conquests, including the annexed French West Indies, save for Trinidad and Ceylon, and also surrender the Cape to Holland, return Egypt to Turkey, evacuate her troops from Malta and restore the island to the order of the Knights of St John.[3] Lord Grenville, now in opposition, denounced the terms as a disgrace and degradation whilst Lord Malmesbury commented caustically, 'Peace in a week, war in a month.' The session of Parliament closed on 28 June, and on the following day it was dissolved. In addressing the king, Mr Speaker Abbot said, 'We now indulge the flattering hope that we may cultivate the arts of peace.'[4] The country did not indulge that hope and began 'at last to apprehend that neither credit, satisfaction, nor even security had been attained by the treaty of Amiens'.[5]

Indeed, when Parliament opened for session on 23 November, there was an ominous passage in the king's speech. He declared that, in his intercourse with foreign powers, he had always been motivated by a sincere desire for the cause of peace but that nevertheless he could not abandon that 'long entrenched policy' in which the interest of other states was necessarily tied to his own: 'I cannot, therefore, be indifferent to any material change in their relative condition and strength.'[6] By this, he was referring obliquely to Napoleon's assumption of dictatorial powers in the Cisalpine Republic and to the 'beneficent dictation' that the Corsican had exercised in the deployment of Ney's army to Berne.

The news of Ney's march into Berne prompted Lord Addington, Britain's Prime Minister, to send an official despatch to the French government remonstrating against the infringement of that canton's sovereignty. As expected, he was dismissed by Napoleon who asserted that the King of England 'had no right to complain of the conduct, or to interfere with the proceedings of France on any point which did not form a part of the stipulations of the treaty of Amiens'.[7] Such 'mild' diplomacy did nothing to assuage Addington's critics at home, who contended that he was a man too incompetent and timid in his treatment with France. In fact, as he revealed to Lord Malmesbury, his maxim was 'to resist or bear all clamour and invective at home till such time as France had filled the measure of her folly and had put herself completely in the wrong'.[8] Events would soon prove him right. But for now, despite these inconveniences to the cause of peace, the country was noticeably relieved, having long suffered the hardships imposed on them by a long and misunderstood conflict, and welcomed the treaty which 'all men were glad of, but no man can be proud of'.[9]

On 8 December 1802, Lord Whitworth was introduced to France's great ruler. To mark this notable occasion, the *curassiers* appeared in armour for the first time since the Revolution. Whitworth's suite drew up to the Tuileries in three carriages belonging to the First Consul. Whitworth sat in the first carriage, attended by a prefect and drawn by six beautiful grey horses, richly caparisoned with servants in shiny new liveries whilst his suite followed closely behind in the two other carriages, again drawn by four equally magnificent steeds.

The First Consul, meanwhile, sat in the Grand Room of the Tuileries with a melancholic countenance. He had lost some of his former dynamism. His cheeks looked more plump, the waistband of his breeches more taut, his skin more sallow. He was placed at the upper end, flanked by the two other Consuls, and the officers of his court, the foreign ministers and an enormous crowd of dignitaries representing all the crowned heads of Europe. He was arrayed in a velvet embroidered suit, the full dress uniform of a French general, half boots with gold embroidery, a military hat of the best beaver with a diamond button weighing 277 carats, a sabre with a Damascus blade and hilt of solid gold, epaulets of the best brilliants and diamonds in the eyes and mouth of the crocodile, altogether valued at a colossal £389,751.[10] Whitworth, conducted by selected officers of the court, bent his steps towards him and, delivering his letters of credence, remained some time in conversation with France's master, during which he lost no opportunity to express George III's earnest solicitude for the preservation of peace.

Between the First Consul and the English Minister there was the most complete contrast that could possibly be. Whitworth's person was tall, elegant, charming and as Napoleon himself described, a '*fort bel homme*'. He had a long, pointed nose that accentuated his intellectual superiority, an effect not wholly dissimilar to Talleyrand's snubbed look. His diplomatic abilities were also of the first order. Indeed, such was his deviousness and resourcefulness that it prompted the ruthlessly ambitious police agent Jean Baptiste Dossonville to claim that it was from this first day at the Tuileries that the perils of state began. In a brief he wrote, 'Lord Whitworth has proved the height to which his genius can soar by the results of his intrigues in Russia with regard to Paul I. He is no ordinary man, such as France has too often sent to foreign courts. He is a clever *politique*, admitted to all Pitt and Grenville's secrets.'[11]

It was quite true that Whitworth had resided many years at the court of St Petersburg as Britain's Envoy Extraordinary and

Minister Plenipotentiary and throughout his appointment had tendered his service with consummate skill. His service, however, was not entirely creditable or honourable to himself or his country. It is supposed that he misappropriated government funds, which he complained were unequal to his needs; had an extramarital liaison with Mme Zherebtsoff, the sister of Prince Zuboff; and, having quitted that court on account of the hostile policies and intemperate conduct of the late and not entirely sane Emperor Paul I, had discreetly disbursed secret service funds to Count P. A. Pahlen, the same military governor of St Petersburg who, leading a gang of inebriated noblemen and officers, invaded the Tsar's palace and squeezed out the Emperor's last breath on the night of 11 March 1801.[12] Indeed, Whitworth was so satisfied on learning of the death of 'that arch fiend Paul' that he vowed to celebrate the day as a festival so long as he should live.[13] So perhaps he was not a man of impeccable morals, and only honest when it was most convenient, but his services nevertheless pleased King George III, who, in recognition of them, conferred on France's new ambassador the Order of the Bath and the barony of the kingdom of Ireland.

Before he set out on his diplomatic mission, Whitworth was furnished with a set of instructions, prescribing therein matters that required 'particular caution and secrecy'. He was told that he would be sent unique ciphers and deciphers for this purpose and was to keep them carefully deposited under secure locks. However, as an added measure, he was to use every other precaution to guard against their being discovered as they pertained to secrets highly prejudicial to Britain's service. He was charged with discovering what plans or hidden designs the government of France had formed, or might have been forming, in respect to the East or West Indies, and to also report on the number of ships of war or land forces that might have been dispatched from the different parts of the French Republic to those quarters.[14] Given Napoleon's restless ambitions, it was presumed that the acquisition of new colonies was always in contemplation and imparting intelligence on such matters was therefore critical to the security of George III's kingdom. So, equipped with his secret instructions,

Whitworth quickly settled down to the business of an ambassador, and, observing all the right methods and decorum, acquitted himself with great skill and sagacity. He and his haughty wife, the duchess, made a handsome English couple and endeavoured to set a very good example in Paris by how they regarded religious observance on a Sunday.[15] They had left England with the best resolutions to show all due reverence to religion, to impart it with dignity and significance in the minds of the Parisians. The duchess had even refused an invitation to a grand assembly given by a Russian princess as it was to be held on a Sunday evening, a time which was reserved exclusively for divine service at their house. The pleasantness of their situation, however, did not last long for on 30 January 1803, an article appeared in the *Moniteur* which was to rouse the fury of the king's ministers and provoke a diplomatic storm.

The article related to an incendiary report compiled by Colonel Sebastiani, a French intelligence officer who was employed as an emissary to the principle courts in Asia and Africa and sanctioned with making a survey of the fortifications and troop dispositions in Egypt. He concluded that, on account of the wretched state of the Turks in that country and the ruinous state of the fortresses, Egypt could be conquered with a French army of 6,000 with no great injury to itself. The report also disparaged the character of the 4,000-plus English soldiers stationed in the cantons around Alexandria and accused General Stuart, commandant of the English forces there, of inciting the Turks to assassinate him. The timing could not have been less propitious, for just when Sebastiani's report was reaching England's shores, a separate investigation was being published domestically, reaching the conclusion that 'Britain was unable to contend with France single-handed'.[16] George III, unsurprisingly, was not in the best of tempers and demanded unequivocal and immediate satisfaction from the Consulate for what he perceived as an unmerited provocation on their part and one that was quite incongruous with the cause of an everlasting peace. He also hastened to add that he would not entertain any further discussion on the difficult subject of Malta until he received a full explanation, an objection which was not altogether inconvenient for him. Matters were thus drawing inescapably to a head, and on 17 February 1803, in a move that departed from established modes of procedure but quite in character with his contempt for customary forms, Napoleon invited Whitworth to the Tuileries to discuss the source of the tensions currently simmering between the two countries.[17]

Talleyrand's note to the English ambassador was sent at the behest of the First Consul, who requested the presence of his company at nine o'clock at the palace. So, in quite deplorable weather, Whitworth left his residence, trundling through the snowy streets to pull up to the grand courtyard of the Tuileries at the appointed hour. Napoleon cordially received the ambassador in his elegantly furnished cabinet and, after briefly exchanging impressions on diverse subjects, motioned him to sit down, meanwhile doing so opposite the table upon which he propped his elbows. He announced that the purpose of this highly unusual conference was to make his sentiments known to George III in a manner which left no equivocation. For the next two hours, he enumerated the many provocations on the part of the English Cabinet and, though scarcely coherent and seldom master of his emotions, he managed to converse in the tone of courtesy due to the occasion.

It was of sad disappointment to him, he began, that the occurrence of peace, instead of having produced a spirit of conciliation and friendship between their two countries, as promised by the Treaty of Amiens, had only been attended by growing mistrust and jealousy. His first point of contention was that Britain's government had deliberately delayed the evacuation of Alexandria and Malta as stipulated by the treaty. However, he cut short the discussion on this matter with the declaration that he would sooner concede the suburb of St Antoine to England than relinquish their rights to the island. He then vented his frustration at the 'diatribes' and 'calumnies' that both the English papers and the French émigré press, particularly one paper subsidised by Lord Pelham, had not ceased to publish against his character and the French government. He confessed that his irritation on this subject increased daily 'since every gale that blew from England brought nothing but enmity and hatred against him'.[18] Indeed, he had already instructed the French Ambassador accredited to the Court at Saint James to make plain his indignation and to demand the repression of these papers, which were 'scandalous' as the liberty of the press, and to ban the émigrés from wearing the order of their ancient government. His dismay at England's goodwill to the émigré community extended to the handsome pension that its government had paid Georges and other leaders of the Chouans, whom he accused of sponsoring his attempted assassination but who had not been removed to Canada as promised. He mentioned in particular two assassins that he claimed had been employed by the Baron de Rolle and Georges for this purpose but who had been apprehended in Normandy and that proof of their treason would be publicly revealed in a court of justice. He concluded by declaring that if England did not instantly fulfil her obligations to the Treaty of Amiens and, in addition, suppress the litany of abuse that never ceased to emanate from the papers in her country, war would be the only alternative.[19]

The interview, having lasted two hours and having been delivered with great speed, scarcely afforded Whitworth the opportunity to interject and propose a few words of explanation. He had listened intently throughout and with the phlegmatic bearing that he was so famed. Indeed, the unflappable disposition of the British ambassador was quite unfavourable to Napoleon's probable purpose which was to bear down on his opponent's reasoning by 'bullying and intimidation'.[20]

The two men then exchanged a few words on some inconsequential questions and then parted with apparent good humour and courtesy. Their relations, however, quickly turned sour, for on 8 March, in response to the military preparations that were taking place in the ports of France and Holland, movements that the French government claimed related to peaceful colonial service but which England feared might in the event of a rupture be brought down upon herself, George III sent a note to both Houses of Parliament recommending counter-measures designed for the security of Britain's dominions. Everywhere – in Parliament, at court, in the city and in every person of 'common sense' – the impression felt by George III's message was that it would surely be the precursor of a rupture. Napoleon was beside himself and, forming a scheme which had no other aim but to bring the protracted negotiations between their two nations to a point, confronted the English Ambassador at a reception of the diplomatic corps held at the Tuileries five days later.

On the evening of the reception Napoleon was with his wife, Josephine, in her apartment playing with the newly born son of Louis Bonaparte and Hortense de Beauharnais. He was all smiles, but when the palace prefect, Monsieur de Rémusat, announced Lord Whitworth's arrival, a visible expression was produced upon his face; relinquishing the child, he grabbed Josephine's hand and spirited her away. Walking through the huge door that led to the reception room, the couple parted ways, with Napoleon passing before the foreign ministers who gathered before him while the latter proceeded to address each of the ladies in turn. Napoleon, spotting the elegant figure of the English Ambassador, waltzed up to him straightaway and accosted him. He began, '*Eh bien* Monsieur Whitworth, are you well? How is Mad Dorset? Do you have any news from London? There are storm clouds over there.' The ambassador replied that he had received letters of instruction from the Foreign Secretary, Lord Hawkesbury, two days ago.[21]

'You are then determined on war!' he observed, deliberately loud enough to be heard by all those circled around. Perhaps guessing this, Whitworth threw back that his fellow countrymen were sensible to the advantages gained from peace. Napoleon nevertheless continued, 'We have been at war for fifteen years – you are determined on hostility for fifteen years more and you force me to it.' The First Consul then broke off and, addressing the Russian Ambassador, Count Arcadi Ivanovitch de Markoff, and the Chevalier Azzara, both of whom were standing just two or three steps away, exclaimed, 'The English wish for war; but if they draw the sword first, I will be the last to return it to the scabbard. They do not respect treaties which henceforth we must cover with black crape!'[22]

The First Consul then continued to tour the room, pausing for a short while to converse with a group of ladies. He was supposed to cross into the adjoining salon where his wife was speaking with the other female guests but returned instead to the presence of the foreign ambassadors and first of all approached the American Minister. The latter was said to be extremely deaf and Napoleon, being too impatient to bear his awkward company much longer, pushed on. He appeared to those whom he addressed to be somewhat agitated, due to the effect which George III's message had on his temper, but still feigned to be attentive, advising the Danish Minister, who was complaining of a cold, to take a stiff drink.

After a few minutes he returned to where the English Ambassador was standing and, to the latter's great annoyance, resumed his attack. 'To what purpose are these armaments? Against whom do you take these measures of precaution? I have not a single ship of the line in any port in France – but if you arm, I too will take up arms – if you fight, I will fight – you may destroy France, but you cannot intimidate her.' To this Whitworth calmly retorted, 'We desire neither the one nor the other. We desire to live with her on terms of good intelligence.'

'You must respect treaties then,' Napoleon shot back. All the time his eyes roved about the room. 'Woe to those by whom they are not respected! They will be accountable for the consequences to all Europe.' Napoleon repeated the last remark twice over and then unceremoniously retired from the hall. He did not wait to have the doors thrown open to him but instead let himself out by one of the folds, forcibly shutting it after him. The whole audience was left to their complete stupefaction, having just witnessed a scene surprising for its extreme 'impropriety, want of decency and dignity'. Whitworth, so he later claimed, was so offended that he was poised to unsheathe his sword if 'in his person the Majesty of England was to be publicly insulted by an actual insult'.[23]

Back in England, the news of Napoleon's behaviour at the Tuileries reception was received with great disfavour. It was held that the country itself, in the person of her ambassador, had been grossly insulted, and in the presence of so many European dignitaries no less. The affair was given its widest possible negative publicity and, playing into the hands of Lord Addington's government, greatly increased the general 'spirit of jealously and resentment'.[24]

17

AN INCIDENT IN CALAIS

Two weeks after this scene at the Tuileries there arrived at the British Embassy an unexpected visitor. John Wesley Wright by now had returned from his peacetime service in the Mediterranean and immediately upon his arrival in London was introduced to England's Prime Minister by his friend Sir Sidney Smith. The latter intended to re-establish his own correspondence with the royalists in France and had requested Lord Addington's permission that his protégé be included in an invitation for Sunday lunch for this end. The invitation, however, proved needless, for by this time Wright had returned to the city where he had once been imprisoned, leaving Smith to beg the Prime Minister's excuses by accounting for him. He had been assigned to HMS *Cynthia*, a sloop built by Wells & Co. of Rotherhithe with the unusual design of a shallow draught and three dagger-boards for stability. At noon on Tuesday 14 September 1802, he joined that ship in the bay of Gibraltar whereupon he read his commission to her company. After remaining moored there for a few more days, they set steering sails fore aft at the Bay of Cadiz, adjacent to the south-west coast of Spain. Before he left, Lord Elgin had requested that he transport some cases of his famous marbles on board the sloop but Wright refused for reasons unknown. Following his adventures in the Levant, he seemed consigned to a humdrum naval existence which saw him command the *Cynthia* as it uneventfully cruised the Mediterranean. He had steered it to Cape St Vincent, the south-westernmost point of Portugal, then through the Tagus River where it remained moored off the town of Lisbon for most of October and November. Thereafter, she sailed around the Cape of Gibraltar and surrounding sea, with intermittent moorings in the bay and again in the Tagus. One of his last commissions before he returned to Spithead was to transport ten army mutineers from Gibraltar to Portsmouth where seven were transferred to HMS *Calcutta* on 21 April for transport to Australia.[1]

Wright's arrival in Paris was greeted without much enthusiasm, especially from Whitworth, who immediately despatched a message to his masters in Whitehall to this effect:

Paris, 18 March 1803

Captain Wright arrived this morning by the way of Havre with your Lordship's letter of the 16th. I shall of course be very happy to avail myself of this gentleman's aid and information: but I fear he is too well known to be of any material service; and I will confess to your lordship that I am not without apprehension that, in a moment of irritation like the present, it may be recollected that he was a prisoner here, and that he escaped from prison. I cannot but think a less remarkable person, however intelligent Captain Wright may be, might have been equally useful, without incurring the risk of adding another *Pierre d'achoppement* to the many which we may expect to find in our way. I have, however, told him that he might remain here for the present, and see his old friends, if they were willing under the present circumstances to renew their acquaintance- which I very much doubt. For the rest, he has seen nothing at Havre which can be construed into an armament; and I verily believe this is the case in every port of France ...[2]

In Whitworth's defence, Wright's appointment as an embassy attaché was highly injudicious given his reputation but even the

English Ambassador was forced to regard his stupendous feat with 'considerable admiration'.[3] He had snuck into the country without a passport and breached the city gate's undetected, entering the embassy in disguise. From there, he set about scouring Paris for former royalist agents and somehow had managed to avoid attracting the attention of the police spies guarding the embassy building. Indeed, a reading of the embassy staff list indicated an operation hardly adhering to the normal forms of diplomacy.[4] The First Secretary was James Talbot, the same rogue agent who had plotted to assassinate the Directory. Even Wright's friend and accomplice in the Temple escape Count Viscovitch was attached to the embassy but he was not quite as artful as the former and was persistently dogged by the police. Everywhere, the city was under the observation of its military guard which, according to the embassy's own intelligence sources, had the capacity to mobilise 20,000 troops within a short summons. It was known that the French government had introduced a system of counter-espionage that was carried to an 'incredible height', making suspicion of the slightest indisposition sufficient cause for citizens to be hushed away at night. Such a system hardly exalted one's opinion of a government which was known by its citizens to have ears everywhere.

Contained in the secret police reports which reached Napoleon's desk each evening was a subsection relating to the general spirit and temper of Paris' population. They dealt with every facet of life from rumours circulated, to acts of brigandage committed to the identities of émigrés returned. The contents therein convinced the First Consul that his popularity depended on the preservation of peace but yet the 'obstinacy and violence' with which he conducted his negotiations with the British government induced a feeling among the population that it was he who was chiefly responsible for the impending calamity that was about to beset the nation. For, according to Whitworth's calculation, the 'moderation and temperance' which England had displayed in her treatment with the First Consul, especially on the delicate question of Malta, had defeated the latter's policy of attributing the approaching breach to the court at Saint James, which he had deigned to accuse of being bent on war by shutting the door to every proposal tending to a peaceful conciliation.[5] Malta was hardly worth a war, especially once its value was made known by its governor, Sir Alexander Bell, but nevertheless Whitworth proposed to bribe Lucien and Joseph Bonaparte as well as Talleyrand £2 million to secure its possession. The first two, notwithstanding their indefatigable efforts, failed to influence their brother and it was only by the most extreme impositions that they wrung from him any concessions on the subject. Indeed, the impossibility of persuading Napoleon to negotiate with Whitworth only served to deflect responsibility away from England. It certainly would have been more chivalrous to have evacuated Malta, but once war was inevitable it made little sense for England to renounce her claim to the island, especially since such a move would have been vociferously attacked for its manifest weakness.

Lord Addington, having long been unfairly chastised for his alleged mishandling of foreign affairs, now reasoned that it would be folly to let Napoleon exploit the situation according to his own timetable; knowing that France was in a state of ill-preparedness, and that her fleet was divided between its European and West Indian stations, he instructed Lord Whitworth to bring the crisis to a head. He was to quit Paris in thirty-six hours if the Consulate did not agree to British terms. Napoleon, however, still wanted to play for time until he had completed his rearmament, particularly of major warships and realignment of alliances. On 10 May he instructed his Minister of Foreign Affairs to send Whitworth another proposal. The British should leave Malta which would then fall under the trusteeship of Russia. The English ambassador saw through this ruse and wrote an exasperated note to Lord Hawkesbury: 'I have been delayed much longer than I wished by the infamous chicanery and difficulties which have occurred.'[6]

The customary diplomatic cue for an impending rupture was the recall of ambassadors, and so it was that at ten o'clock at night on Thursday 12 May 1803, after demanding his passport, which was promptly delivered to him, the English ambassador, Lord Whitworth, quit Paris for good. On 16 May, Parliament was informed of what had transpired. Then, four days later, the

First Consul made the following declaration to the Senate, the Legislative Body and the Tribunate from his favourite residence at Saint Cloud:

> The Ambassador of England had been recalled; Compelled by this circumstance, the Ambassador of the Republic has quitted a country where he could no longer hear the language of Peace ... The Treaty of Amiens had been negotiated amid the clamours of a party hostile to peace; scarcely was it concluded, when it was the object of bitter censure. It was represented as fatal to England, because it was not disgraceful to France. Soon after, alarms were disseminated; dangers were pretended, on which was established the necessity of a state of peace, such as to be a permanent signal if new hostilities. There were kept in reserve, and hired, those vile miscreants who had torn the bosom of their country, and who were intended to tear it anew. Vain calculations of hatred! We are no longer that France, restored to internal tranquillity, regenerated in her administration and her laws, and ready to fall, with her whole weight, upon whatever foreign state may dare to attack her, and to unite with the banditti whom an atrocious policy would once more cast upon her shores to organise pillage and assassination.[7]

Among the first of France's wartime actions was to target the English population. On 22 May 1803, the Consulate decreed that all subjects of the king present in France who were either aged between eighteen and sixty or held a commission from the British government would immediately be deemed prisoners of war in 'answer' for those citizens of the Republic who had been arrested and made prisoner by the Royal Navy previous to any declaration of peace. As Napoleon told General Androche Junot, the dashing Governor of Paris, otherwise known as *La Tempête*, 'I am resolved that tonight not an Englishman shall be visible in the most obscure theatre, or restaurant in Paris.'[8]

The public announcement of this decree naturally brought widespread confusion. At the British Embassy, the First Secretary,

James Talbot, was swamped with applications from the king's subjects but it was only when he arrived at Boulogne that he discovered that the very same law was also being applied to officials normally protected by diplomatic immunity. He was so astonished by this extension of the law that he demanded Citizen Masclet, the *sous préfet* at Boulogne, hand over a copy of the official order. Upon reading it, he begged his excuses and, returning to his carriage, removed all the embassy papers from its luggage compartment. After sifting through them, he found a secluded spot by the roadside whereupon he burnt all the documents that incriminated any individuals or contained secret information injurious to his government.[9] At about the same time, another official, James Mandeville, had returned to Paris from Calais with the disagreeable news that he and the staff at the British embassy had just been refused permission to board a packet for Dover. The ambassador's belongings were also seized at the port but were only returned when the English cabinet threatened to retaliate by confiscating those in the possession of General Andréossy in London.

Indeed, the seizure of possessions nearly had mortal consequences for Wright: when he left Paris with Robert Clifford, a noted cartographer, they happened to be smuggling a box five feet long, two feet broad and a foot high. The trunk contained 100 kilograms of maps, plans, including of La Vendée, manuscripts of France and its environs and which would in all probability of landed them in the Temple prison and, in the present conditions, have 'authorised any legal Government, even any subordinate authority to have executed them at the instant'.[9] Before the resumption of war, Wright and Clifford had spent many a pleasing hour in the company of friends in Paris. When they were not socializing, they spent their time collecting intelligence on the country's topography, its fortifications, etc. As the Napoleonic threat grew more acute, Clifford produced a set of 'skeleton' military maps, newly suited to campaigns of movement, covering the whole of southern England as far north as a line joining Anglesey to the Walsh. He had, in anticipation of the ratification of the Treaty of Amiens, obtained a *permis de séjour* which invited him to circulate freely in the commune. He registered staying at the Hôtel d'Orléans on the rue des Petits-Augustins in Paris where he passed *le printemps à Paris* indulging his appetite for the mathematics of minerals and, acquiring a reader's card, frequently rendered visits to the Bibliothèque Nationale where he read and transcribed primitive alphabets. He also searched for and copied maps. He considered Napoleon's ambition to be unbounded and claimed that the object of his rule was directed to the destruction of England, *per fas aut nefas*. So, he devoted his talents to counteracting the impending invasion that he warned would be 'attempted from every port' in France.[10]

Wright and Clifford had planned to quit Paris on Saturday 14 May, but because of a scarcity in the number of post horses they could not acquire a diligence before the following Tuesday. On Thursday 19th, after a journey that took two days and two nights, they arrived in Calais. They were allowed to embark for England the following day at midday, it being a mail day and all other passages not being allowed. The mail packet, however, departed two hours before schedule and all the registered passengers were advised to make haste and sprint on board before the ship cleared the port. By quite ill-considered timing Clifford chanced to lose his passport, and by the time he had obtained a replacement one from the port commissary the ship had already set sail, its captain unwilling to accept any baggage separated from its owner. A few hours later, Clifford found his original passport and returned to the commissariat with the duplicate. The commissary was evidently impressed by the Englishman's sense of rectitude and rewarded his honesty by permitting him and Wright to board an English vessel that was scheduled to dock for the purpose of collecting Whitworth's horse the same evening at eleven o'clock.

To their extreme bad luck, an official at the commissariat happened to recognise Clifford when he entered the office later that evening. The official had encountered the cartographer when he had formerly served as an officer of Dillon's regiment, an expatriate force in France consisting of both English and Irish Catholics. He was immediately escorted away for interrogation and among the many questions asked was when he intended to set sail. Clifford responded evasively to the effect that due to the French government's regulation, he and his friends were only allowed to sail on mail packets, implying that if they missed Friday's packet, they would be obliged to hang about until the following Monday when the next was scheduled to depart. The officer, supposing that Clifford would be trapped on the mainland till the Monday anyway, granted Clifford his temporary freedom. Seizing the opportunity, he and Wright escaped on the same vessel that was scheduled to depart at eleven o'clock that night. They were both lucky: as it transpired, all the passengers of English nationality who were booked on Monday's packet were apprehended and committed to the prisoner-of-war depots. Their trunk also arrived safely in England, and as they had an order to let their belongings pass at Dover from the Treasury, it arrived at their secret destination without being opened since it left Paris.[11]

News of this incident in Calais quickly reached England, but for one reason or another the newspapers reported that the Englishmen who had been apprehended at the quayside had been hanged straightaway as spies. The opposition party in Parliament, in any event, pounced on the incident in an effort to discredit the government. On the morning of Monday 23 May they secured a debate on the subject, but owing to the sensitivity of the motion the doors of the House were closed from 8 a.m. to 3.30 p.m. to all strangers and gentlemen. The leader of the opposition, Charles James Fox, expiated at considerable length on the virtuous government of Bonaparte, describing him as 'the most stupendous monument of human wisdom' and stating that 'the execution of the unfortunate Gentlemen, the subject of the debate, ought in no shape be attributed to a cruel and savage temper in the Chief Consul but to Necessity, state Necessity, the law of "The Wise & Good in Every Age"'. A Mr William Smith also rose to speak, and, repudiating the claims that the subjects of this debate were innocent of the crimes, declared that in his considered opinion 'the General Officer at Calais showed a criminal neglect for which he ought to be denounced in not proceeding to summary and rigorous justice; that had the municipality the proper judges ... the heads of these unfortunate Gentlemen would by every law have been borne about the streets and their bodies mangled in a thousand pieces in the Room of the mercy that had now been extended towards them in not severing the head from the body but attaching the *tout ensemble* on the Gibbets in the advanced fort at Calais'. He also asked rhetorically what point there was in springing to the defence of such men when there 'were witnesses of the plans being found in Mr Clifford's trunk' and that 'there could be no doubt that these Gentlemen were spies employed by our ministers ... providentially the vigilance of Bonaparte had foiled the intention of His Majesty's Ministers ... What becomes of the Ministers pretended wish for peace! ... do strict justice between the wretched system of wretched Ministers & the great Man of the People of France, The Liberator of Europe. He therefore Bonaparte acted as Criminals ought to suffer & that his Majesty's Ministers ought to be impeached as their employers & in fact as the murderers of two Gentlemen.'[12]

Ironically, just as Parliament was debating their assumed execution by hanging on a gibbet in Calais, Wright and Clifford were already back safely in London. Within the week, the latter would be dining with Lord St Vincent, the First Lord of the Admiralty, who had just recently been charged with organising the coastal defence of the southern coasts. On 1 June, Wright was in London applying to the Admiralty for employment. He was among the many naval officers who had poured into the stately building in search of a commission. Many, if not most, had been on half pay for over a year whilst others had left their ships at Portsmouth, Plymouth or Chatham in the hope of securing even more desirable appointments or commands. Wright was backed by his influential friend Sir Sidney Smith, who, in his usual high-handed manner, wrote to Lord Addington and applied on his behalf:

With regard to my friend Captain Wright, it is evident, notwithstanding Lord St Vincent's admission of his fair claim to promotion when (rather if ever) he returned from his perilous mission to Paris, that it will not be granted by the *Admiralty* for he has not been admitted to see Lord St Vincent for fear of creating a precedent for a crowd of other captains.

You, who know a little of my friend, and who know the delicate nature of the information he has to give, will say with me that he might fairly have been made an exception secretly.[13]

He did not receive a promotion but was charged with a service altogether more hazardous and important to the country's war effort. His mission had its genesis less than two years earlier and involved, once again, the bookseller of Neuchâtel, Louis Fauche-Borel.

18

THE RECONCILIATION

In 1801, with summer approaching, Louis Fauche-Borel had returned to his home in Neuchâtel after four years on the road to settle down with his wife and children. He had been looking forward to building his dream house on a patch of ground which he had purchased for 500 *louis* just on the outskirts of his town, in a quiet neighbourhood known as *Le Vieux Châtel*. His grand scheme to corrupt Paul Barras had perished on 13 *Brumaire*, and, having no other means to fill his purse, he sailed for England in the spring of 1800 with the intention of soliciting employment from the British government. He fancied that, after having rendered so many services, he would be granted some eminent court appointment, but the king's ministers seemed to have thought otherwise; disregarding his petitions, they commissioned him with bearing inconsequential despatches to William Wickham, who was then resident in Vienna. It nevertheless flattened his illusions to be in the confidence of the English cabinet, and so off he went, to the tune of the postilion's horn, moving from one posting house to another, enjoying the warmest comforts, stuffing his belly with the finest foods and all the time exhibiting the grossest affectations. In this fashion he travelled across Europe, first stopping off in Amsterdam, where he was welcomed by the notables of the city. He had always found the Dutch nation to be most upright and industrious but nevertheless condescended to remind his hosts that they owed their greatest obligations to General Pichegru for having, among his accomplishments, instilled its army with the strictest discipline. He also made stops along the way in Wesel, Frankfurt and Hamburg, and upon penetrating the frontier of Austria learned of that country's defeat at the Battle of Marengo. He was content to repose awhile and enjoy the company of his family, but then on 25 September 1801 a letter landed on his new doorstep requesting his presence in London at a conveniently appointed time, the object of his visit to be revealed on his first arrival. He sensed that it related to the approaching signing of the Treaty of Amiens and so, without further ado, he dropped his construction plans and packed his bags, setting off for England.[1]

Before he left, Borel bade a sad farewell to his father, mother and two sisters, all of whom he was destined never to see again, and pressing to his heart his only son for the very last time, sped off in the carriage that was waiting for him. He passed Geneva and Lyon along the way and, after a short inconspicuous stay in France's capital, made haste to Calais where he encountered Mengaud, the zealous French commissary. His name, it turned out, was proscribed in the list of persons to be arrested but because the hyphenated 'Borel' had been purposely suppressed from his passport, he managed to slip Mengaud's suspicions and safely board the packet for England. On arrival in London, he called upon Sir Charles Flint, the Superintendent of Aliens. Flint informed Borel that the English ministry was presently working on the Treaty of Amiens, of which the preliminary terms had recently been signed but that it had not abandoned its hopes of deposing Napoleon and restoring the Bourbons to the throne. However, to effectuate this transition, it needed to call upon two of France's greatest generals: Charles Pichegru and his former friend General Jean Victor Marie Moreau.

On 5 June 1802, Fauche set off for Paris. Before his departure he met with the chief conspirators, including Sir Sidney Smith, who had invited him to a superb dinner on board his beautiful ship *Le Tigre*, then moored in the Downs. After six days, he arrived in Paris and lodged himself in the Hôtel des Bons-Enfants situated in the street bearing the same name. He made no effort to assume another identity, despite his name and description being still high on the police watch list, fancying that his profession and nationality would save him from molestation. But his double life was already well known to the Consulate police, who in their files recorded him as always having 'a scheme for some conspiracy in one pocket and a manuscript for publication in the other'. He began to sense, however, that he was being watched and so, after a few restless nights at the hotel, he moved to quiet lodging in the rue Saint Hyacinthe, now rue Malebranche, not far from what was formerly Place Saint-Michele. His first care was to write to, and beg the private audience of, the victor of Hohenlinden who was then staying with his mother-in-law Madame Hulot in a charming little house in the rue de Saint Pierre. Naturally, Borel claimed to have succeeded in winning over Moreau's confidence, but the reality seems to have been different for he never hazarded to pay a return visit.[2]

On 1 July, two weeks after his interview with Moreau, Fauche paid a visit to the publishing house Bossange, Masson and Besson and presented to its owners a collection of Jean-Jacques Rousseau's writings. Having concluded business to his satisfaction, he left the house and headed towards the rue du Petit Lion. As he made his way down the rue du Tournon, he was seized by two plain-clothed men who pushed him into a waiting carriage. He was immediately conducted to the Prefecture de Police. Passing the Louvre on the way, he pointed to the colonnade of this magnificent edifice, observing that there had never been anything more beautiful in all of Europe. The commissary responded, 'Yes, it is a monument to the vanity of kings. One should demolish it.' This comment naturally awakened the bookseller's curiosity for he pressed him to explain himself. The commissary rejoined that the space should be made into 'a vast potato field', a comment so 'discreditable' that the prisoner felt that he had been instantly transported back to the era of the Committee of Public Safety. That same night, Louis Fauche-Borel was committed to the tower of the Temple where he was to remain for the next few years.[3]

Undeterred by the failure of Fauche's mission, Lord Addington dispatched a second agent under 'private instructions' to negotiate directly with General Moreau for the good of His Majesty's service. His objective was to incite the general 'to second his partisans, put himself at their head' and then 'march to St Cloud and struggle his Empire' with Napoleon Bonaparte.[4] The agent entrusted with this commission was a 'man of some genius' who before the Revolution was a curate of Pompadour and, since 1789, the curate in La Lozère. He deeply abhorred the republicans' persecutions of the priests, having in 1793 been forced to flee his parish and join the Army of the North, seeking refuge at the quarters of the staff major of his nephew, General Joseph Souham. The agent, who was known as the Abbé David, shadowed the émigré army for a short while but, 'having nothing better do', penned a book concerning his observations which he entitled *Histoire des Campagnes du General Pichegru.*[5] He had, about this time, also lived in Pichegru's house together with his uncle and Moreau, and it was this proximity that made the Abbé David a good choice to facilitate the generals' rapprochement. Indeed Moreau, who had known David in his youth, had, since the *coup d'état* on 18 *Fructidor*, heard no news from him until one day in autumn of 1802 the latter unexpectedly arrived at Moreau's country estate, Gros Bois, announcing himself to the latter's servant and demanding a private interview with the general.

The Abbé David's first objective was to seek an explanation from Moreau as to why he had denounced Pichegru to the Directory four years earlier. The two generals had ceased to be friends after Moreau had sent papers to the Directory found in a captured enemy carriage containing evidence pertaining to Pichegru's treason. David had a personal interest in seeking the truth as his brother, Victor Couchery, who was then living with Pichegru under the alias of Wallis at 12 Brompton Row, was among the deputies violently purged on 18 *Fructidor*. Moreau evinced his distaste for having sent the papers, but he convinced himself of the propriety of his actions. He insisted that it was his soldier's duty to denounce Pichegru and that, as his Chef d'Etat Major counselled, if he had persisted in his silence he would have been forced to reveal everything and, in turn, be denounced a traitor himself. David was evidently satisfied with Moreau's feeble explanation and proposed that an accommodation be reached between the two former friends. He then presented Moreau with a letter from Pichegru which spoke warmly of their former friendship and held the promise of future understanding. With this gesture, the two generals were reconciled.

Having accomplished his mission, David made preparations to sail to England. He applied for a passport but was subsequently arrested at Calais and in October 1802, conveyed to the Temple in Paris. Except for a letter from Moreau, which was concealed in the lining of his hand baggage, all his papers were passed to the Prefect of Police, Citizen Dubois, who on 15 December 1802 carried out his interrogation of the curate. The results of the interrogation supplied Napoleon with the knowledge that a *rapprochement* had been made between the generals but, aside from Pichegru's grant of asylum in England, no evidence yet pointed to that country's involvement.[6]

Georges, meanwhile, was preparing to quit London where he had been residing at 6 New Bond Street under the pseudonym Legros. It had been made clear to him by the former Prime Minister William Pitt that England would readily support and finance his operations against Napoleon on the understanding that Napoleon would not suffer the pain of death but instead be taken prisoner and conveyed to England where Royal Navy vessels would be waiting to transfer him to the distant island of St Helena in the Atlantic. Whether Pitt had really set these preconditions is doubtful. After all, it is quite curious why the two Chouans selected to be the advance guard to Paris were the very same who were evidently complicit in the rue Niçaise bomb attack. Indeed, La Haye St Hilaire, otherwise known as *Raoul* or *Doisson*, had been personally selected by Lord Addington himself as the best constituted among the Chouan leaders to carry out the *coup de main*.[7]

In any case, the Governor of Jersey, the Prince de Bouillon, was uncomfortable with St Hilaire's unexpected presence on the island and requested orders from his superiors in Whitehall as to what to do with him. He knew that there were French spies hiding amidst the émigré community and was therefore anxious to dispose of St Hilaire as soon as possible, preferably as far away from the Channel Islands as possible, as he supposed that the French government would accuse him once again of harbouring 'terrorists'. Eventually, England's prime minister responded to Bouillon's request but instead of disbanding the surviving Chouans as hoped, he assigned several of their leaders to the command of Georges, who was then making arrangements with John Wesley Wright to land in France.

On 21 August 1803, Georges quit London and travelled to the Sussex fishing port of Hastings, the conspirators' rendezvous point. He was accompanied by six other Chouans. They planned to disguise themselves as a detachment of hussars or dragoons and attack Napoleon's escort as it left his residence at either Malmaison, St Cloud or Rambouillet at night. Georges would then put himself at the head of government and assume a provisory title until the transitional phase was complete and the exiled Louis XVIII safely restored to the throne. If Napoleon resisted arrest, he would be put to death. Upon arrival in Hastings, he discovered that St Hilaire, his former aide-de-camp, Jean Marie Hermilly and a third Chouan named Breche had been arrested by the local constabulary after having been denounced by an Englishman with whom they had an altercation. He presented himself at the jailhouse, and after clearing their names, went to meet Captain Wright who was waiting to transport them on board his sloop. At that moment, he was struck down by an excruciating toothache and had to postpone their departure until it had been attended to by a local dentist.[8]

Two days later, Wright's darkened sloop appeared in sight of the cliffs of Biville, approximately four leagues to the north of Dieppe, near the village of Penli. He originally intended to land the conspirators in Brittany, but, knowing that the region's coastline was guarded with greater vigilance than ever, he decided to change course and head instead for a hidden place known as the hollow of Parfonval. A thick mist covered the sea and the obscuration of vision was so complete that Treport's church steeple was first mistaken for a mast of a ship. As the sloop closed on the shore, Georges and his companions lowered a small boat and, pulling on muffled oars, rowed in the direction of the light that was gleaming from the summit of the cliff, 320 feet above sea level. They pulled into an obscure outlet formed in a cleft of rock long known to smugglers, and scrambled onto the sand. An *'estamperche'* was fixed to some piles and, after tugging to see whether it would hold, the conspirators began to pull themselves up the rope by their arms, all the while bumping against the steep wall of rock and clay.[9] Georges, the largest and most powerful of the group, remained behind with young Troche, the son of the former procurer of the commune of Eu. A strong wind began to blow, and with each sudden jolt the two men were thrown violently against the rocks. Once aground, they found themselves at the bottom of a crevice and began to make their way through its natural pathway to the open fields above. Satisfied of the Frenchmen's safety, Wright, accompanied by a detachment of sailors, returned back to the sloop that lay in anchor. The danger of being spotted by roving patrolmen grew by the minute. With the mission now complete, he headed back across the English Channel.

Georges and his gang were meanwhile treading their way through the trackless paths to *La Poterie*, a remote farm, and *'maison de confiance'* (or safehouse) near the hamlet of Heudelimont, about two leagues from the coast. They were led by a handsome young Chouan, about thirty years old with a winning smile and dressed in the fashion peculiar to the time. He had earned quite a reputation for robbing mail coaches conveying government money and using the takings to recruit young royalists to the cause. His name was Raoul Gaillard, but he went by the aliases Houvel and Saint-Vincent.[10]

The next morning, after sleeping on beds of hay, the conspirators made their way through the forest of Eu towards Aumale, the rendezvous point where the twenty-eight-year-old Marquis d'Hozier, a former page to the king with light chestnut hair and green eyes, and Louis de Sol de Grisolles were waiting in a yellow cabriolet to convey Georges to Paris. Just as the mighty Breton stepped in with d'Hozier and de Sol, he reportedly turned to his companions and said to them, 'I do not know the sort of fate that is awaiting us, yet I am sure that if any of us falls into the hands of the Usurper he will accept his fate with courage and give no one away.' He entered Paris unobserved on 1 September 1803 after following the *lignes de correspondence* marked out months before, pausing to rest in Madame Dathy's Hôtel de Bordeaux in the rue de Grenelle-Saint-Honoré. In the evening, as it grew dark, he switched to the famous Cloche d'Or restaurant inn, ensconced on the corner of the rue du Bac and the rue du Varenne, and was joined there by his faithful servant Louis Picot, codenamed Le Petit, with whom he remained there in hiding for six days.[11]

The discovery that the First Consul was not as unpopular as suggested did not discourage Georges or his fellow conspirators from carrying out their plan of attack. It was not as if Georges needed a groundswell of public opinion to deliver his *coup de main*. But upon dispatching his agents to La Vendée to measure the mood in that region, he was dismayed to discover how deeply its citizens had fallen into a 'state of inertness'. The pressure of conscription had not, he learnt, imbued the young with a spirit of rebellion as it had formerly done, and this new generation was just as little inclined to take up arms against the Republic as to serve on its behalf. That the Breton general still commanded their attachment there could be no doubt. Of all the Chouan leaders it was his name alone that stood highest in their estimation. Yet no matter their convictions, the Vendéans were unenthused by a life on the heaths and high roads, preferring to remain at home in peace than depose a usurper who even the priests, despite having encouraged the partisan war in the west, now felt inclined towards. But the indomitable Georges was undeterred, and over the next two months he scoured the countryside for volunteers. He managed to muster just over thirty men who were willing to enrol, but for precaution he kept the nature of their mission a secret, telling them only that the restoration of the Bourbons was the objective and that they should wait for his rallying call.

From his base in Paris, Georges prepared uniforms for his volunteers to wear and arms to bear. However, he remained uncertain as to Moreau's disposition and so dispatched a trustworthy Breton by the name of Fresmière to sound out the general, who soon returned bearing news that reaffirmed Georges' suspicion that Moreau was 'chickenhearted' and unreliable.[12] Georges, nevertheless, pressed his sponsors in the English government to act, reminding them that it was he, not they, who ran the greatest risks, having been left alone in the centre of Paris for the past couple of months vulnerable to exposure.

As Georges scoured La Vendée for volunteers, Wright was employed in spying on France's naval build-up and tightening the lines of communication with the royalists in the interior. He was under no Admiralty instructions, having been, on the recommendation of Smith, personally entrusted with this secret and important commission by the Prime Minister, Lord Addington. Ever since his return from Paris, he and Smith had been arranging a correspondence of their own, facilitated through the mediation of the latter's uncle, General Edward Smith, and the general's link with the Prime Minister's brother, Hiley. The general lived at Walmer Castle, formerly a Tudor fort in Deal, where William Pitt officially occupied residence as Lord Warden of the Cinque Ports and where he and Smith's elder brother, Colonel Charles Douglas Smith, were official recipients of this clandestine correspondence transmitted by the agents in France. Pitt was, by this stage, an ungainly man of forty-two whose insobriety had given him an unhealthy hue, yet he was still privy to Britain's war policy and national defence as well as 'the stiletto of espionage, subversion and assassination'.[13] The chef for the new correspondence, a poor Norman abbot named Julien Réné Le Clerc, had moved to Boulogne following the resumption of war, having selected that town as the headquarters for the royalist's organisation as it was, like its neighbour, the Pas-de-Calais, a stronghold of anti-republican feeling and a relatively safe point of communication with England. The abbé, who was afflicted with a wall eye, had served the Paris Agency and Institut Philanthopique and had, in the months preceding the rue Niçaise explosion, been actively involved in its preparation. It was his presence of mind that had saved the most important papers from being confiscated at the time of Duverne de Presle's arrest in January 1797, having flown to the Hôtel of the Agency and removed the minutes and numbers of many secret letters, notably the correspondence which had been conducted by the king himself. Following these events, he went underground and hid in the thickets of the Bois de Vincennes. Since then, he stood determined to resume his adventurous life as soon as the occasion should arise.

Following his unsuccessful interview with Moreau, Louis Fauche-Borel met him in a house on the rue du Pot de Fer living under the alias *Boisvalon*. The abbé appeared to him au fait with the facts but complained that he was paid a 'pitiful' £16 per month for services rendered to the British government. Despite his dissatisfaction, he was ably assisted by Pierre Marie Poix, a defrocked priest who, during this period, had adopted altogether sixteen different aliases, the principle being *La Rose*. Among his many pseudonyms, the priest chose *La Veille Perruke*, an 'old fogy' or *La Besace*, an old-fashioned purse but his favourite, *La Rose*, was certainly intended to tease the authorities by alluding to the little red flowers on the calling cards that members of the royalist agency were known to be circulating in Paris at the time. He diligently organised the system of landings and guided routes to Paris including the one Georges had just used and for this, was abetted by a fashionable twenty-year-old maiden named Nymphe Roussel de Pléville, who otherwise passed as a man by the name of Monsieur Dubuisson. Pléville aka Prime-Rose was quite a beauty, so it was told. She was petite with an oval face, seductive blue eyes, auburn hair that was neatly tucked under a lace bonnet and a tender complexion. When not sporting breeches she was teasingly dressed in a white tunic striped with blue. She would ride into the Norman countryside on a fast horse named 'La Blondine', which had been stabled at British expense for the purpose of carrying confidential letters.[14]

Being employed off the coast of Boulogne, Wright had occasion to forge links with this network and also engage French fishermen to facilitate communications. His observations led him to conclude that there were at least 100 gunboats in Boulogne and that they might be extremely troublesome. He was also lent the use of Smith's private yacht for his cross-Channel communications until he had been supplied with an adequate number of vessels to perform the 'particular service' he was charged with. From

July to September, he passed and re-passed England's stations without hindrance or molestation, having received permission, if not official authority, from the Secretary to the Admiralty, Sir Evan Nepean, and the support of Rear Admiral Robert Montagu, second-in-command to Admiral Lord Keith, Commander-in-Chief in the Downs station.

In fact, Sir Nepean was issuing orders to Wright without having been himself vested with the authority from the First Lord, St Vincent, and without also informing Admiral Keith of Wright's crossings. In September, however, Sir Nepean finally was relieved of the necessity of bypassing them when St Vincent, on the insistence of Lord Hawkesbury, the Foreign Secretary, told Admiral Keith that 'it is of the utmost importance that Captain Wright should be indulged in the fullest latitude'.[15] Equipped with these instructions, Admiral Keith accordingly transmitted the following orders to Captain Carpenter to that effect on 6 September 1803. By then, of course, Wright had already landed Georges and his accomplices on the coast of Normandy:

> Whereas Captain John Wright of H.M. Navy is employed on a secret and delicate service and I have thought fit that he should embark in HM Armed lugger, *Speculator* under your command, you are hereby required and directed to receive Captain Wright on board and to proceed with him from place to place as he may require, furnishing him with boats and chosen me for the accomplishment of his object, vigilantly attending to his safety and protection, and that of any persons who may be with him; and keeping your vessel in constant state of preparation for resisting any attack that the enemy make upon you.
>
> You will victual Captain Wright during his continuance on board in the same manner as the rest of the crew, and when the service on which he is employed shall be affected you are return for further orders into port'.
>
> Given on board the *Monarch* in the Downs[16]

Wright was clearly no favourite of Lord Keith's. Among the reasons, it was said that he and Smith made a point of disregarding the orders issued by their superior officers and that the general opinion circulating the Admiralty's halls was that these two insufferable men had become 'too big for their boots'. The Commander-in-Chief did not approve of anyone, especially naval officers under his command involved in workings of espionage, and he particularly resented Wright and Smith's personal ties with the king's ministers. He knew that secret orders emanating from the Foreign Office had been issued to them but he was not alone in believing that the Foreign Secretary, who was desperately trying to stave off the impending demise of Addington's ministry, was being 'led away' with their talk and doubted if the former had not placed mistaken trust in their assurances. Though holding no particular regard for Wright, the Foreign Minister was prepared to tolerate him as a convenient instrument to be used as occasion demanded but he viewed with extreme disfavour the party of royalists, which he described as 'a rascally gang of frogs'. In any case, Lord Keith complained that orders had been issued to the two about which he knew nothing, prompting him to describe them as 'infernal gadflies flitting hither and thither giving a man devilish small chance of catching them at their antics'.[17] He was not the sole Sea-Lord in the Admiralty to be set by the ears. Lord St Vincent, it was said, had 'a rush of blood to the head' whenever either of their names was mentioned. Indeed, a spate of furious letters flurried between the Commander-in-Chief in the Downs and his deputy, Admiral Markham, in which the insubordination of Wright was the principal subject. Wright was not only employing vessels such as the *Basilisk*, of which they knew nothing, but was also 'talking large of being sacrificed', having nearly been taken by enemy's cruisers. He complained that he had not been given a sufficient force and that the execution of his mission depended on (an early version of) the Royal Navy's Special Boat Service being put at his disposal:[18]

From Walmer Castle, he wrote to Rear Admiral Montagu

21 November 1803

Sir, I have the honour to enclose a letter addressed to Lord Keith the object of which is to procure me the means of executing a particular and delicate service, of very high importance to the interest of this country. You would greatly contribute to the success of this service if you could have the goodness to place the Lively revenue cutter at my disposal immediately, to supersede the necessity of my personally waiting upon his Lordship at Broadstairs; and to enable me to embark and proceed upon this service with the next ebb tide.

His Lordship's attention to this object on a former occasion, and the handsome manner in which the best means within his reach were instantly applied upon my application to him, leave me no doubt of his Lordship's ready sanction to this measure.[19]

Lord Keith was naturally unaccustomed to being addressed in such a high-handed manner, especially by a junior captain with no official appointment, and so, with Admiral Markham on his side, he took his immense displeasure to the First Lord of the Admiralty, Lord St Vincent. The latter was no less astonished by Wright's audacity, and so evidently put out by it that his head was 'too bad to write' to Sir Evan Nepean demanding an explanation. He did endeavour to obtain all the directions that Sir Nepean had given to Rear Admiral Montagu concerning Wright's service, with the added stress that it was 'absolutely necessary that the whole dark business should be cleared up'.[20] His feeling of exclusion was not helped by the surreptitiousness of the Foreign Secretary, Lord Hawkesbury, who signified to him, via a Mr Hammond, that Wright be furnished with one or more vessels 'as occasion might require them on a very urgent mission'. The lords of the Admiralty were by now beyond restive and in their attempt to regain some mastery of the situation succeeded in effectuating the replacement of Rear Admiral Montagu, whom they defamed as 'that Prince of Intrigues', with Rear Admiral Philip Patton, supposedly 'a plain honest man'.[21] However, they appeared unable to rein Wright in, who continued to make matters worse by his incessant provocations. On 19 December, the unruly officer wrote to Admiral Markham complaining that that he had been off the Boulogne coast for some days and that, although he met with enemy cruisers almost every night, he had not seen one of their own, though the wind had been off the enemy's coast all the time. The tone of his letter elicited Lord Keith's rage, who in his mounting impotence demanded to review the logs of the cutters *Hound*, *Griffin* and *Basilisk*, which though officially under his command were being employed by Wright on his clandestine missions. His enquiry seemed to have been readily answered but it evidently surprised him that Wright and his 'clique' were still being intended as spies'.[22] According to his understanding, as an officer of the Royal Navy, the admiral owed the discharge of his duty to the public and not to party or politics. It was not that he expected to be privy to government secrets – indeed, he wrote to Admiral Markham on Christmas Eve acknowledging that, on the subject of the cutters being employed under the authority of the Secretary of State, he saw no reason why he should be informed of the intelligence they may contain – but it only seemed decent to him that he should be acquainted with the vessels so employed and not be told by his inferiors such vessels were absent. In fact, so unsure of his ground was he that he supposed that if there were any branches of the government that had lost confidence in him he would duly request to make way for the man whom they preferred.

The arrival of Christmas Day did not put him in any more festive spirit. Wright's shenanigans had, by all appearances, put him in a permanent state of ill humour and it bothered him no less that the small ships laying at anchor offshore were being directed by a clique at Walmer, who behaved without the least hint of integrity and without suffering anyone to 'check their nonsense'.[23] He had learned from a Lieutenant Stuart that Wright had been at Walmer the last few days, where it appeared from Stuart's impressions that things were not quite right; it was only with the royalists' acquiescence that any cross-Channel communication took place.

In the second week of December 1803, General Lajolais landed on English shores. After quitting Moreau's country estate he had headed straight for Alsace, where he was detained for several months on account of his debts. With no means to subsidise his passage to England, he was compelled to accept a lowly occupation which, though poorly paid, at least bore the promise of an honest living. After having made a short stopover in Schleswig-Holstein, he sailed to England disguised as a Teutonic merchant.

The port authorities at Harwich, however, were expecting his arrival. Despite the strict enforcement of the Aliens Act, he was permitted to proceed on his way without further inconvenience to himself. Everywhere he turned he could sense the country's alarm at the threat of invasion, but at the same time he saw how the people of England were also resolved to teach the First Consul a lesson once and for all. He exploited this national fermentation, telling his employers beyond what he may have imagined to be true and what was certainly beyond truth itself. He did not make any concrete proposals but, like many of the intermediaries who fancied their own talents and importance, he imagined that just one word would suffice to 'decide' Moreau and that this decision would determine the fate of the conspiracy. He fancied that the most eminent royalists would flock round the standard, believing that France would soon be restored to her ancient dynasty, and in his imagination he was created a duke or marquis, rewarded with a château and adorned with riches for his unshakeable devotion. It is just how the plots of this period were woven – by secret agents who at once cheated themselves and their employers.

Having gained admission to the princes' circle, Lajolais represented Moreau as being favourable to a restoration of the Bourbons now that he was excluded from public affairs. Though retired, he still commanded the loyalty of his armies and the support of the French princes. He had, in fact, already considered removing Napoleon (who at that time was assembling in Boulogne the most formidable army ever yet seen in Europe) by petitioning allies in the Senate who were sufficiently powerful to effectuate the reestablishment of the Bourbons on the throne of France. The king's intemperate younger brother, the Comte d'Artois, joined the councils of the conspirators, and upon hearing Lajolais' recount the words that Moreau was supposed to have spoken – that Pichegru need only show his person in France and their friendship could be reformed – apparently burst out, as if unable to suppress his enthusiasm any longer, 'If our two generals are in a perfect understanding, I shall soon be on my return to France.'[24] His excitable behaviour drew the attention of all those present, who, having formerly not known his true identity, were now left with this unflattering first impression. The French princes, in any case, were encouraged by Lajolais' disclosures and for the next three weeks he enjoyed the abounding confidence of the king's ex-ministers, chief among them William Windham, William Pitt and Lord Grenville.

Though they had committed no evidence to paper, it was certain that they had encouraged Pichegru to embark upon his expedition, having informed Lord Keith on 9 January, in a correspondence marked most secret, that it had 'been judged advisable that an officer of rank and consideration should be landed in France as soon as possible and that it was of great importance to His Majesty's government that he should not fall into the hands of the enemy'. Pichegru, evidently believing Moreau to be favourably disposed to the same cause when in fact he was not, accepted these men's encouragements as he did the assurances brought to him by his friend Lajolais. He was living in quiet retirement with Victor Couchery, the Abbé David's brother, on a tidy pension of 100 *louis* per month in a small house at Brompton Row in the capital, where he was said to have passed his time reading all the articles from the *Courrier de Londres* before their actual publication, communicating little with the outside world and pretending to have no correspondence with France. He was apparently unhappy with the measure of consideration that he was accorded but nevertheless agreed to enter France, without further delay, in order to hasten the execution of this grand project and join Georges who, standing alone in the midst of the Consul's police agents, might suppose himself abandoned.

On 10 January 1804 General Pichegru left London in the company of Lajolais and Captain Wright. Together they journeyed to Deal where the latter's sloop was moored, ready to transport them across the Channel. Their companions, who either preceded or followed them to Deal, were men altogether more privileged than the two detachments of emigrants whom Wright had conveyed to Normandy in August and towards the end of September. Besides the two above, the party consisted of the ex-Swiss guardsman Major Rusillion, Louis XVIII's aide-de-camp the Marquis de Rivière and the brothers Polignacs, with whom the Comte Jules would later help bring about the abdication of the king's brother in 1830. They boarded the *Basilisk* and on the following day, 11 January, they set sail for the cliffs of Biville to the same spot where Georges and his conspirators had scaled its heights. They were delayed by contrary winds and it was not before the night of the 16th that the party arrived, on rising tide, at the point of disembarkation. Once put to shore, they tackled the smuggler's rope and scrambled up the same cliff path, being met by a guide who led the party to the lonely farm, *La Poterie*. They were welcomed there by Georges, who had made the journey from Paris, and under the convivial shelter they huddled by the cosy fire, on which a pot of stew was gently simmering. Having accomplished his mission, Wright put his helm on and set a course to the Downs, pulling a mile to the south off Deal Castle and its adjacent naval yard. Once ashore he walked up the steep shingle beach and short passage to the squat, rounded Walmer Castle. Entering a low-ceilinged room occupied by William Pitt's cousin General Edward Smith, Wright reported the successful accomplishment of his mission.[25]

Wright continued to make Channel crossings over the following weeks, landing a number of French royalists along the Breton coast. The secrecy with which he made these trips was undoubtedly necessary but nevertheless grated with his commanding officers, whom he insisted in treating in his usual cavalier manner. Markham remarked to Keith how he had 'never saw a man with more pretensions than Captain Wright and he talks it very well; but I should suppose that to be the extent of his abilities in our line'.[26] To be sure, Wright was a navy officer of the second order but his calibre as a spy and intelligence officer was of the highest level. He was, however, prone to exaggeration, no doubt to elevate his own importance and the mission with which he was charged. According to Keith he claimed that France was 'ripe for insurrection', or at least pretended to think so. Either way, his incessant 'mummery' did not abate throughout the month of January. As Keith again complained:

13th Jan This Captain Wright has come to Deal in the night and called on Admiral Patton for two cutters (Speculator and Flirt) with which vessels he had set off. Thus he has the Admiral Mitchell, Hound and Griffin doing he only knows what, whilst I have only two small vessels of all those belonging to the Downs station to watch the coast from Ostend to Calais...I am at a loss what to do about the Champion; he only mentioned the subject to me at a distance but promised to wait upon me when he returned from the coast of France but which he has not done.[27]

Keith avowed, or so claimed, that Wright's requests would be granted if he was more forthcoming. That same day he wrote the following letter to his subordinate in terms admitting of no equivocation.

Monarch, off Ramsgate, 13 January, 1804

Sir- I have written to Lord Hawkesbury that I have appropriated the Admiral Mitchell hired cutter and the Hound revenue cutter, in addition to the hired vessel which is at your disposal to enable you to perform the service on which you are employed, there two being as many as I can possibly spare at the present moment. You will, therefore, not consider the Flirt, Speculator, or any other of the vessels, than the two before mentioned, as being subject to be employed by you. The Champion is now at Spithead ready to proceed to carry into effect the service which you mentioned to me when here: but your sudden departure from Deal, without any communication whatever with me, renders it impossible that she can remain idle there, when the important station to which she is attached is so slenderly provided for. I take this opportunity of repeating my opinion that Ramsgate seems much better calculated for a place of secret embarkation than Deal, where the surf is frequently too great to be passed.

I am, &c, &c,

Keith[28]

Despite Keith's reasonable objections, Wright was still dissatisfied with the level of cooperation that he was receiving from his superiors and demanded unfettered access to station's squadron:

23rd Jan, Captain Wright had two of the largest cutters and seems content, but he wanted a power to direct any ships or vessels on the station at pleasure. He shall want for nothing if he will ask, but he cadgels [*sic*] with General Smith and the colonel at Deal, added to the old father at Dover; they are all mad with vanity and hold no terms in their abuse of all such as do not hold up their nonsense, to call it by worse name.[29]

That same day, in bleak winter conditions, Pichegru and Georges entered Paris by the Porte Saint-Denis and were quietly lodged on the second floor of a private residence in the rue du Puits-de-l'Hermite. They were dressed in green greatcoats and each had a pair of pistols tucked away. They had left *La Poterie* farm after having paused a short while and travelled by night, sometimes on foot or horseback and sometimes in a carriage. They were accompanied on the first leg of the journey by Rousillion and Picot, a native from Brittany with thick black hair, a small beak nose, black eyes, round chin and an oval face scarred heavily from smallpox. In the meantime, Lajolais, who had taken a different road, reached Moreau's residence and announced Pichegru's arrival in Paris. Moreau, however, was not prepared to welcome Pichegru to his home but agreed to meet his former friend at the Boulevard de la Madeleine at nine o'clock on the evening of 25 January. It is not certain what actually transpired in their first encounter, but at a second meeting Pichegru presented Georges to Moreau and revealed their joint plans for the 'overthrow of the tyrant'. At first, Moreau was displeased to find himself in the presence of the notorious Georges, the perceived mastermind behind the rue Niçaise bomb attack. He himself was struck by the impression of the meeting, apparently saying that 'this will do mischief'.[30] Moreau was not entirely indifferent to the overturn of the government but evinced his displeasure at plotting for the Bourbons' restoration. He was, in other words, happy to oversee Napoleon's downfall but felt that only he and Pichegru, and not Georges, were worthy of the great task. Indeed, at their third interview, which was again attended by Georges, Moreau's attitude was still more intractable and, whilst agreeing that Napoleon must be overthrown, he argued that the Senate alone could decide as to what form the superseding government should take. At the same time, he intimated that during the transition period he should be invested with supreme power. And thus, Moreau's secret ambitions to govern were revealed. Pichegru apparently left in despair, uttering, 'It seems that fellow has ambition too! He would, in his turn, govern. Poor man! He knows not how to govern France for twenty-four hours!' Georges too was exasperated, decrying, 'Usurper for usurper! I love him that now governs better than Moreau, who has neither head nor heart!'[31]

The three conspirators met for a final time at Chatillot, but despite minor compromises it was evident that an impasse had been reached and no agreement could be made as to the precise mode or speed that the new government would take. They thus parted ways, uncertain of each other's ambition but surely suspecting that they had made a grave mistake in engaging in such a foolhardy enterprise.

Above left: 1. An enthusiastic proponent of the underground war against revolutionary France, Britain's Prime Minister, William Pitt the Younger. (Courtesy of the Library of Congress)

Above right: 2. Charles Maurice de Talleyrand-Périgord by Jacob Ernst Marcus, 1812. (Courtesy of the Rijksmuseum)

Right: 3. Louis Stanislas Xavier de France by Louis Marin Bonnet. (Courtesy of the Rijksmuseum)

4. Patriot or traitor? A contemporary portrait of the dissident republican General Jean-Charles Pichegru by Charles Howard Hodges, 1795. (Courtesy of the Rijksmuseum)

Above: 5. Republican troops commanded by Pichegru cross the Rhine near Düsseldorf on 20 *Fructidor* an III (6 September 1795). (Courtesy of the Library of Congress)

Below: 6. The famous 'whiff of grapeshot'. Rebellious sections are mowed down on the footsteps of St Roch Cathedral on the historic journée, 13 *Vendémiaire* an IV (5 October 1795). (Courtesy of the Library of Congress)

7. William Sidney Smith by Johann Carl Schleich. The maverick commodore relished his career in espionage, referring to it as an occupation 'of a superior sort'. (Courtesy of the Rijksmuseum)

8. The only known portrait of the gallant Captain John Wesley Wright, after G. Galleia. (Public domain)

9. First Consul of France, the great Napoleon Bonaparte by Louis Bouilly. Below the medallion, Napoleon is depicted reviewing troops in the courtyard of the Tuileries palace. (Courtesy of the Library of Congress)

10. Napoleon's nemesis: the legendary Chouan leader, Georges Cadoudal, in a book released on the centenary of the French Revolution. (Public domain)

11. The ambitious turncoat, General Jean Victor Moreau. Moreau's rapprochement with his former friend, Pichegru, would form the basis of the 'Great Conspiracy'. (Courtesy of the Rijksmuseum)

12. 'Armed heroes'. A satirical portrait of Britain's neglected Prime Minister, Lord Henry Addington, by the caricaturist James Gilray in May 1803. Despite the earnest desire for peace, Addington suffered a storm of criticism once the terms of the Treaty of Amiens were announced. (Courtesy of the Library of Congress)

13. *Desespoir des Ennemis de la France à la decouverte de leurs Complots*. Printed by order of the French government, this propaganda piece contains forty-two bust caricatures of the principal conspirators, including no. 8, 'Mr Vic-kam', no. 12, 'Mr. Adington' and no. 18, 'Lord How Kersbury'. (Courtesy of the Library of Congress)

14. The end of the Revolution. With the conspiracy unraveled, Napoleon found the pretext to crown himself Emperor of France. The coronation took place on Sunday 2 December 1804. (Courtesy of the Library of Congress)

19

CONFESSIONS

At about the same time, an elaborate deception was being carried out to entrap the British government and distract the French one. The centre of this intrigue was a double agent named Chevalier Jean-Claude Hippolyte Méhée de la Touche, a former Jacobin whom the English thought to be 'a very clever fellow'.[1]

The son of a quack surgeon from Meaux, Méhée began his career as a secret agent in Poland spying on behalf of the republicans but was expelled from the territory by the Russian government and returned to France, where he joined in the assault on the Tuileries on 10 August 1792. As a reward for his zeal he was appointed secretary of the Paris Commune that same night, and subsequently put his signature on the papers sanctioning the infamous September massacres at l'Abbaye prison. He afterwards became the secretary of Jean Lambert Tallien before being appointed to the Ministry of War under the Directory in November 1795. He held the same function in the Foreign Department under Charles François Delacroix, but in the aftermath of the coup of 18 *Fructidor* was deported to Guyana together with Pichegru and the other prisoners.

Following Napoleon's usurpation of power, Méhée edited a newspaper secretly funded by Joseph Fouché criticising the Consulship. He was accused of complicity in the attack on Napoleon's life of 3 *nivôse* and was subsequently included in the list of suspects condemned to deportation. Napoleon, it will be recalled, imputed the assassination attempt to the Jacobins. After enduring a gruelling year in exile, Méhée was reported to have escaped from the Ile d'Oléron in an American merchant ship. In fact, his friends in Paris had interceded on his behalf and secured his liberty in exchange for the promise that he would spy on England for France. He thus set out for Guernsey, where he hoped to seduce the émigrés and the British officers of the garrison.

Posing as a repentant Jacobin, Méhée managed to enter into friendly relations with General Doyle, the island's governor, and Sir James de Saumarez, the admiral stationed there. He also tried to win over Lord Addington's ministry in London by sending them classified documents from the Ministry of Foreign Affairs purporting to reveal Napoleon's designs on Egypt and Turkey. The English cabinet just ignored him, so, hoping to appeal directly to them in person, he confided to Doyle that according to his sources Napoleon was devising a means of fomenting rebellion in Ireland. Doyle and de Saumarez were so alarmed by the news that they enjoined him to hasten at once to England and relay this information to the government in person. The ministers authorised his entry into England and advanced him £20, although half the sum would have sufficed, as well as issuing him with a passport to enable him to depart forthwith.[2]

In London, Méhée had an audience with George Hammond, the Under-Secretary for Foreign Affairs. Unlike Mehée, who was handsome and charming, the Englishman was described as a 'disagreeable person of ugly appearance, who was inclined to be suspicious'.[3] Hammond received him in his usual haughty manner but nevertheless promised to show his papers to Lord Hawkesbury, who would then decide upon his employment. A few days later, Méhée was summoned again to the Foreign Office where he found Hammond in a more genial frame of mind. The news which the English minister had to impart, however, was still disappointing. Hawkesbury was suspicious of Mehée's story and instructed Hammond to dismiss him on the grounds that the government could not accept his espionage services as they had just concluded peace with France, but that should war reignite they may reconsider their position. Méhée consequently presented himself to Bertrand de Moleville, the former Minister of Marine and Colonies for Louis XVI; repeating the story he had recently told to Hammond, he solicited his assistance. The two men agreed to revive the ploy of making Mehée's former friends, the Jacobins, the instruments of a royalist restoration. But when Méhée alluded to his financial difficulties, Moleville made his excuses, and after staving off the eventuality for three months, Méhée was arrested at the suit of his landlord for a debt of £47, and committed to a sponging house. He remained a prisoner for only a few days when the news arrived from Paris that Britain's ambassador, Lord Whitworth, had asked for his passports following the rupture of peace negotiations.

The outbreak of war brought an immediate change in Mehée's fortunes. Bertrand de Moleville intervened on his behalf and, settling his debts, gave him £50 and told him that the British government was prepared to allow him £10 per month to be withdrawn from a discretionary secret service fund. Shortly afterwards, he was informed that he would be dispatched to France on an important mission. The plan of uniting the republicans and royalists against Napoleon was submitted to the English Cabinet and a copy was sent to Louis XVIII. It was claimed that he never took part in the 'great crimes of the Revolution' and that on 10 August, he was actually helping to procure passports for the victims and had even contrived to save the king from the assailants.[4]

In London, Hakwesbury finally relented to Moleville's pressure and issued the following instructions. Méhée was 'to concert with his friends, measures for overthrowing the existing government in France in order that the nation might have an opportunity of choosing the form of government the most calculated to ensure its happiness and tranquillity.'[5] On his way to France, the wily Frenchman paid a visit to the British Minister, Francis Drake, then resident in the Bavarian capital so that he could conduct his secret correspondence with agents operating in France with greater facility. Méhée was awarded £700 and a salary of £50 per month. On 9 September 1803 he set out for Munich bearing two passports, one in which he was named Stanislaus Jablouski and described as a Polish nobleman, and the other in which he was simply Mehée, a French national who had been expelled from England as a Jacobin under terms of the Alien Act. He was also provided with a bottle of sympathetic ink, despite supposedly not knowing how it was made or rendered legible.[6]

In Munich, Drake gave Mehée precise instructions as to the object of his mission as well as bills of exchange to defray his own, and his agents', expenses. He was charged with stirring disaffection in the army, sabotaging factories devoted to the manufacture of war supplies and gathering intelligence on Napoleon's military plans, particularly his secrets relative to the descent on England. Mehée, meanwhile, remained in secret communication with the French government, and on arriving in Paris relayed Drake's instructions to the *Grand Juge*, Claude Ambroise Régnier. His patriotic conduct earned him the approbation of Napoleon who hailed him 'a good Frenchman'.[7] And so, from that moment on, Mehée's correspondence with Drake was continued under the direct supervision of Napoleon's police. Drake was furnished with bad information about France's naval movements and the activities of the camp at Boulogne. The First Consul wished to trick Drake into disclosing information which might implicate the English minister and thus furnish him with grounds for levelling accusations of espionage against the British government. Mehée, now based in Frankfurt, maintained simultaneous correspondence with Fouché, the *Comité Secret des Jacobins de Paris*, Moleville and Drake. The latter was not deceived by Mehée but appears to have remained ignorant of the existence of the 'Great Conspiracy'. He knew, however, that he would be sacrificed by Hawkesbury, who had agreed to this charade with Mehée in order to divert Napoleon's attention from what was happening in Paris.

As it turned out, Napoleon was not distracted for long. For the past few weeks, reports had been reaching the Tuileries of an upsurge of royalist activity in the west including rumours pertaining to mysterious landings on the Breton coast and plots to assassinate him. The reports, though seldom in agreement, were sufficiently troubling to Napoleon. According to a British informant, he was already becoming 'more morose, more choleric and more reserved' each day on account of his diminishing popularity.[8] With no victories to boast of, the war had, as Fouché correctly predicted, brought a universal change of mood. So, on 17 January 1804, in an address to the senate on the state of the republic, Napoleon did not spare an opportunity to denounce the 'odious conduct of the British government which has been attempting to throw on our coasts several of these monsters'.[9]

It was not until 25 January, on the very day that Moreau and Pichegru held their first meeting, that Napoleon conceived a plan to penetrate the mystery himself. He had reason to doubt the effectiveness and reliability of his secret police, supposing that if a serious plot was afoot then some of his own agents must have known something about it but were deliberately keeping him in the dark. He was also persuaded that the men who manufactured the rue Niçaise bomb would have strong reasons for preparing a similar surprise under existing circumstances, telling Joachim Murat, the Governor of Paris, 'The emigrants are certainly at work. Numerous arrests are taking place; some of the individuals taken must be sent before a military commission, that will condemn them, and then they will confess before they suffer themselves to be shot.'[10] So, he turned his investigation to the state prisoners who were detained by the police as spies or political undesirables and ordered General Moncey, the *Premier Inspecteur Général of the Gendamerie Nationale,* to lay a list of their names, together with the dates and circumstances of their apprehensions, before him.

Having examined the particular services attached to each of them, Napoleon identified five individuals from the list who were ripe for interrogation. Turning to Pierre François Réal, he asserted, 'I am very strongly deceived or there are here some men who will not be wanting in making revelations.'[11] Of the five men, two were brought before a military commission seated at the rue des Capucines and acquitted of the charges of conspiring against the state.[12] The next pair, Louis Pierre Picot and Charles Le Bourgeois, were not so fortunate.

They were arrested by the police on 8 January 1803 at Pont Audemer in Normandy thanks to the intelligence received from a French agent in London codenamed 'Laubeypie'. 'Laubeypie' had been sent to England during the Amiens interlude ostensibly as a representative of the Bank of France to investigate the printing of fake tender. After making a number of enquiries he had reported to the French ambassador to the court of St James, Comte Antoine-François Andréossy, that a tailor named Roulier, who was then resident in London, had informed some agents that he had designed uniforms for Picot and le Bourgeois and that whilst being fitted they boasted that they were leaving for France to bring to an end the First Consul's rule of power. Andréossy forwarded the report to Paris and also issued a formal complaint to Lord Hawkesbury, citing the two men's ties with Georges. Picot and Le Bourgeois were suspected of being complicit in the rue Niçaise bomb and held *au secret* in the Temple where they were repeatedly tortured. Such was their distress that they wrote letters begging to be shot rather than to continue being subjected to their ordeal. 'Death, yes, Death,' cried le Bourgeois, 'is preferable to the horrible situation to which I am reduced. Send me to the plain of Grenelle or to the Scaffold, have me taken to a fortress, have me deported ... the First Consul could never authorise such tortures for a Frenchman ...' The two men had confessed only to knowing that five generals, whom they named as Pichegru, Willot, Danican, Cadoudal and one other, would land in France when circumstances permitted. In mid-January, after numerous appeals, their solitary confinement was lifted. On 25 January, their fellow prisoner Ferdinand Christin, a Swedish diplomat, invited them to dinner. While they were dining the warders entered and violently seized the two men. Garrotting them in front of their host, they bundled them down the stairs and into a waiting carriage. They were then brought before the military commission and shot before a firing squad that very evening.[13]

The last of the five was Jean Pierre Querelle, a former apothecary and native of Lower Brittany. He had served under Georges in La Vendée and, having arrived at Paris two months before, had been denounced by a creditor whom he could not repay and was arrested by the police. On Napoleon's orders, he was interrogated over a number of days and nights by Fouché but managed to maintain his silence. He was thereupon transferred from the Temple to the military prison of l'Abbaye where he was brought before the newly formed Council of War of the First Military Division, commanded by Joachim Murat, and at 3 a.m. was condemned to death. Unlike Picot and Le Bourgeois, who were both executed *sur le champ,* he was left the whole night in his dungeon to reflect on his precarious predicament.[14] At the break of dawn, as the appointed hour drew near, his jailers perceived that the prisoner's courage was about to break and accordingly removed him to another cell on the ground floor to witness the preparations for his execution. A gendarme belonging to the firing squad jolted his nerves further by tying his horse to one of the bars of his cell. At the same time, a mounted escort was brought to the prison courtyard to conduct him to the plain of Grenelle. Faced with the terrifying possibility of death, he broke down. Calling for the prison warden, he pleaded that someone in authority might be summoned to listen to a statement which he wished to make.[15]

Napoleon was immediately alerted of the incident. Signing an order countermanding the death sentence, he dispatched Réal, the Counsellor of State, to the prisoner's cell. When Réal arrived at l'Abbaye, he found Querelle, a little man with a thin, pointed nose and pockmarked face, in such a state of abject terror that he had to be administered with brandy to restore his speech.[16] His appearance in the prison cell was hardly reassuring, given his reputation as one of Fouché's most notorious henchmen, but he assured Querelle that his life would be spared, provided he made a frank statement.

Querelle confessed to having been a surgeon aid on board *Duguay-Trouin* and of having landed with Georges at Biville four months prior. He also disclosed the identities of all the conspirators who were now in France, the exact spot at Biville where they landed and the route which they took to Paris. All of the conspirators, he revealed, had returned to France for the purpose of deposing Bonaparte. He could not be sure where Georges was concealed, having been incarcerated *au secret* for the last several months, but nevertheless he was most certainly hiding in the capital.

Stunned by the revelations, Réal rushed to the Tulieries Palace where, visibly blanched and panting, he communicated to Napoleon the alarming news that Georges and his accomplices had been present in Paris for the last four months, supposedly without the police's knowledge. The news produced a flurry of activity. The police were urged to redouble vigilance, yet no clue was known as to the direction from which the danger emanated. Every night, Querelle was visited in his cell by Réal or Desmarest who questioned him with increasing severity. Their interrogations revealed little. On 3 February, Querelle was extracted from his prison cell, escorted by Citizen Pasque, the giant inspector of the police, and a detachment of gendarmes commanded by a republican zealot named Lieutenant Manginot. They left surreptitiously at dawn, passing through the Saint Denis gate and taking the road to L'Isle-Adam.[17] For forty-eight hours they scoured the suburbs of Paris and village surroundings of Taverny, Pierrelaye, Franconville, Ermont and LePlessis-Bouchard. On the third day, as the troops returned to Paris, they traversed the village de Saint-Leu, when Querelle thought he recognised a cluster of trees, a turn of the road and a house. After resisting at first, the proprietor, a vine dresser named Denis Lamotte, confessed to having boarded a party of seven strangers who had arrived at his house at 2 a.m., two of whom were on horseback. He noticed that they all carried pistols, and appeared much fatigued. In his description of the guests, he identified a 'stout man' conforming to Georges' appearance. Lamotte also disclosed the individual routes that they took, assuring his interrogators that his confessions were not the fanciful product of his imagination.[18]

Meanwhile, in Paris, a number of important arrests were being made. On 6 February, Louis Picot, Georges' servant, was apprehended with Rubin de la Grimaudière and Coster St Victor. Picot had been recognized foraging for food and conveyed to the Prefecture de Police. He was promised his liberty in exchange for disclosing Georges' hiding place. He was also offered 1,500 *Louis d'or* which was counted before his eyes. Prior to his association with the Chouans, Picot, an uncouth lad, had been a post-boy at Lorient and doubtless had never seen so large a sum of money before. He nevertheless refused to betray his master, to whom he was lovingly devoted, and suffered the pain of torture. The concierge of the depot, Bértrand, who was reputed for sadism, undertook the grim task entrusted to him by Réal. Picot's fingers were crushed by a musket and a screwdriver. Yet he revealed nothing. 'He has borne everything with criminal resignation,' the 'judge-inquisitor' Jacques Thuriot wrote to Réal. 'He is a fanatic hardened by crime. I have now left him to solitude and suffering; I will begin again tomorrow; he knows where Georges is hidden and must be made to reveal it.'[19]

On the following day, the soles of Picot's feet were put to fire. His spirit finally left him and, begging that his torment come to an end, he provided the police with a description of Georges' appearance as well as style of dress. Furthermore, he gave them the address at Chatillot, on the rue Careme-Prenant and rue du Puits de l'Hermite. The police rushed there, arriving only to find the residence abandoned.

It was at this time that General René Savary, the commandant of Napoleon's special police protection, was summoned to the Tuileries. The First Consul was in his private cabinet, leaning over a large canvas and measuring with a pair of compasses different points of the coast of Normandy to Paris.[20] Dissatisfied with the efforts of General Moncey's gendarmerie to police the coastline, he ordered Savary to leave in great haste for Dieppe in order to intercept a fresh landing of royalists whose arrival was expected soon. The intelligence was obtained from a young Gaston of eighteen or nineteen named Troche. His father, a watchmaker, was named in a list of police suspects in the neighbouring towns of Eu and Treport who had participated in civil commotions or robbed diligences. He was said to be a former emissary of the party, but, being too elderly, his son was apprehended in his place by the gendarmerie and brought to Paris for interrogation.

Troche was instantly recognised by Querelle. He exhibited none of Picot's courage, making no attempt to deny his association with the conspirators. He also confessed to having conducted the brothers Polignacs to La Poterie farm, their first resting place en route to Paris. He declared that three disembarkations had already taken place and that a fourth was planned the evening of the next day. Equipped with Napoleon's instructions, Savary set off in plain clothes at seven o'clock in the evening accompanied by Troche and a detachment of gendarmes *d'élite* transported on a wagon borrowed from the First Consul's very own stables.

Throughout the night, and most of the following day, the cavalcade rolled across north-west France, passing numerous disaffected areas along the way. It arrived in Dieppe on 7 February at eight o'clock in the evening, twenty-four hours after its departure from Paris. On orders of the Ministry of War, all coastal troops, from Dieppe to Saint Valery, were now placed under Savary's authority. Savary instantly demanded the signals of the coast and was informed, to his surprise, that the only activity belonged to an enemy cutter hovering off Treport. He communicated this to Troche, who relayed how it was customary for such a boat to be kept in this position so that, with a single tack, it could reach the foot of the cliff where the conspirators could be put ashore.[21]

That evening, in disguise and armed with a hunter's knife, a pair of pistols tucked in his belt and a two-shot rifle thrown over his shoulder, Savary with his men rode on horseback in the snow, with Troche trotting alongside. After an hour and a half they arrived at Biville in the Manche. They were guided to La Poterie farm, situated at the extremity of the village facing the sea. Having ordered the gendarmes to hide in the orchard, Savary knocked on the door. An old lady turned the latch and, recognising Troche, voluntarily recounted how Pagot and Laurent, the two Normans charged with greeting the conspirators at the foot of the cliff, had just rejoined their post.

Upon learning this, Savary and his party headed for the coast. Trudging through the snow, they arrived at the bend of a hedge, a few minutes' walk from the shore. There, they encountered Pagot and Laurent. The two confessed to having just returned from the coast and said the boat had not been able to land because the surf ran too high. They had been trying to land for the last few days, but with the sea being rough and the foot of the cliff studded with reefs a boat could only approach during flood tide, when the water was calm.

At daylight, after having let their two captors go, Savary and Troche went to observe the enemy cutter's position. As soon as the day began to dawn, the vessel bore away from the shore and took its position opposite a signal tower on the coast, in a deep and wide ravine, at the extremity of which was fastened the same 'Smuggler's Rope' which Georges and his accomplices had scaled. For six or seven nights, they kept watch and ward. The sea, however, was too rough for a landing to be attempted; the cutter eventually sailed off, and after several weeks' vain observation Savary received orders to return to Paris. It was during the passage to Rouen that he received the stunning news that General Victor Moreau, the Victor of Hohenlinden, had been arrested.[22]

With suspicion at its height, the Consulate passed a law obliging France's citizens to declare the names of any individual lodged at their home who was not a relative. The death penalty was also pronounced against anyone who was harbouring Georges' accomplices. These measures, which were intended to produce important disclosures, led to one such discovery. On 9 February, in the rue Saint Sauveur, at the house of his mistress, Madame de Saint Leger, Alphanse Hyacinth Bouvet de Lozier, one of Cadoudal's principal confidants and former adjutant-general of the army of the princes, was arrested. Unlike Picot, who made a stout resistance, Lozier bore himself calmly when police raided the house. He initially denied all knowledge of the conspiracy and refused to impart any information that was pertinent to the investigation. But on the night of 13/14 February, in an attempt to extricate himself from guilt, he attempted to commit suicide. The Temple's concierge, Louis-François Fauconnier immediately reported the incident to Réal:

I placed Bouvet de Lozier *au secret* in the guardroom. He profited from a moment of absence when the guard spent in the neighbouring room. It was six thirty in the evening. He took a handkerchief and a tie. He attached one to his neck and the other to the pommelle of a brache (fiche) of a wardrobe. He climbed on his bed and jumped down. The guard, who had the habit of smoking, met a detainee who he asked for some tobacco. He returned to his room to get his pipe. As it was dark, he did not see the detained. He called him and saw him hanging and wriggling. Scared, he called for help and demanded a knife. Also, the names Prunes, Nicodeau, Fouche and Lourdin rushed up. Citizen Nicodeau cut the handkerchief and injured the guard in the arm. The last tried to lift Lozier but he fell as a mass on the ground. He scratched his nose and front, rested a small moment without consciousness but also that the handkerchief which served to tighten the neck was slackened. He gave a great sigh, and fell to awful convulsions of nerves. We lay him on the mattress where he agitated horribly. The health officer arrived, sedating him and returned him to his normal state. During the bout, he testified to those surrounding him, a violent morose that they had recovered his life. Returning entirely to himself, he instantly begged to make known to the *Counseillor d'État* Real that it was urgent that he see him straightaway which Fauconnier did. Also, he asked not to be alone and from this time, he is guarded *à vue* by three guardians.[23]

Finding himself restored to life, Lozier delivered a 'spontaneous declaration'. In the presence of Réal, he revealed how Moreau had dispatched General Lajolais to London and had also met Pichegru in Paris on three separate occasions. Napoleon was naturally incensed and immediately summoned a secret council at the Tuileries in which the two consuls, Jean Jacques Régis de Cambacérès and Charles François Lebrun, as well as Joseph Fouché, were in attendance. To them, Pichegru's involvement in the conspiracy was incontestable evidence that both royalists and republicans were in collusion. Yet they remained undecided as to the precise extent of Moreau's complicity. Napoleon was generally astonished that he was involved. 'Moreau!' he cried. 'What! Moreau in such a plot! Nothing can equal the profound stupidity of this whole plot unless it is wickedness. The human heart is an abyss that is impossible to predict; the most piercing looks cannot gauge it.'[24] Despite his incredulity, Napoleon demanded the arrest of the dissident general. As he argued, 'They will say that I am afraid of Moreau. It will not be found so. I have been the most merciful of men, but I will be the most terrible, when it shall be necessary. I will strike Moreau as I would strike any man when he enters into conspiracies, odious in their object, and disgraceful by the party reconciliations which they imply.'[25]

A second, more pressing need entered his calculations. As it was pointed out, most of the conspirators remained at large and were undoubtedly preparing to deliver the *coup de main* at once. Napoleon therefore ordered the investigation to be expedited and that the principal parties be seized as this would invariably lead to further discoveries. But the question of jurisdiction still needed to be resolved. Cambaçérès, who possessed intimate knowledge of the law, cited the danger of invoking civil authority in an affair of this order and proposed that as Moreau was a military figure he should be sent before a council of war. Napoleon, however, was opposed to the proposition. 'They will say,' he remarked, 'that wishing to disembarrass myself of Moreau I have had him assassinated, judicially, by my own creatures.'[26] In consequence, the council agreed upon a middle course in which Moreau would be sent before the criminal tribunal of the Seine. The constitution permitted the suspension of the jury in certain cases and it was decided that this suspension should be immediately pronounced for that same department.

The council next ruled that the Grand Judge Régnier should draft a detailed report on the conspiracy, citing the reasons for the arrest of Moreau, and present it to the senate, the legislative body and the tribune. The deliberations lasted the whole night and on the following morning, the 15th, Lajolais was seized at his apartment on the rue Culture-Sainte-Cathérine where he was hiding under the assumed name Levasseur. At eight o'clock that same morning, on the bridge of Charenton, as he was returning from his country seat at Gros Bois, Moreau's carriage was surrounded by a unit of elite gendarmes. As he was taken into custody, further arrests were being made in a concerted police operation. The next day, Napoleon ordered Generals Jean-Jacques Liébert and Joseph Souham to be included in the raids. They were suspected on account of their close affiliation with Moreau but were subsequently exonerated and reinstated to their former positions.

The news that Moreau had been detained produced no remark from Pichegru, but witnesses relate how he could not conceal his grief and astonishment. The news spread quickly across Paris, and on 17 February, before the *Corps Legislatif*, the *Grand Juge* Régnier read out a statement laying bare the conspiracy and the complicity of the British government:

> New plots have been hatched by England; this was the case even amidst the peace which she swore to maintain, and when she violated the treaty of Amiens, she counted less on her strength than on the success of her machinations. But government was vigilant; the steps of the agents of the enemy were followed by the eye of justice: the people of London were no doubt expecting to hear the explosion of that mine which had been dug under our feet. At any rate, the most ominous reports were spread, and they were indulging the most criminal hopes; on a sudden the agents of the conspiracy were arrested; proofs have accumulated, and they are so strong and so evident, that they carry with them convictions to every mind. Georges had his band of assassins had remained in the pay of England; their agents were still traversing La Vendée, Morbihan, the Côtes du Nord, and were endeavouring, but in vain, to find partisans of whom they were deprived by the moderation of government and of law.[27]

In conclusion, Régnier made it plain to the assembly that the most vigorous measures would be taken to assure the apprehension of the remaining conspirators who were still at large. The proceedings were subsequently related by Napoleon to General Soult, the commandant of the Camp of St Omer, two days later:

> You must not attach more importance to the affairs of Paris than they deserve. Moreau, misled by I know what passion, called Pichegru to Paris. Pichegru has arrived, and with him Georges and forty other brigands. Moreau and

fifteen brigands have been arrested. The police seized fifteen horses and uniforms which were to be used in attacking me on the road between Paris and Malmaison. I have had the examination read to the Senate and the Council of State, who are indignant. Moreau shall be tried before the tribunals; during his examination he showed the greatest consternation. This is one more ungrateful traitor that France has to punish.[28]

He followed with a letter to Joachim Murat, the governor of Paris:

Citizen General, - The Bishop of Orleans will send you a man called Piquantin, from La Vendée; you will employ him as a secret agent, and give him a suitable salary. You will promise him 2,000 francs for each *chouan* whom he delivers over, and more for Georges.[29]

During this time, Pichegru frequently changed hideouts. After entering Paris through the Saint-Denis gate, he spent his first night at Denands, a wine shop situated at the corner of the rue de Bac and the rue de Varennes, before switching addresses two more times. Then, on 28 January, he and Georges installed themselves in a charming house perched at the bottom of the hill of Châillot, near the River Seine. The house was rented by Lozier's mistress, Madame Gostard de Saint Leger, and was exquisitely decorated with Indian mousseline curtains from India, ottoman sofas, armchairs covered by blue and white velours from Ultrecht and bergères in brocaded silk. Pichegru laid his sparse belongings in a fine room with two windows draped with curtains of plain white dimity and lacquered furniture upholstered in blue and white velvet.[30]

At Châillot, the two conspirators first learned of Querelle's betrayal of silence. Whilst expressing a 'pious wish' that the man was dead, Georges affected to treat the news with indifference, declaring that no harm could befall them as their accomplices did not know their hiding places in Paris. Nevertheless, after a day or two it was decided that they would switch quarters than risk a police raid. Georges returned to the house in the rue du

Puits-de-l'Hermite while Pichegru accepted the hospitality of Henri Rollard, an army contractor friend, who maintained the Hôtel du Cercle on the rue Richelieu. His room, however, was partitioned by a very thin curtain which meant that at night, as he lay in bed reading, the hotel guests could see him clearly as they walked up and down the corridors. He therefore instructed his aide-de-camp, Victor Couchery, to find him another hiding place. His change of quarters took place just in time. A guest had observed him reading in bed and reported to the authorities that Rolland had an unknown visitor. From the informer's description by a sketch artist, for which he received a reward of 3,000 francs, the police concluded that it bore a striking resemblance to Pichegru. They accordingly repaired to the Hôtel du Cercle but failed to find a trace of him there. Rolland was nevertheless placed under arrest on suspicion of harbouring one of France's most wanted men.[31]

Acting on his instructions, Couchery petitioned a man named Janson, the ex-mayor of Besançon, a friend of Pichegru's in former days, for help. He initially declined to involve himself in the affair but only agreed when Couchery made him an offer of 1,800 francs.[32] Janson put him in secret communication with a milliner named Madame Gille who owned an apartment on the rue des Noyers. According to later claims, she was initially told that her lodger was a bankrupt tradesman named Prevot who was desirous of avoiding his creditors. But on the second day of his stay, Couchery arrived bearing the alarming news that Generals Lajolais and Moreau were in police custody. That same evening, after having been warned by Janson of her lodger's real identity, Madame Gille intimated to Pichegru that he could no longer stay with her.

For the next ten days Pichegru remained out of public sight. He appeared to have found his predicament intolerable and was said to have drawn his pistol on occasion, declaring his intention of taking his own life. In desperation, he appealed to the goodwill and generosity of a businessman named Treille who, in turn, put him in touch with an intimate friend and daily messmate named Leblanc. Leblanc agreed to place his rooms in the rue de

Chabanais at Pichegru's immediate disposal, but before making final arrangements he procured an interview with Murat, who agreed to pay 100,000 francs in exchange for Pichegru's delivery to the police.[33]

After supper that evening, Pichegru, the Treille family and Leblanc headed surreptitiously to the rue de Chabanais. They took the rue Colbert, passing the Opera house before arriving at the rue Neuve des Petits Champs. They then turned right and a few metres further on, changed direction, entering between two large, seven storey buildings which formed the rue de Chabanais. Under the building's *porte cochère*, numbered 39, the Treilles bade Pichegru farewell and headed home. Leblanc thereupon led Pichegru up a wooden staircase to his rooms on the second floor. He explained to his guest that as there was only one bed, he would spend the night at the lodgings of a friend but that the maidservant would ensure that all his comforts would be attended to in the morning. Left to himself, Pichegru locked the door and drew a chest of drawers across it. He then placed a pistol under his pillow and, before a lamp burning beside him, lay to rest.[34]

Leblanc, meanwhile, headed to the office of the *Grand Juge*, Régnier, where he found the police inspector, Pacques, the police commissary, Comminges, and a detachment of gendarmes *d'élite* commanded by Lieutenant Noireau waiting for him. An hour or so later, the whole party headed for the rue de Chabanais. Quietly mounting the stairs in single file to the second floor, they positioned themselves before the bedroom where they supposed Pichegru lay asleep. Leblanc continued to climb up the staircase and, reaching the attic, awoke the maidservant and demanded the key to his apartment. Putting on an underskirt, she handed him the key and, following Leblanc with a candle in her hand, descended the staircase and rejoined the eight gendarmes. Taking the key, Pacques turned it gently in the lock. The door resisted. Kicking it in unison, the policemen burst into the room, pushing past the chest of drawers which barred their way, and flung themselves upon Pichegru.[35]

The general was at that moment lying in bed reading a book. His first impulse was to grab the pistol under his pillow but he was prevented from doing so by one of the gendarmes who reached the bed first, overturning the table upon which a candle was standing. A violent struggled ensued lasting more than fifteen minutes. Pichegru's left hand was cut by a sword thrust. He managed to overpower four of the gendarmes, such was his tremendous physical strength, but a fifth seized him by his testicles, eliciting a cry of excruciating pain. He fell down groaning and in an instant was covered by the gendarmes. As one of the arresting agents later reported, 'The struggle was severe and was only ended by violent pressure on the most tender part of his body, causing him to become unconscious.'[36] The drapes were torn from his bed. Pichegru was then garrotted, borne to the ground and firmly secured with a rope.

Before their prisoner's eyes, the gendarmes next conducted a rigorous search of the rooms, seizing the concealed weapons as well as a watch hanging in the chimney on a small gold chain. Frisking his clothes, which lay on the bed, they extracted four letters of exchange from London, two bills from the Bank of France for 150 francs each, ten pieces of gold worth twenty francs, one piece for 80 francs and a second pistol loaded like the first. Having drawn up a *procès-verbal,* they prepared to leave. Wrapped in a blanket and bound hand and foot, Pichegru was carried down the stairs past a gathered crowd and thrust into a cab. He was immediately conveyed to the police headquarters at the Quai Voltaire whereupon he was interrogated first by the Prefect of Police, Dubois, and then Réal. At first, he refused to answer the questions put to him, alternately hurling deprecations at them but finally, having seemingly exhausted himself, submitted to Réal's interrogation:

'What is your name?'

'My name is Pichegru.'

'Your first names?'

'I have one. Charles.'

'What is your age?'

'Forty-three.'

'What is your last domicile?'

'Paris.'

'Which persons did you see habitually in London?'
'Everybody.'[37]

The initial questions were innocuous enough. But when Réal began referring specifically to the conspiracy, and in particular the roles played by Abbé David, General Lajolais and the Comte d'Artois, Pichegru stoutly denied their accusations, employing both bravado and mockery in turn. He also refused to sign the *procès-verbal* once the preliminary investigation concluded, declaring that his examination had been conducted in an insidious and insulting manner.[38] He was nevertheless permitted to dress himself. Meanwhile, orders were sent to the Temple prison to prepare for the prisoner's reception.

During this time, Pacques and Comminges were conducting their own interrogations. Following Leblanc's denunciations, Pacques' gendarmes stormed Treille's home on the rue Vivienne at the break of dawn. Having ransacked the place, the gendarmes conveyed the Treille family to the police station where they were compelled to sign an attestation promising their liberty in exchange for their confessions. The next day, an official note appeared in the *Journal de Paris* stating that a person named Treille, after having found a hiding place for Pichegru at the residence of his friend Leblanc, denounced the general to the Chief Justice's agents. 'Leblanc,' added the newspaper, 'is at present in flight and is actively being sought for.'[39] For the next decade, Treille would be made to account for his betrayal. As for Leblanc, he promptly claimed his award of 100,000 francs and packed his bags for Germany.

At the police bureau, preparations were made for the prisoner's departure. After throwing on a brown tailcoat, Pichegru was led down the staircase, shadowed by Pacques, and manhandled into a fiacre, surrounded by an escort of gendarmes. Heading in the direction of Pont Neuf, they trundled along the Quai de la Mégisserie, across the Place de Grève and down the rue du Temple until they stopped in front of the prison's central tower. The registry bell was then rung, signalling his arrival. Through the wrought-iron prison bars of their second-floor cell, Louis Fauche-Borel and his nephew Vitel watched as the 'Victor of Holland' tottered in, surrounded by Savary's gendarmes. That same night, as Pichegru tossed and turned in his cell, Réal was roused by his servant and handed the following bulletin:

> Report of the concierge of the Temple. Night of the 8th to 9th of Ventôse, Year XII. General Pichegru has been brought to this prison, placed in close confinement, and is under strict surveillance. He is calm.[40]

Meanwhile, a number of precautionary measures were taken in anticipation of the arrest of the last conspirators, notably Georges, now known to be at large in Paris. The prison's surveillance was confided to General Savary who, having arrived within hours of Pichegru's arrest, hurried there with two of his best officers, Colonel Ponsard, an old captain of grenadiers, and Lieutenant Manginot, to occupy the prison with 100 infantrymen and 15 gendarmes *d'élite*. Seeing his registry fill day by day the prison concierge, Fauconnier, was given 14,287 francs to facilitate the reparations and improvements for the fortification of the Temple and its dependencies. At the same time, a description of the notorious Chouan was printed in the journals and affixed to all the bridges, crossroads and street corners of Paris. On 28 February, the senate suspended trials by jury and the Governor Murat ordered the gates to be closed from 7 p.m. to 6 a.m. Orders were also issued to the gendarmes patrolling the barriers and ramparts to fire upon anyone attempting to cross without authorisation.

Overnight, a tight cordon was thrown around the city. Anyone leaving Paris, whether on horse or in carriage, was stopped in search 'for Georges who is still hidden in Paris with fifty of his accomplices with the intention of assassinating the First Consul'.[41] Laundry carts, barrels and even hearses were rigorously examined. On the Seine, officers of the marine guard, stationed on skiffs, searched river barges and boats and stopped all town embarkations before conducting them to the corps of guards on the shore.

In England, meanwhile, the news of Moreau's arrest had thrown the government into disarray. On 6 March, the day after it reached London, a Privy Council meeting was convened. William Marsden, the newly appointed Secretary to the Admiralty, was ordered to superintend the safe recovery of the conspirators. He immediately instructed the commanders of cruisers 'to stand in as close to the coast of France as may be consistent with their safety, in order to favour the escape of Generals Pichegru and Georges, or other Persons who have lately escaped from Paris'.[42] Wright assumed command of HMS *Vincejo* and was given instructions to transport his nephew, who bore the same name, and Jean Marie Hermilly to the west coast of Brittany to search for survivors. On 10 March, they set sail for Quiberon bay.

Two days earlier, after a week of failed efforts, the French police obtained a clue which led them to believe that Georges was hiding somewhere not far from the Panthéon. For the past three weeks, he and two of his companions had been concealed in the attic of a grocer's shop in the rue de la Montagne-Sainte-Geneviève. The police immediately placed the area under surveillance. By then, Georges had already made the decision to switch hideouts after the brother of one of his aides-de-camp, Louis Léridant, had observed suspicious figures following him on his errands. But on 8 March, an officer of the peace named Petit, who knew Léridant, saw him by chance strolling with a woman on the Boulevard Saint-Antoine. Shadowing him a little while, he also recognised an individual whose face struck him to be similar to a sketch of Joyaut's which were then posted all over the walls.

The sudden appearance of strangers making enquiries in the neighbourhood prompted Joyaut to switch quarters. Prevailing upon Caron, a royalist hairdresser, to hide him in his shop in the rue du Four, he then instructed Léridant to find him a cabriolet to convey him there. Léridant, in turn, asked his Parisian friend and flatmate, one Goujou, to hire the vehicle. He was not to know that the latter was being blackmailed by Fouché into spying for him.

At seven o'clock in the evening, the following day, Léridant pulled up before the Place Saint Étienne-du-Mont, near the rue des Sept-Voies, in a cabriolet with the number 53. All of a sudden, Georges entered the square, in disguise and flanked by three of his faithful Chouans. They were followed by a young girl who was carrying a large parcel stashed with 35,000 francs in foreign exchange which the English Treasury had given them.

Just as he climbed into the fiacre, two police inspectors, Petit and Destavigny, emerged from the shadows, followed by two more, Buffet and Caniolle, and sprinted towards the cabriolet shouting, 'Georges! Stop! Stop!' The Chouans turned on them, stabbing Destavigny in the shoulder with a dagger. The cabriolet meanwhile sped off before the little girl had time to toss them the parcel. The policemen started in pursuit. Through the fiacre's back window, Georges could see that they were gaining on them. Turning to Léridant, he ordered him to whip the horse into a faster gallop.

The cabriolet continued to rattle down the hive of narrow and crooked streets with the policemen running close behind, shouting, 'Georges! Georges! It's Georges!' Just as it pulled out from the rue Monsieur le Prince onto the Place de L'Odéon, Caniolle made a lunge and managed to cling to the back of the hood. Buffet, in turn, flung himself in front of the cab, seizing the reins of the horses. Reaching out of the window, Georges shot him with his pistol and then jumped out of the cabriolet. Caniolle raised his heavy stick but Georges fired again, wounding him in the side. Caniolle nevertheless managed to scramble to his feet and catch up to Georges, striking him hard on the head as he entered the rue de l'Observance. At the same time, two local butchers and a clerk in the lottery office rushed to the scene, thinking that the police were chasing a common criminal, and threw themselves on the mighty Breton.[43]

Bound with rope, Georges was dragged to the Prefecture de Police where he found waiting the cynical figures of Louis Dubois, the first prefect of police of Paris, and Pierre Marie Desmarest, the head of the secret police. His responses to their questions were firm and frank but calculated not to incriminate any of his accomplices. He declared that he intended to attack Napoleon with as many men as protected him, take him prisoner and then proclaim Louis XVIII, King of France:

'Where did you stay in Paris?'

'Nowhere.'

'Was Pichegru one of the conspirators?'

'I have no idea.'

'Moreau?'

'Don't know him, never met him.'

'Was Louis Picot not your servant?'

'I have no servant.'

'Where were you lodging when you were arrested?'

'In a cabriolet.'

'What prompted you to fire at a policeman?'

'The necessity to repulse force by force.'

'Are you aware that you killed a family man?'

'You should have had me arrested by bachelors.'

'When did you come to Paris?'

'I think five months ago, but I did not stay all the time in Paris. I moved about, but I will not tell you where I went. Anyway, you have me, and there are enough victims without adding to their number.'[44]

He was then committed to the Temple. Before he left, Georges did make one important disclosure. He confessed that he had only delayed delivering his *coup de main* as he had been awaiting the arrival of a prince in Paris, the identity of which he would under no circumstances reveal. This naturally begged the question: which prince?

20

THE D'ENGHIEN AFFAIR

On the morning after his arrest, Georges' two servants were brought before the Prefecture de Police and questioned vigorously. During their interrogation, Léridant avowed that every so often, a mysterious man appeared at his master's home at Châtillot and although he did not know his identity, he supposed that he was of some importance because everyone would stand up, including the brothers Polignac and the Marquis de Rivière, and not resume their seats until he had left. The description given by Georges' servants corresponded neither with the age of the Count d'Artois nor with the person of the Duke of Berri, his second son. Also, both of them were known to be far away in England. Nor could the mysterious man have been Louis XVIII and his nephew the Duc d'Angouleme as they resided in Warsaw and, besides, were personally known to them. This left Louis Antoine Henri de Bourbon, the Duc d'Enghien, the handsome thirty-one-year-old grandson of the ailing Prince de Condé.

Following the signing of the Treaty of Amiens, and the subsequent disbandment of Condé's army, the Duke d'Enghien had moved to Ettenheim, a small village near the Rhine, about nine kilometres from the frontier, to be close to Princess Charlotte de Rohan, the niece of the notorious Cardinal de Rohan, to whom, it was rumoured, he was secretly married. There he rented a small but quaint house under the protection of the margrave of Baden where he lived modestly, drawing on a pension which he had been receiving from England since August 1792. He passed his days indulging in his favourite pastimes, tending to his small flower garden and hunting in the Black Forest. It was rumoured that every so often he crossed the bridge of the Rhine and travelled as far as Strasburg where he would attend the theatre.[1] Alarmed by the rumour, his grandfather reprimanded him on the subject in a letter dated 16 June 1803:

> You must admit it was useless to risk your liberty and your life ... Your position may be useful in many respects, but you are very near; take care and do not neglect any precaution to get warning in time and make a safe retreat in case the Consul should take it into his head to have you seized. Do not think there is any courage in acting in defiance in this respect. It would be a rashness unpardonable in the eyes of the whole world and could only have the most frightful consequences.[2]

D'Enghien was seemingly piqued by his grandfather's admonishment for he no sooner wrote back assuring him that the rumours had no merit:

> One must know me very little to be able to say or seek to make others believe that I have put my foot on republican soil, except with the rank and station to which the chance of birth entitles me. I am too proud basely to bow my head. The First Consul can perhaps succeed in destroying me, but he cannot humiliate me. One may travel incognito among the glaciers of Switzerland as I did last year, not having anything better to do; but as for France, when I travel there, I shall have no need to conceal myself.[3]

Yet despite his protestations of innocence, d'Enghien kept in secret touch with the political underground from Ettenheim. Living in proximity to the frontier, he was well placed to maintain correspondence with disaffected persons in France, little imagining that Napoleon would regard these innocuous letters as proof of his complicity in 'The Great Conspiracy'. The British government, for example, had sent him a note requesting that he inform the émigrés in his neighbourhood that they were to receive an increase in their pensions. In turn, on 15 January 1804, d'Enghien sent his own note via the English envoy at the Austrian court, Sir Charles Stuart, petitioning the government for a military commission in the campaign which was projected to commence on the German frontier:

> [He] begs His British Majesty to employ him, no matter how nor in what position, against his implacable enemies in case a continental war breaks out; whether in allowing him to serve in the armies of the Powers allied with England; or to join the English troops on the continent wherever they may land; or in deigning to confide to him some auxiliary troops in which he could appoint some old faithful French officers and the deserters who might join him. There will be many of them at this moment in the troubles of the Republic; of this the Duke d'Enghien has convinced himself in a most positive manner by a two year's residence on the frontiers of France.[4]

Napoleon had another source in the double agent, Méhée de la Touche. Having received reports that royalists were operating on the right bank of the Rhine, Méhée set off for Offenburg, a small town in Baden some six miles north of Ettenheim, to confirm the reports himself. He arrived there towards the beginning of March and was promptly informed by the Comte de Musset, an émigré who led a small band of malcontents, that several old officers in the Prince de Condé's army were organising themselves in breach of the Treaty of Amiens and attaching themselves to the person of the prince himself in accordance to instructions from the English cabinet. Méhée thereupon reported the intelligence to Réal at Strasbourg.[5]

Napoleon was evidently agitated by the report and directed Réal to write to Citizen Shée, the Prefect of the Lower Rhine at Strasburg, to ascertain if the Duke d'Enghien was still at Ettenheim. At the same time, the police commissioner Citizen Popp reported on the presence of émigrés surrounding the prince:

'One sees there a number of French émigrés, among who there must be some persons of distinction. But from the information which I have managed to procure, it does not appear that this assemblage is dangerous; however, the government may judge that it deserves some attention.'[6] The commandant of the division at Strasburg, General Leval, thought otherwise, writing to Régnier, 'You have undoubtedly been informed of the intrigues which are being hatched at Offenburg by the six or seven hundred emigres who are living there.'[7]

Due to these letters, Régnier wrote to Napoleon alerting him to the existence of a committee of French émigrés in Offenburg which was subsidised by the British government and exciting new troubles in France. Alarmed by these reports, the chief inspector of the gendarmerie dispatched an emissary to Ettenheim to spy on d'Enghien up close. He claimed that his observations led him to doubt the prince's love of hunting or love affair and hurried back to Paris reporting, instead, how he led a 'mysterious life', was frequented by emigrants, and was oft absent for up to eleven days for reasons unknown. Upon receiving this report, the chief inspector of gendarmerie submitted it directly to the Napoleon, instead of presenting it to Réal first, as was the normal protocol.

The report related how it took sixty hours to travel from Ettenheim to Paris by crossing the Rhine and another sixty to return, totalling five days. It would also take at least five days to make the necessary observations in Paris. This length of time, so it was deduced, was consistent with the duration of d'Enghien's purported absences and the time needed to travel back and forth to Châtillot where the mystery personage, who was the object of such veneration, appeared. Napoleon was enraged: 'This is beyond a joke. To come from Ettenheim to Paris to plot an assassination and to fancy one's self safe because one is behind the Rhine! I should be too simple to suffer it!'[8]

That evening, he held an emergency council in which the three consuls as well as Talleyrand, the Grand Judge Régnier and Fouché were in attendance. The purpose of the discussion was to decide whether d'Enghien should be arrested. Régnier opened the meeting citing the many 'proofs' of the prince's guilt. Talleyrand

and Fouché followed suit, repeating their own reasons for severity. Cambaçérès, however, was alone in opposing d'Enghien's arrest, anticipating a backlash in public opinion which had already expressed sympathy for Moreau and which might turn in favour for the prince as well. He also argued that the memories of the Terror were still raw and that their cause was best served by waiting for d'Enghien to re-enter France in which eventuality, no one could then dispute the Consulate's right to arrest and sentence him to death. His arguments nevertheless failed to persuade Napoleon, who by then had already made up his mind to settle accounts with the Bourbons.[9]

Talleyrand thereupon read out a long report purporting to the conspirators' activities abroad. It detailed Francis Drake's artifices, as related by Méhée de la Touche, and supported by certain officious correspondence concerning the emigrants residing in the electorate of Baden. Then, in his capacity as Minister of Foreign Affairs, he signed a number of state documents, two of which were sent to the French representative in the state of Baden, justifying the violation of territory and a letter of instructions to the arresting officer.

With the majority of the council in agreement, Napoleon convened a cabinet meeting that same day and dictated the order for a small armed force of 1,000 men to be deployed across the Rhine for the purpose of kidnapping the prince. He summoned his secretary, Meneval, the Minister at War, Berthier, and his aide-de-camp, General Armand de Caulaincourt, and, showing them his maps of the Rhine frontier, pointed to the route which the arresting party were to follow. Caulaincourt, who was charged with executing the operation, accordingly ordered General Ordener, commandant of the *gendamerie à cheval*, to repair to Neuf-Brisach, a commune in Alsace, and organise the necessary provisions to transport 300 dragoons and three or four brigades of the gendarmerie across the Rhine at Rheinau on pontoons and proceed expeditiously to Ettenheim Château, where they knew d'Enghien to be residing.

D'Enghien, it appears, dismissed the secret warnings which he had received of his impending arrest.[10] But on 13 March, having learnt of the sudden detainment of the Baronne de Reich on the frontier he instructed his loyal servant Caronne to keep watch and ward during the night. He was also informed of troop movements in the neighbourhood and that boats had been dragged to the left bank of the river as if to convey French troops aboard. The information prompted the prince to take a range of security precautions. He had two beds placed next to his own, his arms placed on a nearby table and the doors of the house bolted shut. That night, he went to bed around eleven o'clock. At about 2 a.m. Lieutenant Schmitt thought he heard the stamping of horses and the rattling of arms and woke Baron Grunstein. The noise stopped but then a little after five, just as it was dawning to the east, the sound of the horses' clattering hoofs was heard again. Opening the windows, they saw French gendarmes scaling the walls and soldiers amassing in the courtyard. D'Enghien stood gripped by indecision. Caronne implored him to flee through a back window, but before he could take any precipitate action the gendarmes had come bursting through the door.

Having seized all of the papers they could find, Colonel Charlot, the chief of the gendarmes, ordered d'Enghien, his friends and domestics to be put in a peasant's cart and conducted back to the Rhine by way of Graffhausen and Kappel. From her window, Princess Charlotte de Rohan saw her lover dragged past her house wearing nothing more than a pair of loose trousers, slippers and a waistcoat. They reached the citadel of Strasbourg about four in the afternoon. A courier was meanwhile dispatched to Napoleon to announce the news of the arrest. In the afternoon of Friday 16 March, after suffering days of uncertainty, Charlot and the Commissary of Safety, Popp, entered his cell and in his presence opened the papers which they had removed from his residence. They read them cursorily and then, having arranged for the letters to be tied up in separate bundles, left d'Enghien to understand that they were being sent to Paris. On the following afternoon, Charlot repeated his visit and instructed his prisoner to sign a *procès-verbal* attesting to the opening of the papers. Charlot did, however, give the prince permission to add an explanatory note making clear his intention to have done nothing more than to 'serve in war and make war'. His statement, which contained no violent intent, was rendered more insidious in Charlot's final report. According to him, 'The Duc d'Enghien esteems Bonaparte as a great man; but being a prince of the Bourbon family, he has vowed an implacable hatred to him, as well as to the French, against whom he will make war on all occasions.'[11] Together with the *procès-verbal*, this report was then sent by express courier on horseback to Napoleon who, without summoning any other minister to witness the action, sat down to examine the contents. Disquieted by what he read, he forwarded the reports to Réal, instructing him and Desmarest to file them away in absolute secrecy and not to let the slightest news of what they disclosed be made available to public scrutiny.

After an evening's rest, d'Enghien was suddenly roused in the middle of the night. Scarcely being afforded time to dress, he was hustled alone into a carriage, his loyal pug, Mohiloff, jumping in after him, and transported under escort of the gendarmerie on the highroad to Paris under the assumed name Plessis. Travelling steadily toward Paris in the bitter coldness, they approached the city barrier about 4 p.m. on Tuesday 20 March, after sixty-three hours on the road. Napoleon, who had retired to Malmaison, was informed by a courier of their impending arrival. He immediately issued an order that the prisoner's carriage head instead for the Château de Vincennes, an ancient Gothic fortress about a mile beyond the walls of the city. The news appeared to have plunged him in a state of unrest. Earlier that morning he was paid a visit by Fouché, who found him walking agitatedly in the grounds. According to Fouché's version, which is not altogether reliable, Napoleon greeted him with the words, 'I can tell what brings you here ... I shall strike a great and necessary blow today.'[12] Suspecting Napoleon's intentions to be sanguinary, Fouché protested that public opinion in France, and indeed throughout Europe, would cry out in revulsion if he took any un-precipitate action without contestable proof. 'Proof! Isn't he a Bourbon, and the most dangerous of the lot?'[13] Turning away, Napoleon thereupon hurried back inside but before disappearing added, 'You and your friends have said a hundred times over that I should end up as the General Monk of France and bring back the Bourbons. Well, there'll be no turning back now. What stronger guarantee could I give to the Revolution that you cemented with a King's blood? In any case, I've had enough; I'm surrounded with plots; I must strike terror into them or perish'.[14]

That very afternoon, the commandant of the château, Monsieur Harel, was notified by letter from Réal that a 'prisoner, whose name must not be known ... will probably arrive at the castle of Vincennes tonight ... It is the intention of the government that everything shall be kept very secret about him and that no questions shall be asked as to who he is or why he is detained.'[15]

As the armed escort was drawing near Paris, Napoleon drove from Malmaison to the Tuileries in order to attend to the affairs of state. He was joined by Talleyrand and two of his Consuls who drew up in front of the portico in separate carriages. By now, he had already made the fatal decision of having d'Enghien secretly handed over to a court martial and not tried by a court of justice. His reasoning, despite its moral ambiguity, was quite sound. Essentially, he doubted whether a regular court could be induced to pass a sentence on d'Enghien that was concordant with his prejudices. In the first place, the prince's lawyers could safely argue that the kidnapping and violation of neutral territory was an illegal act. Also, as Cambacérès earlier argued, public opinion in France, which was always fickle, could turn in d'Enghien's favour any moment. A long-drawn-out trial was therefore highly unfavourable especially as 'the solemnity of condemnation' might revive the aspirations of the émigrés, who had returned to France, and lead them 'into temptation', as he later said. But probably the greatest concern was the evidence itself. Having examined d'Enghien's papers himself, and finding so little compromising proofs in them, Napoleon feared that a regular court of justice, with its balanced and measured procedure, would never convict him on that same basis.

Convening a Council of State, Napoleon then issued the following decree:

Article I. The heretofore Duke d'Enghien, accused of having borne arms against the republic, and of having been, and still being, in the pay of England, for taking part in the plots contrived by that power against the internal and external safety of the Republic, is to be brought before a court martial, composed of seven members appointed by the governor of Paris, which court will assemble at Vincennes.

Article II. The Grand Judge, the Minister of War, and the Governor of Paris are charged with the execution of the present decree.

Bonaparte.[16]

On Tuesday afternoon, at about five o'clock, Savary was summoned to the cabinet of the First Consul. He had just returned from his mission to Biville in Normandy and was ordered to send a brigade of infantry and a strong detachment of its cavalry to keep garrison at Vincennes. He was also told to deliver a sealed letter with orders that he carry it to the governor of Paris, General Joachim Murat. A true sycophant, Savary could be depended upon to execute the ruling of the court-martial without scruple or delay. He accordingly repaired to the castle, arriving there about eight o'clock in the evening. Having posted the infantry of the garrison on the esplanade and next to the park, he observed the seven members of the court-martial arrive in separate carriages. They were escorted to Harel's room where, gathered around a bristling fire, they waited upon Brunet, Murat's aide-de-camp, who soon arrived bearing the government's decree of accusation. Everything was now ready.

That same night, as the dawn approached, d'Enghien was roused from his sleep and summoned before a military commission for interrogation. Napoleon himself formulated the questions to be laid before the prince. He acknowledged that he had received money from the English government but that it was in the form of a pension and in no way was to pay for the sinews of war. He also disdainfully refuted the allegation that he had played any part in the conspiracy or had ever set eyes on Pichegru. But when asked whether he had borne arms against his country, d'Enghien answered in the affirmative. Unbeknownst to him, it was to spell his doom: in conformity with the law and Napoleon's explicit instructions, the death sentence was to be applied forthwith. The interrogation ended, the Judge Advocat, Captain Dautancourt, major of the gendarmerie *d'élite*, enjoined d'Enghien to sign the *procés-verbal* of the responses he had just given. Handed the document, he wrote:

> Before signing this *procés-verbal,* I earnestly request that I may have an interview with the First Consul. My name, rank, my way of thinking, and the horror of my situation, lead me to hope that he will not refuse my request.
>
> L. A. H. De Bourbon[17]

When the interrogation was over, d'Enghien was taken unshackled into the room where the military commission had assembled. It was a little after midnight. The light of a few flaring torches fell across the faces of the seven harbingers of death. Brunet stood at one side. In the president's chair sat General Hulin, a violent and ardent patriot who had stormed the Bastille. Behind him loomed Savary. The prince still had no notion of the seriousness of his predicament for he answered his accusers without evident regard of the consequences. Hulin pointed this out:

> Sir, you seem not to be aware of your situation, or are you determined not to answer the questions which I ask of you. You shut yourself up in your high birth, of which you take good care to remind us; you had better adopt a different system of defence. I will not take an undue advantage of your situation, but observe that I ask you positive questions, and that, instead of answering, you talk to me about something else. Take care, this might become serious. How could you hope to persuade us that you were so completely ignorant as you pretend to be of what was passing in France, when not only the country in which you resided, but the whole world is informed of it? And how could you persuade me that with your birth you were indifferent to events, all the consequences of which were to be in your favour? There is too much improbability in this for me pass it over without observation;

I beg you to reflect upon it, that you may have recourse to other means of defence.

After a moment's pause, the prince replied gravely:

Sir, I perfectly comprehend you; it was not my intention to remain indifferent to them; I had applied to England for an appointment in her armies; and she had returned for answer that she had none to give me but that I was to remain upon the Rhine, where I should soon have a part to act, and for that I was waiting. I have nothing more to tell you, Sir.[18]

The president of the commission then declared the discussion closed and ordered all those who had been present during the debates to leave the room, convening a close session of the council to deliberate. Approximately two hours later, the commandant of the infantry of Savary's legion informed him that the commission had passed sentence and that a picket was required for its execution.

Two hours after that, the commandant of Vincennes, Monsieur Harel, appeared before d'Enghien, his face visibly blanched. From the prison cell he conducted the unfortunate prince down the winding stairs leading to the subterraneous quarters of the castle. As they descended with his pug, Mohiloff, loyally by his side, the prince naively inquired, 'Am I to be immured in a dungeon?' Harel did not answer. At the bottom of the stairwell they reached a postern which opened into a large, makeshift ditch which had been hastily dug. A detachment of soldiers and gendarmes *d'élite* stood by the flickering light of torches, brandishing muskets. An adjutant then stepped forward and read out the commission's sentence.[19]

The hour struck six o'clock in the morning. The sun had risen and a heavy mist lay on the ground. D'Enghien demanded a priest but was refused. He also asked for a pair of scissors, which he employed to cut off a lock of his hair. Removing a ring from his finger as well, he handed them both to an officer who promised to deliver them, together with a final note, to his beloved Charlotte.

He then knelt down for a few minutes, and, commending his soul, rose to face his executioners. His last reported words were, 'How awful it is to die this way and at the hands of Frenchmen!'[20] The order was given, the soldiers fired, a bullet pierced his heart and he fell to the ground. The soldiers then tossed his corpse into the prepared hole and covered it with earth, all the while trying to muffle the sound of Mohiloff's howling. The prince's dog was later adopted by Gustav IV of Sweden. On his collar were inscribed the words, 'I belong to the unhappy Duc d'Enghien.'

That night, Talleyrand was playing hazard at the house of the Duchess of Luynes. In the early hours of the morning, he pulled out his watch. Giving it a furtive glance, he asked whether the Duke of Bourbon had any other son beside the murdered prince. The guests replied that, as he knew only too well, d'Enghien was his only son. 'Then,' Talleyrand observed, 'the House of Condé is no more.'[21]

The news of the d'Enghien's execution was quickly spread abroad. A number of reports circulated that were injurious to Napoleon, but whatever his private feelings he made no effort to justify the deed. It was said that upon hearing of the prince's death he appeared 'troubled, preoccupied, sunk in thought', and that he paced up and down his apartment, his hands clasped behind his back, his head sunk low. Another observer claimed that he murmured under his breath a passage from Voltaire's play *Alzira*, although this sounds less plausible:

> Of the Gods that we worship the difference see:
> To avenge and to kill is enjoined unto thee;
> But mine, when I fall 'neath thy murderous blow,
> Only bids me feel pity and pardon bestow.[22]

In any event, except for the official report which appeared in the *Moniteur* the morning after the transaction, the French government never recurred to the subject. The Court of St Petersburg and the Swedish government lodged official protests against the violation of Baden's territory but were only greeted by Talleyrand's laconic replies denying their right to interfere. None of the other Continental powers made such a remonstrance. The Duke of Wurttemberg congratulated Napoleon on foiling the plot. The Duke of Baden expelled all the émigrés from his territories. Charles IV of Spain, a blood relative, approved of the execution. His Prime Minister, Godoy, applauded the Ambassador of France, observing that 'when one has bad blood, it must be spilled'. Hearing this, Louis XVIII returned to his cousin in Spain the collar of the Golden Fleece, an earlier gift, in disgust. In his letter to the younger king he added, 'In the present century, it is more glorious to deserve a sceptre than to carry one.'[23]

Thirty-four hours later, the government of Karlsruhe was informed of the daring raid. The Elector, Charles Frederick, a venerable old man with 'an amiable philosophy of life', was generally alarmed by the news but, having taken up arms against revolutionary France, he was now at peace with the Consulate and no act of servility was too abject for him or his timorous ministers. All of Napoleon's demands, no matter how humiliating, were obeyed. No sooner had he received Talleyrand's diplomatic note before he issued a decree banishing all French émigrés from his soil. The only statement his government dared to make that could be construed as a complaint was one that the arrests in Baden's territory had been made unexpectedly and without its prior knowledge. Napoleon's heavy-handed treatment of the Elector was an integral feature of the continental system that he pursued in 1804. Now that he was master of Belgium and Holland, he too regarded the patchwork of German territories, such as the Rhine provinces and Hannover, as annexed to his system of bullying. They were all expected to display unequivocal attachment to France's imperial interests. And an incident was shortly to reveal in the clearest light their subservience.[24]

With public outrage at its height, Napoleon judged that the time had come to denounce England to the world and to make public the secret correspondence which Francis Drake had been carrying on with Méhée de la Touche. On 25 March 1804, less than a week after d'Enghien had been executed, the *Moniteur* printed the written indiscretions which Méhée had extracted from Drake together with the secret instructions issued by the

British government. A long report from *Grand Juge* Régnier was published along with these documents holding Addington's ministry to account. It made clear that the true object of Drake's mission to Munich was 'to recruit agents of intrigue, of revolt, of assassination, to make a war of brigandage and murder against the French government, and to injure the neutrality and dignity of the government to which he was accredited'.[25] A copy of his correspondence was also sent to every member of the diplomatic set affixed with a note which denounced the perfidious character of Britain's ambassador. It wasn't long before the tremulous courts of Germany expressed their outrage at the startling revelations. The Bavarian minister deemed no words too strong to condemn 'the disgraceful and criminal proceedings of Mr Drake'. Count Beust, the Elector of Ratisbon's special envoy, professed his 'profound indignation', while Abel, the agent of the free towns, represented the plot as having been principally directed against the person and government of Napoleon, 'whom all the inhabitants of the free towns of the Empire regard as the generous protector who has saved their independence, and for whom they are penetrated with the highest veneration and the most perfect attachment'.[26]

At the same time, Napoleon ordered Talleyrand to demand the immediate expulsion of Drake from Munich. The Elector was also commanded to seize his papers and arrest the Bishop of Châlons as well as two other royalist conspirators who had been implicated in the correspondence. Just three months before, in a complete volte-face, the Elector had confided to Britain's disgraced minister that no one abhorred the principles of Jacobinism or the egregious misconduct of the usurper more than he did. Now the tables had turned. Napoleon's incursion into Baden had struck terror in his heart. Without even affording him an opportunity to explain himself, the Bavarian Prime Minister, Baron von Montgelas, told Drake that the Elector could no longer engage in communications with him or permit his presence in his palace. And with this, Drake's mission had come to an ignominious end. Without awaiting instructions from his masters in London, and perhaps out of fear that he might meet the same fate as the Duke d'Enghien, Drake took to flight with the utmost precipitation.

Not long afterwards, on 11 April 1804, Régnier published a second report in the *Moniteur* revealing that Drake was not the only English agent complicit in 'vile intrigue'. Sir Sidney's brother, Spencer Smith, who was accredited to the Court of Wurttemberg now that his diplomatic mission to the Ottoman Porte had ended, was declared guilty of similar indiscretions. Like his compatriot Drake, he had spent time acquiring information on the internal arrangements of France, engaging actively in the intrigues of the royalist conspirators, and promoting disaffection in the army against the person and government of Napoleon. He had also unwittingly entered into a correspondence with an agent of the secret police, a certain Captain Rosey who was stationed at Strasbourg and who had, following Méhée de la Touche's instructions, posed as an aide-de-camp of a pretended dissident French general. Not one of Smith's letters were included among the papers appended to Régnier's report, but the *Moniteur* did publish a narrative report of his transactions with Rosey. Alarmed by the damning contents of the article, the Court of Wurttemberg ordered, upon Napoleon's insistence, the immediate recall of Spencer Smith. Anticipating a confrontation, Smith made secret arrangements to leave Stuttgart. Leaving behind his stately carriage, which had long been the object of observation, he set off on foot, a pistol tucked under his belt. Taking a myriad of crossroads to avoid being apprehended by French gendarmes, he managed to cross the frontier safely.[27]

21

MIDNIGHT MURDER I

Back in Paris, meanwhile, Pichegru continued to deny his complicity in 'The Great Conspiracy'. Separated from his fellow prisoners and confined strictly *au secret*, he was only permitted to leave his cell to undergo the frequent examinations to which he was subjected. He comported himself with great dignity throughout, refusing either to retract his original testimony or sign the *procès-verbal*. He was nevertheless spared the petty annoyances and humiliations visited upon the other state prisoners. Two days after his arrival, Réal, who officiated as investigating magistrate, even agreed to reassign the two sentinels who were posted in his cell.[1]

Despite granting this small concession, Réal refused to relax the severity of Pichegru's confinement, supposing that the attendant deprivations would weaken his resolve. He soon grew frustrated by the prisoner's obstinacy, and, heading one late afternoon to the Temple prison, ordered Pichegru to array himself in the clothes seized from General Lajolais' domicile: a green outfit, frockcoat and pair of boots. Pichegru was then removed from his cell and paraded before his fellow conspirators, Bouvet de Lozier, Louis Picot and Troche le Père, all of whom he pretended not to know.[2] At the same time, Réal instructed his agents to question known acquaintances of the general. They knocked on the door of his relatives and interrogated former officers in the Jura. In Arbois, the authorities interviewed his former mistresses, including one whom they dubbed 'the belle butcher's wife', but not before sending a missive to the First Consul shamelessly denouncing the very man whom they had fêted as a hero ten years earlier:

> We do not dissimulate to you, citizen Premier Consul that in the midst of the general indignations that all the French have suffered at the news of an apparent attack, a sentiment more painful still have effected lively our hearts. It is that our commune which was in other times glorified to have given one day a soldier of liberty who conducted often his brothers in arms to the field of victory and now has reddened to be counted among the stipends of England and the vile instruments of her rage. Already on 18 *Fructidor* an V, we deplore his association with the henchmen of the royalism and to ward off with contempt the shameful privilege that he has stipulated in favour of his natal soil for price of his treason. Today, we cannot see but with horror the continuity of his crime and the certitude of the implacable hatred that he carries for his country. England alone belongs the right or rather the shameful employment of fomenting the troubles, organizing the plots, of giving asylum to the traitors and beyond all to nourish and protect the assassins.[3]

Although denied all intercourse with the prisoners and society, Pichegru knew only too well that Georges, the brothers Polignacs, the Marquis de Rivière and all the chief conspirators had been captured. It was intimated to him that he could expect lenient treatment should he confess. Napoleon even dangled the possibility of despatching him on a colonial mission, as he supposedly told Réal that despite 'having committed a misdeed, he had served well and honourably his country. I do not need his blood. Say to him that it is necessary to regard all this as a battle lost. He cannot stay in France, Present him Guyana. He knows the country. One could make him a handsome position there.'

In any event, no threats or promises could induce Pichegru to betray his partners or effect the great object in view, implicating General Moreau in 'The Great Conspiracy'.[4] He threatened, on the contrary, to speak out on his impending trial, to reveal the methods by which he and his companions had been entrapped by the police and to reveal what he knew of Napoleon's flirtations with the Bourbons. 'When am I before my judges,' he exclaimed defiantly, 'my language shall be conformable to truth and to the interests of my country.'[5] The Consulate was evidently troubled by such expressions, but whether they were responsible for what would transpire next remains, more than 200 years later, a deep mystery.

At about noon on 6 April 1804, the same day that the barriers of the capital were finally opened, a carriage came rumbling over the cobblestones of the Temple's courtyard and five grim-looking men dressed in red stepped down, shadowed by a sixth man in a black robe cloaked beneath a crimson coat. A sentinel then ushered in the sombre procession. Within the prison walls, a gloomy silence prevailed. After a few moments, a hussar from the tribunal arrived and informed them of what had come to pass during the night. The men in red were judges of the criminal tribunals of the Seine and they were accompanied by the government's public prosecutor, André Gérard. At around ten o'clock, the night watchman reported looking into Pichegru's cell as he did his rounds before returning at seven o'clock the following morning. After having lit the fire and run some errands, he approached the prisoner's bedside only to discover that his body was lying lifeless.[6]

Pichegru had been dead for hours. His body was accordingly examined by the district police commissary, Pierre Dusser, the prison surgeon, Francois Soupé, and his colleague Fluery.[7] He lay on his left side. A black silk cravat was tightened around his neck and through it was inserted a small stick, forty-five centimetres long and four or five centimetres in diameter. His face and body were discoloured. The muscles of his hands were contracted, his tongue pressed between his teeth.[8]

Not long after, four members of the tribunal were sent to the Temple to formally investigate the manner. They took the depositions of a few witnesses, including one of Savary's gendarmes *d'élite* who reported hearing coughing and spitting coming from the prisoner's cell about three hours after midnight.

Having compiled their *procès-verbal* of the visit, Pichegru's body was then transported from his cell. It was attested by one of the judges, Rigault de Rochefort, that no trace of injury or contusion other than a minor scratch on his left cheek, produced by the stick being twisted, could be found. Later it was claimed – though no inmates ever bore witness to such allegations – that he had been tortured, his thumbs pinched in the hammer of a gun. His cell was also examined. An inventory was made and it was admitted into evidence that a volume of a French translation of the works of Seneca, published in 1752, lay on the chimney stand within arm's reach of his bed. It was lying on its reverse side and conveniently opened at the passage in which the philosopher discourses on the suicide of the younger Cato: '*Non, je ne crois pas que Jupiter ait jamais rien vu de plus beau que Cato invincible ... Allons, mo name, commence l'entreprise que tu médites depuis si longtemps!*'[9]

The news of Pichegru's death quickly circulated the prison cells. In spite of the pains taken to prove that he had perished by his own hand, few doubted that he had been foully murdered, especially so soon after the execution of the Duke d'Enghien at Vincennes. It was claimed that his death deprived Napoleon of his most important *piéce de conviction* against Moreau and that it was the publication a few days before of the Comte de Montgaillard's pamphlet titled *Memoire concernant la trahison de Pichegru* (*Memoir Concerning Pichegru's Treason*) which induced him to put an end to his own existence. Naturally, Georges didn't believe such feeble explanations and with sublime irony told Fauconnier, his keeper, 'Citizen Turnkey, I here deliver to you my cravat; and I solemnly promise to make oath before any public notary as I now do before you, that I will never strangle myself, nor make any attempt on my own life.'[10] The day after his death, the *Moniteur* published the following article:

The proceeding evening Pichegru had copiously dined according to his custom, for he loved the pleasures of the table. He was full of meat, had a short neck, was sanguineous, and the want of exercise predisposed him the more to apoplexy; in the evening, too, he had asked for a Seneca, and opening the book at the page where the philosopher discusses the miseries of life and the easy passage to eternity, Pichegru had prepared himself for suicide. He had concealed a stick taken out of a fagot of firewood, and that, with his cravat, sufficed for the strangulation. Thus Pichegru has escaped the disgrace of the scaffold by suicide.[11]

It was hardly a dispassionate obituary.

Reading the article, one foreign diplomat resident at Paris reported to his court, 'It is evident that Pichegru has been selected as a victim. The history of the Roman emperors of the Lower Empire presents the picture of this country and government!'[12] The Consulate tried to deflect public rumour by pivoting attention to England's role in 'The Great Conspiracy'. On 16 April Lord Addington stood before the House of Commons, repudiating the repeated accusations levelled against the British government:

Mr Speaker, I rise to express my unfeigned obligation to the noble lord, for affording His Majesty's ministers an opportunity of repelling the foulest and most infamous charge that has ever proceeded from a government, claiming to be considered as part of the civilised world; a charge, the most unfounded and diabolical, urged by a government the most sanguinary and tyrannical, for the sole purpose, I implicitly believe, of giving a colour to the commission of crimes, the most heinous and atrocious that has ever disgraced and blackened human nature. As to the imputation that the author and perpetrators of that foul crime have attempted to throw on his Majesty's government, it is almost beneath their dignity to condescend to refute it; but I think it my duty to state to this House and to the civilised world, that no authority has been given, that no instructions have been transmitted to the English minister at the court of Munich (Drake), to engage in or undertake anything that was not strictly consistent with the most scrupulous observance of the rights of nations and, what is paramount to them, the duties of humanity.[13]

Hawkesbury, Britain's Foreign Minister, followed suit by issuing a circular on 30 April 1804 to the Ministers of Foreign Courts resident in London:

> His Majesty has directed me to declare that he need not be reduced to the necessity of repelling with merited scorn and indignation, the atrocious and utterly unfounded calumny that the government of his Majesty have been a party to plans of assassination; an accusation already made with equal falsehood and calumny by the same authority against the members of his Majesty's government during the last war; an accusation incompatible with the honour of his Majesty and the known character of the British nation, and so completely devoid of any shadow of proof, that it may be reasonably presumed to have been brought forward at the present moment, for no other purpose than that of diverting the attention of Europe from the contemplation of the sanguinary deed, which has recently been perpetrated, by the direct order of the First Consul in France, in violation of the right of nations, and in contempt of the most simple laws of humanity and honour...Under these circumstances his Majesty's government would be unjustifiable if they neglected the right they have to support, as far as is compatible with the principles of the laws of nations, which civilised governments have hitherto acknowledged, the efforts of such the inhabitants of France as are hostile to the present government. They ardently believe, as well as all Europe, to see an order of things established in that country, more compatible with its own happiness, and with the security of the surrounding nations; but if that wish cannot be accomplished, they are fully authorised by the strictest principles of personal defence, to endeavour to cripple the exertions, to distract the operations and to confound the plans of a government, whose system of warfare, as acknowledged by itself, is not only to distress the commerce, to diminish the power and to abridge the dominions of its enemy, but also to carry devastation and ruin into the very heart of the British empire ... A minister

in a foreign country is obliged by the nature of his office and the duties of his situation, to abstain from all communication with the disaffected of the country where he is accredited, as well as from any other act injurious to the interests of that country; but he is not subject to the same restraints with respect to countries with which his sovereign is at war. His actions to them may be praiseworthy or blameable according to the nature of the actions themselves but they do not constitute any violation of his public character, except in as far as they militate against the country, or the security of the country, where is accredited.[14]

Despite England's flat denials, Napoleon had found the pretext he needed to confer legitimacy on himself. For some days he had been engaged in drafting a new constitutional instrument with the input of his Privy Council which, as he told Marshal Soult, would finally put an end to the hopes of the Bourbons and prevent a counter-revolution. It was approved by the Council of State on 13 May, three days after the fall of Lord Addington's administration, and submitted to the Senate three days later. After a short debate, the senate passed the measure which thus became the 'Organic Senatus Consultum of 28 Floréal, year XII' (18 May 1804). Clause 2 had historic dimensions. It stipulated firstly that 'Napoleon Bonaparte, now First Consul of the Republic, is Emperor of the French'. Secondly, 'the title of emperor and the imperial power be made hereditary in his family, in the male line, according to the order of primogeniture'.[15] Then, to give sanction to the Imperial Constitution, a fresh plebiscite was ordered by decree the following day.

The drama was not over. On 28 May, the long-awaited trials of Moreau and Georges began. Of the 356 'brigands' arrested in connection with the conspiracy, forty-five were also arraigned before the court. The air was electric. For the full twelve days over which the proceedings took place, the avenues around the Palais de Justice were thronged with enormous crowds. Anyone of any importance in the capital, including all the foreign ambassadors accredited to the Court of St Cloud, attended. Napoleon, however, was not at all optimistic about the effect that Moreau's appearance would have on the army, where a serious undercurrent of discontent remained. The signs were ominous enough. He had been receiving reports from General Moncey, the Premier Inspecteur Général of the Gendamerie Nationale, that he could no longer rely on the allegiance of his men. Outside the Palais de Justice, the same soldiers who had been charged with crowd control raised their arms and cheered, '*Vive Moreau*!' as the prisoner was led inside. General Lecourbe was even seen placing his hand on the hilt of his sword to indicate his preparedness to draw if Moreau gave the nod of assent.[16]

At ten in the morning, arrayed in their long red robes, the twelve handpicked judges of the criminal court passed solemnly through the crowd and entered the Palais de Justice, assuming their seats. Once assembled, the president, Hémard, ordered the prisoners to be brought in. They entered in a single file and took their positions in the dock, each sandwiched between two gendarmes. Moreau walked calmly in, dressed in the uniform that he wore during the Battle of Hohenlinden. Of all the defendants, only the tall and pale Bouvet de Lozier wore shame on his face, his eyes never leaving the floor.

The acts of indictments were then read out. The crimes alleged against Moreau were:

1. Not having denounced Pichegru in the year 5,
2. A reconciliation and culpable relation with Pichegru, in England, through the agency of David and Lajolais,
3. Having engaged to re-establish the Princes of the House of Bourbon on the throne of France,
4. Having had interviews with Pichegru at Paris, and rejected certain overtures, but substituted others, which had for their object the overthrow of the Consular government,
5. Of not having denounced the conspiracy.[17]

Napoleon hoped that the destruction of Moreau's reputation would greatly diminish the violent expression of dissent that was sure to follow his condemnation from the senior officers of the army. To the first charge, Moreau retorted: 'If I erred, it was an error against the Directory; which has since been sufficiently expiated by my having gained thirty battles, and saved two armies.' Throughout the trial he sat on the beach looking sedate, having the appearance, as Napoleon's secretary related, 'of one led by curiosity to be present at this interesting trial, rather than of an accused person, to whom the proceeding might end in condemnation and death'.[18]

To plead his defence Moreau selected the service of Claude François Chauveau-Lagarde, a man of great eloquence who had earlier pleaded the cause of France's unfortunate queen, Marie Antoinette. Having been rigorously vindicated by the lawyer's ingenious arguments, Moreau expounded at great length, and not without eloquence of his own, on his life and accomplishments, concluding before the magistrates, 'Such has been my character, and such the tenor of my conduct through life. I solemnly call heaven and earth to witness the innocence and integrity of my intentions. You know your duty. France awaits your decision; Europe contemplates your proceedings; and posterity will record them.'[19]

Georges was not as 'chicken-hearted' as his fellow conspirator. Appearing with a miniature of Louis XVI hung round his neck, he freely admitted before the Tribunal that he had come to Paris 'to attack the First Consul by main force, and to put his lawful King in the place of an Usurper'.[20] He also expressed his profound regret, not that he had been captured but that his captivity prevented the realisation of his objective. Throughout the twelve days of proceedings he amused himself with punning on the name of Thuriot, whom he jocularly called *Tue-roi* (kill king). He also requested brandy so that he could rinse his mouth after pronouncing the judge's name or answering any questions. His insolence did not stop there. Appearing one day without the miniature of the king, he was asked by Thuriot what he had done with it. 'And you,' he replied, 'what have you done with the original?' At this laconic reply the crowd burst into shouts of applause, inciting Thuriot, whose cheeks flushed red with embarrassment, to order in a faltering tone that the prisoner be conducted back to his cell. Georges also did not deign to reply to some questions, telling the court to interrogate the brothers Polignac instead; 'For they,' he exclaimed, 'wish to live, but death has no terrors for me.'[21]

He would soon find out. On 9 June, the President made known the final determination of the court. Georges, Bouvet de Lozier, Roussillon, d'Hozier, de Rivière, Picot, Lajolais and Armand de Polignac were all sentenced to death and their properties confiscated. The latter's brother, Jules, offered to take his sibling's place but his request was denied, an instance of fraternal affection which drew the tears of a number of ladies in the room. Jules Polignac, Léridant and Roland received a two-year sentence, 'the same that one gives a handkerchief thief', as Napoleon scoffed.[22]

Moreau was also sentenced to two years' imprisonment. He was found guilty of only two minor counts in the indictment, the first that he failed to denounce Pichegru in 1797 and the second that he did not report the conspiracy when he first became privy to it. There was, in reality, little evidence stacked against him. The chief witness against him, Louis Picot, recanted his testimony, declaring in court that the accusations which he had levelled against Moreau had only been obtained under violent duress, and to prove his point he raised his bruised hands for everyone to see. Out of the twelve judges before whom Moreau appeared seven were in favour of an acquittal. The sentence was thus a compromise. He nevertheless challenged the verdict, claiming that it stood contrary to all common sense. 'If,' he said, 'I played the part of a conspirator, I should be condemned to death as a chief. No one will believe that I acted as a corporal.'[23] In any event, Moreau's punishment was not even carried out. His sentence was subsequently commuted by Napoleon, who banished him from the empire. He set sail for the United States, where, resting on his laurels, he purchased a beautiful country residence on the banks of the River Delaware at Morristown opposite Trenton. Surrounded by his friends and family, he lived in perfect tranquillity until 1813. He subsequently returned to Europe, falling in battle in the service of Russia near Dresden that same year from a round-shot fired from a French gun.

Georges, on the hand, was prepared for his end. On the day before his scheduled execution, he requested a bottle of excellent wine to be brought to him. Having tasted its contents, and finding it of inferior taste, he complained to the gaoler that it was not the vintage he desired. The gaoler told him that the quality would do for a miscreant like him. Without deigning to reply, Georges corked up the bottle and then hurled it at the gaoler's head with such poise that the gaoler sank prostrate to the floor.

The following morning, on 25 July 1804, exactly two weeks after Fouché was reinstated to the position of Minister of Police, Réal appeared before Georges' cell and offered him Napoleon's pardon. He refused on the grounds that his companions were not included. At eleven o'clock that morning he arrived under heavy guard at the Place de Grève before the Hôtel de Ville, where the guillotine loomed ominously. A profound silence prevailed. As the tumbrel rolled towards his place of execution, passing an ocean of heads, he quipped, 'We have achieved more than we intended. We came to give France a King; we have given her an emperor.'[24]

Hugging two of his friends, Georges mounted the scaffold. To the end he displayed extraordinary insouciance. He was assisted by the Abbé de Keravenan, a family acquaintance, who, at the Restoration, became the parish priest of Saint-Germain-des-Prés. Reciting the *Ave Maria*, Georges stopped after 'Holy Mary, Mother of God, pray for us sinners now …'

'Go on,' said the Abbé, 'and in the hour of death.'

'No need,' he replied. 'This is the hour of death.' He then stepped on the scaffold. With one drop of the blade, Georges' large head tumbled into the bloodstained basket.[25]

22

MIDNIGHT MURDER II

Something was troubling Captain Wright, for on the day before his capture he was observed pacing up and down the quarterdeck of HMS *Vincejo* plunged in a gloom. In pursuance to Admiralty orders, he had been cruising the French coast between the Loire and Lorient searching for wanted royalists and annoying the enemy. Between 28 April and 4 May he successfully harassed several large convoys. On boarding one Spanish brig he discovered some musty old American newspapers, in one of which he noticed an address to Great Britain from *Alfred, an Epic Poem*. He seemed to have been much affected by the last lines of the stanza for he was observed muttering them repeatedly as if in a reverie, 'Return victorious or no more ... return victorious or no more.'[1] The chronicles of the time supposed that he was shaken by a presentiment of the fate that awaited him, and the experience of his fellow conspirators at the hands of the enemy was sufficient to account for it. He always knew of the personal risks, having famously braved so many dangers, but on the eve of this occasion he was overheard talking loudly of how he and his crew were being sacrificed. Wright was originally assigned the *Favourite* sloop of war, but being out of dock he was assigned this old Spanish prize packet that he would complain was 'one of the most inefficient vessels that ever hoisted an English pendant'.[2] He typically protested vigorously against the appointment, incensing many of his senior commanders. Among those annoyed was Lord Keith, who moved to silence him.

On the evening of 4 May, Wright spotted a large corvette of 18–pounders with a convoy of thirty sail at the entrance of Lorient. He directed his course to intercept her on his approach to Belle Isle, a steep and strongly fortified island south of Quiberon, six and a half leagues long and two broad. The following day, he chased a convoy from the Teigneuse Passage to Le Palais where it was kept under observation till the morning of the 6th. That same evening, Wright, accompanied by the brig's surgeon, Mr Lawmont, landed on shore of the Isle of Houat on a mission to assist wanted royalists. Being unsuccessful in their search, they made their way back to the *Vincejo*, which swung quietly at anchor.[3] It was a dark and hazy night, but the brilliant moonlight cast a spotlight on their silhouettes and guided them through the winding paths that led back to their little boat at oars. They had almost missed the brig after falling foul of the treacherous rocks and shoals that tangled the foot of the island, but with some forceful strokes of the oars, their blades biting into the water, they managed to pitch and heave their way towards the *Vincejo*. At daylight, Wright observed the same corvette from Lorient getting under weight in the bay of Quiberon. He kept a close eye on its motions but by daylight on the 8th the *Vincejo* found herself becalmed close to the mouth of the Morbihan, with the ebb tide carrying her so close to the Teigneuse rock that they were forced to anchor to avoid it.

The *Vincejo* was now stuck in a narrow and intricate passage without a pocket of wind and with a strong tide against her. Wright now depended on chance. Determined not to be driven into the harbour, he ordered his men to sweep to. The sailors scrambled about, breathless, but despite their exhaustive efforts they could not stop the floodtide pulling the brig ashore again. The enemy flotilla, meanwhile, was rapidly gaining ground. By 8.30 a.m., it had reached within firing range and then, all of a sudden, a tremendous booming sound echoed in the distance and bursts of smoke billowed into the air.[4] The first broadsides were fired, rumbling like thunder. Yards from the *Vincejo*'s starboard quarters, fountains of water sprang up. Wright stood resolutely on the quarterdeck, every few moments raising his spyglass to observe the distant cannon. The *Vincejo* was already in a brittle condition; the greatest part of her keel had fallen apart and only constant pumping could prevent her from sinking.[5] The officers, who held a special affection for their captain, implored him to transfer to the *Fox* cutter, which was then sweeping out of the bay. They knew that his life would be endangered once the republicans found out who he was. Opposing their importunities, Wright boldly gave the order to sweep her broadside and engage the enemy. The French gun boats now began encircling the brig, their portside gun ports opening up before the eyes of the beleaguered crew. They scrambled on deck, and though exhausted by hard labour at the oar they frantically manned and heaved upon the brig's starboard sweeps and larboard guns in desperation. The air was filled with billowing smoke as the ships traded blows. With devastating accuracy, the enemy's broadsides tore through the *Vincejo*'s hulls and masts, ripping the yards and rigging, whilst the eddying smoke filled the air as round-shot and grape were discharged with equal intensity. The crew began to fall fast. A grape-shot slashed Wright's thigh just inches from his groin, and though wincing in pain he summoned the strength to remain on deck. The unequal contest raged for two hours, and by the end the *Vincejo* was torn asunder, her firing capacity reduced to one gun, the others disabled or damaged by the falling yards. The vessel was about to sink fast and the enemy's marines, towing up alongside, their swords flashing in the sunlight, were poised to board en masse. With the imminence of blazing death, Wright had no choice but to hail that he had surrendered in time to spare the lives of the few men that remained. John Wesley Wright, naval commander and agent of His Majesty's secret service, was once more in enemy hands.

The enemy's commanding officer, Lieutenant Laurent Tourneur, appears to have admired Wright's display of bravery, for upon receiving his sword he was reported to have declared, 'Sir, you have nobly defended the honour of your nation and the reputation of your navy: we like and esteem the brave and will treat you and your company with all the regard possible.'[6] The *Vincejo* was then towed into Porto Navallo, a small harbour lying in the mouth of the River Vilaine. During this time Le Tourneur treated his opposite with the greatest respect and courtesy, in the evening sending him and his officers upstream by boat to the little town of Auray accompanied by a single soldier. Ashore, the English officers were held in private houses under guard whilst the wounded were conveyed to hospital. As they passed the streets women rushed from their homes and offered the famous prisoner victuals. Wright was so little guarded that upon his arrival at the residence of Monsieur Le Grand, the naval commissary, he was left unattended except by a domestic servant. Le Grand, who was wearing a blue uniform and sporting a gold braided tricorne, received Wright cordially and, mistaking him for the commandant of the French flotilla, congratulated him for his marvellous victory. It was only once Wright corrected him that he realised who his guest was.

After a few days, Wright's captors received orders to take him to the French interior. Along with the on-board surgeon, Lawmont, he was transported in a cart guarded by a detachment of gendarmes and National Guardsmen under the command of a Swiss officer. Just before leaving, the mayor of Auray came to express his deepest gratitude to Wright for having liberated his son from the slave dungeons of Constantinople. In front of the town's dignitaries, he handed Wright a letter thanking him for his past humane actions towards those Frenchmen who had fallen in his captivity. It read: 'Yes, Sir, we will never forget that it was thanks to your kind concern that Citizen Thevenard, son of the Maritime Prefect of the port of Lorient, and the crews of two French boats condemned at Rhodes to hard labour, obtained their release; even more recently in cruising our area, we have learned with feeling that you released fathers of families, old men and children that fate of war had made fall into your hands.'[7] The inhabitants of Auray also evinced their respect by accompanying the celebrated prisoner a little while along the journey.

On the road to Vannes Wright struck up a conversation with the officer commanding the escort, during which he expressed his wish to see Citizen Julien, the prefect of the department of the Morbihan with whom he had become acquainted during the campaign in Egypt. The latter received Wright as an old acquaintance and invited him to dine with him that evening. The fatigue of the journey, exacerbated by the inflammation of his wound, however, prevented his attendance. Instead, that night he lodged in an inn, but this time he found himself closely guarded by a sentinel in his room and a second posted at the front door of the house.

The next morning, Wright was summoned to Julien's residence. In the presence of General Chambarlhac, the commandant of the department, he was told that he was being sent to Paris by the stagecoach for his comfort. Wright, of course, saw through this artifice, having heard similar fictions before, and protested that it would be too painful for him to quit his officers and seamen with whom he was duty bound to share the burdens of the journey. At this, Julien dropped the charade and, adopting a different tone, frankly told Wright that it was his intention that the French government be afforded the opportunity to extract from him information respecting the 'conspirators and assassins' whom, he charged, Wright had landed upon the French coast, adding cynically that 'those persons would probably wish to claim his acquaintance'.[8]

In reply, Wright told Julien that he owed no account of his services to any authority but his own government and that he had no intention of divulging any information to his enemy. He then warned Julien not to depart from the customs of belligerent nations in their treatment towards prisoners of war. The interview ended there. Once the prisoner left his sight, Julien wrote a letter to the *Grand Juge* Régnier notifying him of the high-profile arrest:

Vannes, May 15 1804

Citizen Grand Judge,

An English Corvette was taken a few days ago by our Gun-boats, at the entrance of the Morbihan; and having yesterday learned that the Officers and crew of this vessel had reached Vannes, on their way to Espinal, I had an interview with the Captain, with the intention of obtaining by artifice some admission, or accounts, relative to the Traitors who might it aiding him on the coast; or of the accomplices in the conspiracy, who might have secreted themselves aboard his Vessel, to escape, as I suspected, to England. I soon discovered this Captain to be a person of some importance; he is a Mr Wright, who landed Georges, Pichegru and their accomplices on the coast of Dieppe. I knew him well in Egypt, where he was Lieutenant of Sir Sidney Smith, and charged by that Commodore with all his negotiations with the French Army. I thought he might make some useful discoveries, or at least might acquit himself, by avowing that it was by order of his Government, that he disembarked on our coast that band of assassins; and might thus furnish a new and authentic proof of the participation of the British Cabinet in this atrocity. I have, therefore, sent him off by the Diligence, and under the escort of the *Gens d'Armerie*; recommending you, however, to pay him the respect due to a prisoner of war. Mr Wright is the same person who, some years since, escaped from the Temple with Sir Sydney Smith; he is very reserved and cunning; a fanatical enemy of the French; vain enough to consider himself destined to play a considerable part; and so insolent as to believe that his situation secures him from danger. But as this may fail, if he is placed in the alternative, of throwing the blame of his mission upon his Government, or of passing for an ostensible Conspirator, and so liable to justice; I thought proper to state my own opinion on this subject. He will set off this evening in the Diligence from Rennes, and will arrive at Paris almost as soon as my letter; he is accompanied by a very young Nephew, and his domestic, whom I did not think proper to separate from him.

Although I wished to conceal from him the motive of the extraordinary measure adopted towards him, he was not to be duped; and I have reason to believe, from my conversation with him, that he studied his part; and is determined to remain silent, on the principle, that he ought only to render an account of his military operations to his own Government. Nevertheless, whatever measures you may take respecting him, I thought, at all events, it would be importance to send you a man, who has acted so conspicuously in the frightful Conspiracy which has struck all of France with alarm; and which Providence, always propitious, seems to have thrown as a new example of its benevolence towards Buonaparte on the coast of Morbihan; where his well armed ship was destined to be taken by gunboats, and himself to be discovered amidst a crowd of prisoners, amongst whom, in any part other than here, he might have remained undiscovered. I hope, Citizen Minister, you will approve of the measures I have taken.

I have the honour to salute you,

Julien.[9]

Conducted by two soldiers, one on either side of his carriage, and the third perched upon the coach box, Wright arrived in Paris after a painful ten-day journey, accompanied by his nephew John Rogerson Wright and his faithful servant. The journey's discomfiture had extended the inflammation of his wound to the bladder and produced an excruciating strangury that interrupted his passage and almost forced him to pause at Haudan, near Paris. His officers were sent to the prisoners' depot at Verdun whilst the sailors were conveyed to Givet in the Ardennes. Upon his arrival, he was transferred from Réal's police office to the Temple whereupon he was conducted, under military guard, to a heated and crowded room, and in the presence before the notorious judge, Jacques Thuriot.

The judge's 'countenance and brutal demeanour' brought to Wright's mind 'the savages who ... rushed upon Paris to massacre thousands of innocent victims confined in corroding prisons, without trial or even examination. He appeared, like another *Jefferies*, panting for blood, and cumulating insult, artifice, falsehood, and menace, to disconcert, betray and intimidate the weak or unwary.'[10] To the preliminary questions Wright answered that, having been taken in arms, he had perfectly satisfied all these points to his captors upon his surrender. He followed by saying that, as the interrogations stood contrary to what he deemed 'received principles and the practise of civilised nations toward their prisoners of war', he was determined not to accord it the least legitimacy by answering any questions. An animated conversation followed relating to the laws of nations and customs of war during which Thuriot levelled a number of accusations against the British government, declaring at the end that the laws and customs of France *alone* should be applied to him. In response, Wright pointed out the injustice of applying to him the laws of France with which he was wholly unacquainted and to which he owed no allegiance. At this point, Thuriot erupted in anger and accused Wright of having disembarked 'conspirators and assassins' in France under orders from the British cabinet for the purpose of murdering Napoleon, overthrowing the government and fomenting civil war. He also declared that he would compel Wright to answer his questions or he would send him before a military commission whereupon he would be shot as a spy *sur le champ* if he persisted. To this, the prisoner responded contemptuously that he had never been afraid of his enemy's shot and that, as his person was in the judge's hands, he may well dispense with him as he so pleased. The interrogation lasted almost five hours, by the end of which Wright had lost all concentration, being exhausted by the fatigue of six days' travel, the pain of inflammation and the barrage of insults and provocation.[11]

After the interrogation, Wright was installed in one of the upper turrets of the little Temple. Though confined *au secret*, he was able to communicate discreetly to a friend and fellow inmate through a small casement in the roof adjoining his chamber. He was also permitted to walk freely in the gallery opposite the gateway whilst his comrades were permitted to exercise for one hour a day in the garden or the upper galleries of the tower. Soon after, Wright was informed that Napoleon's stooge, General Réné Savary, desired an interview with him. The two men had met during the Treaty of El Arish negotiations but what began with mutual professional courtesy had now turned into a visceral animus. After a vain attempt to draw from him some confession injurious to the royalist conspirators, Savary launched an attack on the private character and politics of his close friend Sir Sidney Smith. Seeing that Wright was unyielding and unprepared to concede on any point, Savary shifted his ground and directed his attack towards his friend's brother, Spencer Smith, to whom he seemed resolved to give no quarter. He also declared France's intention to prosecute the war against England without pity or restraint and with 'all imaginable means'.

Two days after the first examination, Wright was again brought before Thuriot and subjected to a renewed interrogation during which he dozed several times in his chair, having found the first round already so tedious. This time, Thuriot declared that Wright would be treated as a leading actor in the conspiracy and be made to stand trial for his life. He also accused Wright of having landed the 'conspirators and assassins' in France without any authority from his own government and that it would no sooner disavow him than associate themselves with a hired mercenary.

To this, Wright replied that he was prepared to meet the very worse consequences of his patriotic duty and felt no apprehension of being disavowed by his government. He was then confronted with a number of the conspirators whom he had landed but again refused to recognise them or respond to any questions concerning them. As a last ploy Thuriot threatened him with criminal prosecution for having escaped from the Temple in 1798 by means of the surreptitious transfer order, but when this failed he ended the interrogation by declaring, 'It is useless interrogating you,' to which Wright shot back, 'Perfectly so.'[12]

Napoleon's police agents were forced to admire Wright's firmness. Besides resisting the succession of threats, he also spurned the offer of a large purse and a commission of admiral in the French service if he would betray the British government. He was then threatened with execution for being an accomplice with Georges and Pichegru, to which he responded, 'If such a violation of the laws of war and of nations take place, I shall recommend my soul to my Creator and the vengeance of my death to my King and Country; but I hope that you will remember the many thousands of your own countrymen prisoners in England.'[13]

Following the interrogation Wright was re-confined *au secret*. After a few days, the sentinel posted in his cell was withdrawn but to his immense displeasure, he was paid a second visit by Savary. The general, who was accompanied by two senior officers, began by voicing his disappointment that Wright had not written to him, insinuating that his predicament was now critical. He saw, however, that Wright could not be cowed by the implied threat and, switching tact, said, 'I know that you do not fear death but you have dishonoured yourself before all of Europe, which regards you as an accomplice of assassins, your reputation is blackened.'[14] He also pretended to doubt Wright's character as a British officer. Ridiculing this folly, Wright declared that he was born in Ireland and pointed to his naval uniform which, according to the prison's inventory, consisted of an old blue cloth coat, ornamented with gold epaulettes, a white shirt, single breasted waistcoat, blue pantaloons and a cocked hat bound with black silk of the old oak pattern looped with four bright gold bouillons, the central two twisted. Savary remarked that it was not proof of his commission in the Royal Navy, for the brigands which he had landed in France also possessed uniforms. He offered, however, to restore Wright to his full liberty if he would confess to England's complicity in 'The Great Conspiracy'. He was met with this typically stiff response:

> Tell your master, Savary, that I had you on board ship in Egypt- that I did you the honor to admit you to the same table, and was far from imagining then that you could ever allow yourself to make a base proposal to a man who has the honour of being a captain in the navy of his Britannic Majesty. Had you any native military spirit in you, you would know that the sentiments professed by a soldier restrain him from making or accepting a dishonourable proposal, that must stamp an indelible stigma both on those who make it, and on those who listen to it without indignation.

Days later, the prison concierge informed Wright that Savary intended to repeat his visit. Wright told him not to bother, telling his keeper that, 'of all the despicable wretches it had been his misfortune to meet with', Savary 'was the man for whom he had the most sovereign contempt, that his conduct was a disgrace to a military uniform'.[15] Savary seems to have got the message for he never again deigned to appear before the prisoner.

Shortly thereafter, Wright received a summons to appear before the tribunal as a witness against the conspirators, stipulating that he would suffer severe punishment should he not comply. Nevertheless, Wright protested against the authority of France's courts declaring that as a British officer he could not be compelled to give any evidence before it. He added that, despite being a prisoner, he was still subject to martial law and naval discipline, and therefore could not possibly comply with the summons without being guilty of high treason against his king and country. Moreover, he would prefer to be shot by the enemy than be executed by his own countrymen for violating both his public duty and code of honour. The scene ended with the messenger leaving the summons with the prison guardian but with Wright pointing out the absurdity of being summoned judicially to give evidence before the court at the same time that he was being detained *au secret*.

On the day that the trial began, Wright was removed from his cell and placed in the same apartment that he had occupied years earlier. His servant was permitted to attend him. Under a brick in the floor, he found some files, spring saws and other instruments for cutting the iron bars which he recalled having deposited there during his first confinement. He was also able to communicate freely with a handful of other prisoners unconnected to the conspiracy who, without the knowledge of his keeper, managed to procure for him some small comforts including wine, rum and brandy.

Hours later, Wright was brought before a messenger who was waiting with a gendarme to conduct him to the court. Again, he rejected the summons and refused to accompany them. The messenger told Wright that he was under orders not to use violence but to treat him with respect. The messenger furthermore told him to address his protest in writing to the president. Again,

Wright refused, rejecting the authority of the court. Upon this, the messenger left to compile his report. He returned not long after accompanied by an officer and a guard, announcing that he had orders to take him before the court by force if necessary. Seeing the futility of resisting, he finally relented. He was then handcuffed, handled into a hackney coach, and conveyed to the Palais de Justice.

Upon entering the courtroom the gendarmes removed the manacles from Wright. He insisted, however, on holding them in his hands to show everyone that he was being compelled to appear against his will. After hearing the *Acte d'Accusation* read out, he was remanded to custody. He was compelled again to appear before the criminal court one week later, and again he protested in the same manner. This time, he was deposited in an antechamber where the other witnesses were assembled and listened as they exchanged accounts of how they had been tortured by Napoleon's secret police in order to confess to the public the existence of the assassination plot. They described how they had their thumbs screwed together by the cock of a musket while lighted gunpowder was applied to their nails, how burning coals or hot embers had been applied to the soles of their feet. They also recounted how they had been threatened with execution, how their homes were rifled through in search of evidence, their furniture destroyed, their families routed.

Wright's arrival in the courtroom produced a something of a stir in the audience. He slowly shuffled in, but as he had trouble standing erect a chair was offered to him. He sat himself perfectly at ease, with one leg in a resting posture across the opposite knee, and darted his eyes all around the hall, examining its structure and the audience within it. The president of the court then called him by name and enjoined him to answer all the questions that would be posed, 'without partiality, hatred or fear'. Wright replied that, in the first instance, military men knew no fear; that he was a British prisoner of war and had surrendered in battle against a superior force. He added that, in accordance to his sworn duty to his king and country, he would not answer any of the questions that might be put to him. He also claimed the rights and customs of war, the very same ones which he had never failed to extend to the many Frenchmen who had fallen under his power. The last declaration created such uproar that it elicited cries of silence from the vergers of the court, forcing him to suspend his speech until order was restored.

The transcripts of Wright's interrogations by Thuriot were then read out. The secretary, however, had not finished the preamble when Wright interrupted him by saying that he had one observation to make. Granted the parole, Wright declared aloud that the written records were incomplete as, amongst other omissions, they did not mention the threats to send him before a military commission to be instantly shot as a spy if he did not betray his government. At this moment Thuriot rose from his seat, scarcely able to contain his composure, and addressed the president, gesticulating wildly. But despite interrupting Wright the latter still insisted and succeeded in expressing himself loud enough to be heard by everyone in the galleys. The witnesses being ordered to withdraw, Wright descended the first few steps from his seat. Turning around, he bowed to the man who had offered him a chair, saluted the prisoners and retired, bowing first to the counsel and then to the audience as he passed by. He never once faced the court.[16]

Wright was subsequently transferred back to the Tower, where he was permitted to stroll in the garden for two hours a day and fraternise with the other prisoners, including General Moreau, who occupied the chamber adjacent to his. He was, however, separated from his nephew John, who, after embracing him in the garden, tearfully lamented, 'I shall never see my uncle again; Buonaparte is going to kill him.' The young lad had also appeared as a witness during the great trial and tried to answer each question with caution. He was asked if he knew 'in England, of a conspiracy against France' to which he replied only, 'I have heard it talked of in the province of Kent, at Greenwich, about six months ago.' But he let his guard slip when Judge Thuriot asked, 'How often have you seen men disembarked upon the coast of France from the corvette, which you sailed in?' to which he admitted not having witnessed any disembarkations 'since within two months, or thereabouts'.[17]

Wright was also brought face-to-face with a former friend and inmate, Jacques Jean Marie François de Tromelin. Tromelin had landed at Moraix towards the end of March and had returned to his old château of Coatserho where he intended to pass the rest of his days in peace and tranquillity in the company of his loving, devoted wife. But three weeks later, on 11 April 1804, at approximately eleven o'clock at night, a detachment of gendarmes, together with the police commissioners of Brest and Moraix, knocked on his door and spirited him away in a post-chaise before the startled household. The gendarmes, under the command of Captain Ravoeu of the department of the Seine and Oise, ransacked the château in search of evidence linking him to Spencer Smith and his brother, Sir Sidney. They were acting upon intelligence from the *agent provocateur* Captain Rosey, who reported to Napoleon that Spencer Smith had confided to him in a conversation that Tromelin was a close acquaintance. The gendarmes found nothing incriminating among his papers except a letter that he had written, but had not yet sent, to an officer posted at the garrison of Brest, inquiring if anyone there possessed a carriage for sale because 'he had lent his to an Englishman who had not returned it'.[18] When Ravoeu demanded to know who this Englishman was, Tromelin replied that he was a physician by the name of Dr Scott who had travelled to France legally. The police subsequently made background checks on this individual and discovered that he had arrived from England to wait upon Lady Elgin while her husband (of Elgin marbles fame) languished in prison. Examining the police surveillance records they found that de Tromelin had called upon her 'assiduously' in Paris. He explained that he had visited Lady Elgin often because he had frequently enjoyed her generous hospitality in Constantinople when she was in happier circumstances and also hoped 'to lessen her antipathy for France'. Undeceived, the police commissioners charged him with 'being in communication with the *enemies* of the state', a capital offence, and, upon Napoleon's orders, confined him *au secret* in l'Abbaye.[19]

A week later, Tromelin was interrogated in his cell. At first his answers were laconic and monosyllabic. But after a while, for motives which are unclear, he decided to give a full account of his misadventures since his emigration from France thirteen years previous. For the first time, the French police learned the true identity of John Bromley, Sir Smith's 'Canadian' servant in the Temple, the same young cockney lad whom they had 'repatriated' in 1797. He also told his interrogators how they had managed to stage their famous escape but was cautious enough not to incriminate anyone whom the secret police could still possibly punish. The only Frenchmen whom he did name were Louis de Phélippeaux, who was long dead, and the Abbé Ratel, who was in England. For a week or two he heard nothing, then one day he was suddenly removed from his cell and taken under armed escort to the Court of Criminal Justice where the great show trial of Georges and his accomplices was in progress. He was brought before Wright and was asked to identify him. Seeing no harm in stating what was already patently known, he declared that Wright was the very same English sailor with whom he had been incarcerated in Paris years earlier. Somewhat naively, Tromelin did not realise at first that the French authorities were actually trying to incriminate Wright in 'The Great Conspiracy', and through him the British government. He also had not known that thirty-eight of the alleged conspirators, who were on trial for their life, had in fact refused to identify Wright as the captain who had landed them along the Breton coast. He at once wrote to Régnier, making it clear that the only time that he had contact with Wright after their imprisonment together in the Temple was when he served as an officer of *Le Tigre* during the Egyptian campaign and in London as a friend of Sir Sidney's. He also emphatically denied any knowledge of the assassination plot.

He heard nothing afterwards, but then several months later he was paid an expected visit from Monsieur Crepy, the police commissary assigned to the district of Brest. Crepy advised Tromelin to petition Napoleon for a commission in the Imperial Army; otherwise, as he said, his case was 'hopeless'. When asked, he told Tromelin that the reason why he was trying to help him was that during the Egyptian campaign he had been imprisoned by the Turks in the dungeons on the Island of Rhodes and that, Tromelin had, as Sir Sidney's emissary, managed to secure him and his fellow comrades better treatment. He also told Tromelin that he had already written to Réal and Régnier on his behalf, telling both of them that their prisoner was very well known to the army of Egypt for his humanitarian efforts, that he had saved many of their lives, and that his arrest had aroused the consternation of the people in the district of Finistère. Tromelin also learnt that another officer whom Sir Sidney and Wright had liberated from the dungeons built under the bagnios in Constantinople, the Chef d'Escadron Calmet Beauvoisin, had also written to Réal and interceded on his behalf. Days later, Tromelin sent for Crepy and, telling him he would accept his advice, handed him a letter to deliver to Napoleon in which he promised his allegiance. In the letter, he suggested that he could best render service in the Levant as he possessed strong command of the Turkish language but that he was unable to serve in an infantry regiment on account of a foot injury which he had sustained whilst on a reconnaissance mission at Aboukir. His wish was only half granted. He was released from prison but dragooned into the ranks of the 112th regiment of the line.[20]

Wright was also reconciled with the surviving officers and sailors of the *Vincejo*. For twenty-six days they had been confined *au secret* with nothing but bread and water to nourish them and not a moment's fresh air. During this period they were repeatedly interrogated at night by police agents regarding Wright's mission. The interrogations yielded no results. Questioned about their movements in the first days of March, the pattern revealed that the *Vincejo* made no disembarkation but once Wright took command of the brick at the dunes they left for Quiberon, having no other links than with the fishermen from the Island of Houat who came each day to sell their catch. They were, among others, interrogated by Fauconnier's young son who had spent some time in an English boarding house and who had come prepared with a questionnaire.

Among the officers was George Sidney Smith, nephew to Sir Sidney and son of the Bishop of Bristol. Along with a young officer named Wallis, he shared the same lower chamber with Louis Fauche-Borel's own nephew, Vittel. With nothing but a basement window opened to the level of the sun, and exposed to the dank and putrid atmosphere, they soon fell ill. They were finally permitted to exercise a little each day in the courtyard, and during one stroll, using a fragment of wood carbon, they drew on the prison walls an image of the gallows and hanging men underlined with the name 'Buonaparte'.

At length, they were permitted to lodge together in one large room where they communicated surreptitiously with Wright. After a month's solitary confinement, the other officers were permitted to walk about the courtyard and converse with him. He superintended the education of two sailors, setting before them each day French grammar and mathematical tasks which he slipped through a small opening in the cell door.

Towards mid-July Napoleon ordered Louis Alexandre Berthier, the Minister of War, to transfer all of the prisoners of the *Vincejo* to Landau, a depot assigned to English prisoners of war. It was announced to Wright that his nephew, his servant and George Sidney Smith would accompany the convoy but that he would remain alone in the Temple as his complicity in 'The Great Conspiracy' and former escape from the prison denied him the status of a prisoner of war. Before their departure they were permitted to see Wright, who, although affecting good cheer, was evidently stuck with a dark foreboding. On taking leave of the surgeon Mr Laumont, he said, 'I hope we may meet again under more favourable circumstances; but at all events, whatever may happen to me in my present position, I will behave, believe me, whatever reports may be sent abroad, like a Christian and a British officer.'[21]

Wright now remained alone. In his correspondence, he lamented how this separation was very painful to him, especially his removal from the three pupils who were so dear to him. He regretted not being able to supervise their education and on one occasion predicted, 'Buonaparte will destroy me; he has not forgotten our proclamations in Egypt, nor what we have written to him, nor the reproaches which we have addressed to him on the subject of his crimes at Jaffa.'[22] He therefore tried to find ways to distract himself from the oppressive prison environment. He requested permission to have a flute for his amusement, but on being refused procured a German one clandestinely. He also petitioned the Temple's concierge, Louis-François Fauconnier, to obtain more books. The concierge denied the request; casting his eyes on the volumes which Wright's officers had left him, he replied that he had already more than he could read. Fauconnier was not being unnecessarily inflexible, most likely just conforming to orders from the Minister of the Interior. He was a family man, in his mid-fifties and father to five children. Sturdily built, with an eagle's beak and brown hair receding from the forehead, he was otherwise jovial, a '*bon enfant*', '*pitoyable à ses heures*' and always a great friend of the bottle.[23] He allowed his prisoners to fraternise when they were not confined *au secret* and receive invitations from friends from outside. He also joined the many feasts that some of them, like Louis Fauche-Borel, did not fail to organise in order to escape the boredom of their captivity. All of this did not prevent Fauconnier from discharging his duties with customary assiduity. He kept the police up to date with information on the behaviour of those same detainees with whom he feasted or played cards. Yet, given his sense of rectitude, he warned them not to disclose in front of him anything that could interest the judges, adding that his sense of duty obliged him to report them. He also permitted Wright to keep up his epistolary correspondence:

Letter to Mr James Wallis, his First Lieutenant from the Temple at Paris

Accept my thanks for your congratulation on my promotion, which is, however, become indifferent to me, farther than to demonstrate the liberality and justice of government, of which I never entertained a doubt. I beg you to bear in mind that I have every proper feeling on the occasion, and the handsome manner in which it has been conferred has not escaped my observation or failed to have due weight. Although it has been in my contemplation to resign my commission, through an official channel here, in order to relieve the government from the embarrassment my extraordinary situation must have placed it under, and to prevent a practise which I forebear to characterise, bearing upon other victims on either side; but I felt, on further reflection, that although I was willing to forego its protection, yet no act of mine, thus situated, could absolve my government from the performance of its duty to a British subject.[24]

Until then, the British government had made no attempt to liberate Wright either diplomatically or by threatening retaliation on the prisoners of rank in their power. His friends therefore petitioned the cabinet, which, through the medium of the Catholic Majesty's ambassador, remonstrated against the 'severity' of his treatment. Napoleon was evidently angered by such 'insolence' and ordered Talleyrand to issue a sly rebuke. The letter, which was dictated by him, was couched in the following terms:

Paris, 10th Fructidor, XII (28 August 1804)

I have laid before his Majesty the Emperor this letter which you have done me the honour of communicating to me. By his order I must recapitulate to your Excellency some facts which relate to the object of that letter. Mr Wright was taken by our cruisers at the very moment he was landing Jean Marie and two of his accomplices on the coast of Brittany. Prior to this he had already landed at three times consequently banditti of a similar description, who have since been brought to judgement, convicted and punished, for having conspired against the state, and attempted the life of the first consul. These species of acts, under whatever point of view they may otherwise be contemplated, certainly do not appertain to war; there is no age nor any nation in which they would be regarded as crimes, and one may with truth aver that it was *flagranti delicto*. Mr Wright was captured by French mariners than officiating as an armed force.

According to accounts, to which full credit must be given, this officer had been demanded from the English Admiralty. The Lords directing this department were of course not ignorant of the kind of service to which he was destined; the shame attached to the premeditation and execution of a project as atrocious and vile as it was cowardly, remains entirely with the men who devised the plot, and with him who undertook to accomplished their views.

I am ordered, Sir, to declare to your Excellency, that his Majesty the Emperor will never suffer Mr Wright to be exchanged. No Frenchman, belonging, with whatever rank he may, to the Imperial Navy, can ever consent to be placed in the balance with that person in a cartel of exchange. But, Sir, the Emperor having heart to do everything which depends upon his Imperial Majesty to mitigate the scourges of war, and willing to prove that in his breast such a disposition preponderates over every motive of useful and just severity, has authorised me to declare that his Imperial Majesty will give orders that Mr Wright be placed at the disposal of the English government. May I beg of you therefore to make known to Lord Harrowby this generous determination of his Majesty ... I shall therefore remain in expectation of learning by your means the place which the English government wish the prisoner of state claimed through your intervention to be delivered over.

I avail myself of this opportunity of renewing to your Excellency the assurances of the most high consideration.

CHARLES MAURICE TALLEYRAND[25]

The letter bore false promises.

William Windham, the former Secretary of War, also brought Wright's case before the Houses of Parliament. A descendant from an ancient Norfolk family, Windham was said to have possessed superior intellectual gifts and oratorical abilities and, though thin, meagre and sallow-looking, his deportment was never less than manly and dignified:

I cannot help calling the attention of the House to another instance of the violation of the laws of nations, fully as atrocious as any to which the Speech alludes; I mean the case of an English officer, Captain Wright, who was taken by the enemy, after gallantly defending his ship against a very superior force; although he was an officer taken in the honourable service of his country, yet the French government had not only thought proper to order him to close confinement as a prisoner in the Temple, but had affected to treat him as a criminal, and to have interrogatories put to him about the orders he had received from his government. This violation of the law of nations, it did not appear that our ministers had taken any steps to prevent; the many weeks and months that had passed over since the imprisonment of that officer, had witnessed no measure taken to redress his wrongs; and yet the measures to be adopted are obvious. We have many French officers taken under similar circumstances, and the law of reprisals alone can secure the proper treatment of those of our officers who have the misfortune to be prisoners in France.[26]

When Windham first appeared before the House, he doubted whether he should move for the papers relating to the treatment or exchange of Wright to be brought to its attention, thinking they would not show the government and the country in an advantageous light. Sidney Smith, occupying the bench behind him, disagreed and voiced his opinion that the production of the papers would be of service to Wright as it would bring the circumstances of his situation to the view of the country and to Europe. He spoke in the highest terms of Wright, stating that the motion would afford some consolation to his friend, who despite being immured in a solitary dungeon knew that he was not forgotten by his country. The motion would also make known to Napoleon the extent of Britain's indignation towards his treatment of Wright. He concluded by reading a letter from an officer at Verdun about the capture of Wright's vessel. The letter ended thus: 'We lament this separation from us, as would the absence of our dearest friend. His manners are those of a perfect gentleman, his abilities of the first class, and his bravery only equalled by his generosity and humanity. In his deportment to his inferiors he appears in the most amiable point of view, it being that of a kind and benevolent father. Indeed, I have not words to express my admiration of his character.'[27] At this point Smith was so overpowered by the weight of his emotions that he was no longer able to speak and, in the end, broke off abruptly.

The Chancellor of the Exchequer raised no objection to the production of the papers moved for by Windham. However, before the papers could be examined before the House it was necessary that some additional ones be presented as well. These papers were accordingly produced and laid before Lord Camden, who proposed that if Wright was treated as a prisoner of war then a general cartel should be established between the enemy nations. The king, impressed by the lengthened captivity of Wright, deemed it reasonable to expect that an honourable redress on these points should precede any establishment of a general cartel. In any event, Windham's motions proved abortive, yielding no results.

Meanwhile, beyond the prison walls, the city of Paris prepared for the coronation of its new emperor, Napoleon Bonaparte. Under the glow of torch lights thousands of workers laboured, tearing down derelict buildings, sweeping the streets and sanding the quays that ran along the Seine. In their workshops, saddlers, carriage-makers, lace-men and embroiderers worked around the clock to fulfil their handsome commissions. Then, at the break of dawn, on Sunday 2 December 1804, a discharge of artillery resounded through the air announcing the commencement of the day's celebrations.

Between ten and eleven o'clock, in tune to cannon salutes and the pealing of church bells, the imperial procession left the Tuileries palace in an especially designed carriage, glittering in gold, and pulled by richly caparisoned bay horses, formerly belonging to the King of England. Napoleon was lavishly dressed in a white velvet costume laced and embroidered in gold on the seams, with diamond fastenings and facings sparkling with gold and gems. On his head sat a black velvet cap with two white aigrettes and ornamented with diamonds. The Empress Josephine was aglitter too, wrapped in a mantle of crimson velvet, lined with white and Russian ermine, and studded with diamonds and golden bees.

Escorted by six cavalry regiments defiled between double lines of infantry, the cortege passed slowly along the quays of the Seine

before the immense crowds of Parisians who, more from curiosity
than enthusiasm for the new regime, had turned out to witness
the grand spectacle. At about midday, the procession pulled
into the great archiepiscopal court. A dense fog hung in the cold
air but suddenly, as Napoleon descended from the coronation
carriage, the clouds dispersed, the fog dissipated and a brilliant
ray of sunlight appeared. There, Napoleon arrayed himself in the
imperial robe studded with golden bees and fastened with a gold
cord and tassel whilst the venerable Pope Pius VII pronounced the
traditional prayers in a low voice.[28]

Invested with his imperial ornaments, Napoleon proceeded to
the porch of the Cathedral of Notre Dame through a long wooden
gallery especially erected for the occasion, and from which hung
the banners of the sixteen cohorts of the Legion of Honour. He
bore the coronation ornaments of Charlemagne whilst, behind
him, Marshal Kellerman carried the emperor's crown in the form
of a tiara, and Marshal Perignon his sceptre. Upon entering the
great court the choir began chanting the anthem *Tu es petrum*.
Napoleon advanced with great dignity along the middle of the
nave, passing the different bodies of state and deputations ranged
along the ancient tapestry walls according to their ranks. His
brow was girded with a simple wreath of golden laurel recalling
the crown of the Caesars. The Pope, preceded by the master
of the ceremonies, and accompanied by the cardinals, followed
the emperor to the throne erected in front of the grand altar,
equidistant from the centre of the church. Before taking possession
of the throne he fell to his knees and then, rising back on his
feet, propped himself in an adjacent chair. The Pope bestowed
him a triple unction, on the head and two hands. Then, just as
he motioned to lift the crown from the altar, Napoleon seized it
and, removing his laurel wreath, placed it on his own head. At
that precise moment a small particle of stone about the size of a
nut fell from the vaunted roof and landed just inches away from
his person. Pretending not to notice this curious omen, Napoleon
placed the crown over Josephine's tiara of diamonds, playfully
removing it before balancing it on her head again. He then
mounted the throne whilst his brother supported the skirts of the

imperial mantle. Josephine took her place beside him, shadowed by the assembled sovereigns of Europe. The Pope proceeded to the foot of the throne and recited the prayer *In hoc Imperii solie*. After having pronounced these words, he kissed the emperor on the cheek, and turning towards the audience, proclaimed in a loud voice, '*Vivat Imperatorin eternum*!' To which the congregation, now on their feet, their plumed hats tossed in the air, repeatedly exclaimed '*Vivent L'Empereur et l'Imperatrice*!'[29] With this, the Revolution and the First French Republic had come to an end.

Shortly afterwards, on 18 February 1805, a gendarme arrived at the Temple bearing a release order for Louis Fauche-Borel. After thirty-one months' imprisonment, his release had finally been granted. Taking leave of his fellow inmates, he reserved a few words for Wright who told him, 'My dear Fauche, if you are not able to return to England, I ask you in all grace to go see the Knight Jackson in Berlin; make him aware of my position and say to him well that I expect to share the fate of Pichegru. I do not know if one will say that I was strangled with a tourniquet; but I say to you, and tell this to your friends, I have too much principle, faith and strength of heart to kill myself.' He left the prison gates at seven o'clock in the morning and, escorted by an officer of the gendarmerie, bound forth for the frontier. He was accompanied by his brother, François and the prison warden, Fauconnier, who accompanied him as far as Saint-Denis, the first stage of the long journey. There, he was bound with a cord, the ends of which were twisted around the wrists of two gendarmes and continuing on foot, marched eastwards towards Laon where he managed to procure a post-chaise. Trundling through Namur and Aix-la-Chapelle, he crossed the Rhine and on 6 March 1805 arrived at Wesel, just kilometres beyond the frontier of Napoleon's empire. Two and a half years earlier, Louis Fauche-Borel had entered France as a royalist agent in the service of England. He left a spy in the pay of a regicide.

Borel had purchased his freedom. In the aftermath of the great show trial, he had been transferred to La Force prison, a sordid hellhole reserved not for renowned state prisoners, as he fancied himself to be, but for common riffraff. He appeared to be much piqued by this, for after just three days' confinement he was, in police parlance, 'cooked to a turn'. He wrote to Desmarest, Fouché's henchman, repenting for his past and professing his new-found 'attachment to the Government'. 'I place myself entirely in your hands, as I have often wished I might do; you know that I can be of *very special* service to you, and there are at the present time few men who can serve you so advantageously as I. I shall explain my methods to you, and am convinced that I shall merit your confidence by my discretion; it is by attaching myself to those who understand their business, and are able to distinguish between adventurers and upright men, that I hope to effect my own advancement and to benefit my family.'[30] Desmarest did not mistake his meaning. Before indexing the letter among the other documents comprising his police dossier, he scribbled in the margin, 'Wants to be employed a spy.' This was Borel's price for returning to the Temple. Nor was he no longer accused of conspiracy but merely of '*manoeuvres* against the safety of the state', a far lesser crime.[31] It now remained to restore him to full liberty.

Wright was not indulged in the same manner. Yet compared to the debased squalors of early nineteenth-century prison hulks, the conditions characterising his confinement were not terribly severe. Although denied interaction with his fellow inmates, he did enjoy the company of an 'amiable' cat which purred quietly on his lap. Nor was he deprived completely of distractions or amenities. In fact, he had amassed a number of objects which were neatly arranged in his cell. On the mantelpiece sat a tin teapot and coffee pot as well as a case of geometrical instruments, a silver watch, a tin lantern and a box of colours for drawing. He had also managed to procure a total of sixty volumes of bound and unbound books which were piled on shelves and a further twenty-four volumes in a cupboard mostly on marine geography and history. On his desk were rolled twenty geographic charts and a looking glass.

His daily routine suffered no disruption either. Then, one morning in early October 1805, the Inspector General of the Ministry of Police, Pacques, accompanied by the police commissary, Jean François Comminges, and a couple of agents, entered Wright's chamber unannounced. They found him writing a note. He instantly slipped it into his mouth, at which point Comminges threw himself upon the prisoner. Wright nevertheless managed to swallow the note but was overcome by a scuffle. His papers were then removed, as well as twenty to twenty-five *louis* which were concealed under the bottom of his trunk. The police agents retired and visited three other detained parties in succession, taking away their papers which ultimately revealed nothing suspicious relative to Wright's situation. The intrusion greatly agitated the prisoner as he was heard afterwards uttering violent deprecations against Napoleon and the tyranny of Savary's police unit which superintended the prison.[32]

Napoleon read about this incident in one of the police bulletins which Fouché, now back behind his desk at the Quai Voltaire, ensured reached his eyes, even on military campaigns. Collated by a handful of confidential clerks employed in each arrondissement, the bulletins were submitted to the Central Bureau before being bound into a single report by a clerk named François, an ex-barrister and royalist agent whom Fouché had released from prison and given employment in December 1799. The report was thereupon passed to Desmarest, who made corrections before forwarding it to Fouché. Two copies were prepared, varying in length from between fifteen to twenty folios. One copy was filed away, the other returned to the reinstated Minister of Police, who made his final annotations and marginal comments to read by Napoleon only. Tied with green ribbon and sealed by Fouché, the report was then delivered directly to Napoleon by a courier of the State Secretariat or of the military governor's staff:

Police bulletin. Friday, 18th October 1805, Plan of Escape. The Ministry had warning that the English prisoner Wright appeared, by different movements and signals, to be procuring, for the chamber that he occupies in the Temple, some intelligence on the outside. One has presumed that he is contemplating escape. After a few days observation, a search was made of his room. One found there, in the lining of the lid of a boot, the following objects: 10 bundles of string, of 321 feet length, unique for forming a cord; another piece of cord 6 feet long to which we was attached a very solid iron hook, used to be fixed to the top of a wall, a roll of brass wire and iron wire, In a portefeuille a neuf cases numerotees, a small saw, montee en fer, with a steel blade (we tested that it sawed the iron with facility and speed), three other steel blades destined to replace the one attached. In a wardrobe, under the parquet floor, a piece of bent, iron wire of 5 to 5 fingers long. Finally, we found, among the books, in another trunk, two bags containing around 50 pieces of gold.[33]

The articles had actually been hidden during his earlier incarceration and had lain undetected ever since. Yet what began as a routine search of Wright's cell was overblown into the discovery of an elaborate escape plan. In view of his former escape nine years earlier, it was not unreasonable for the French to suppose that Wright might attempt to stage another prison break. The incident nevertheless plunged Wright temporarily into a gloom. His constitution was greatly weakened and over time he grew sickly, nervous and frequently afflicted with pains of the spleen. He was also deprived of exercise other than what could be performed in his cell, the length of which was just eighteen feet. Despite the deterioration in his health, he remained mentally alert and kept attuned to events unfolding beyond the prison walls. He communicated with a friend in the cell below him by striking two blows with a broom handle and dropping messages attached to a string through his casement window. He learned, for example, of Napoleon's march into Germany, followed by the seizure of Ulm, Meningen and Augsburg. He also heard of Horatio Nelson's brilliant victory at Trafalgar, news of which the French government had attempted to conceal. Naturally, Wright could not restrain his enthusiasm, humming couplets which he had composed in honour of England's great naval hero.

That night, on 27 October 1805, Wright stayed up an hour or two past midnight playing the flute. At about eight o'clock in the morning one of the gaolers, François Savard, entered his cell to offer him a breakfast roll. He crossed to the window and threw open the shutters, as was his habit. He then turned towards the figure lying on his narrow bed, situated in an alcove. Wright was positioned on his back with the cotton bedsheet pulled up to his chin. Drawing closer, Savard was struck by the immobility of the prisoner's body. Closer still, he saw how Wright's eyes were wide open and that his face looked 'contorted'. Pulling back the sheet, Savard perceived that his throat had been slashed. He was stone dead. In Wright's right hand, drooped beside his thigh, lay a razor with a white handle … shut.[34]

Two hours later, Pierre Dusser, commissary of police of the Temple division, was summoned to the Temple. He found waiting in Wright's cell Auguste-Juste Ravier, captain of the Seine gendarmerie; Louis-Réne Pousignon, quartermaster of the gendarmerie; Edme-François Soupé, the prison surgeon; and Fauconnier, the concierge. Outside in the courtyard, groups of prisoners were assembled. Pointing towards Wright's chamber, one of them, Sieur Poupart, stretched out his arm and by the action of his hand motioned a person cutting his throat. Inside, the body was examined and an inventory was taken of the room. On the table lay a chart of the Danube and issue 33 of the *Moniteur*, dated Friday 3 *Brumaire* an XIV. Soupé, who conducted the examination, then compiled the following coronary report:

A transversal wound situated in the anterior and superior part of the throat, above the bone termed juxoid in length about 18 *centi-metres*, penetrating onto the cervical vertebra; which wound appears to have been effected by an edged instrument, such as a razor, which in its course has cut the skin, the muscles, the tracheal artery, the *oesophagus,* and the sanguineous vessels of that part, whence has ensued a considerable effusion of blood, and the prompt death of the said Wrigth [*sic*].[35]

The physical evidence was clear. Wright's head was nearly torn off. The witnesses then began to draft a *procès-verbal*. Meanwhile, Pacques, the Inspector General of the Police, had joined. He observed passing and re-passing the door the figure of Abbé Alary, a friend of Wright's, and motioned him in. The abbé bowed and, casting a look at the bed, saw his friend's corpse. When he asked what had transpired, he was told that Wright had cut his own throat. He was then ordered by the police inspector to sign the *procès-verbal* that he had just completed. Alary approached the bed again and, seeing the body motionless, raised the bedsheets and uncovered him. Diverting his eyes downwards, he saw that Wright was still holding the razor in his hand. Filled with horror at the sight, he motioned to retire but was prevented by the police who told him he must sign the *procès-verbal*. This he refused, and in an observation which devastated everyone in the room he indignantly replied, 'The man who cuts his own throat does not shut the razor for the use of another.'[36]

Later that day, the authorities announced that Wright had committed suicide, apparently overwhelmed by the news of Napoleon's victory at Ulm. On 6 November 1805 *The Times* reported on the battle's aftermath. On the same page was written an article under the heading: 'CAPTAIN WRIGHT'. The newspaper quoted two French papers, the *Gazette de France and* the *Journal de Paris*. The report read, 'Capt. Wright of the English Navy, a prisoner in the Temple, who had disembarked on the French coast Georges and his accomplices, has put an end to his existence in prison, after having read in the *Moniteur* the account of the destruction of the Austrian army.' The second read, 'The day before yesterday, Mr Wright, the English officer who last year disembarked the assassins of England on the coast of Brittany and was imprisoned in the Temple, after having read the bulletins in the *Moniteur,* and uttered much abuse against the Austrians, and particularly against General Mack, cut his throat with a razor.'[37]

The Times commented:

We fear there is no doubt of the fact of Captain Wright's decease but we cannot believe that a gallant officer, who has so often looked death in the face and was proverbial for courting danger, fell in the manner mentioned. Those, who order and perpetrated the midnight murders of Pichegru and the Duke d'Enghien, can, no doubt, explain the nature of Captain Wright's death.[38]

Thus was the final act of 'The Great Conspiracy', the expiration of the gallant Captain John Wesley Wright, a forgotten hero of the French revolutionary wars and, along with Sir William Sidney Smith and William Wickham, one of the great agents of Britain's early secret service.

EPILOGUE

PRIVATE INVESTIGATIONS

In the year of Waterloo, there appeared in British-occupied Paris a man who was once a state prisoner of the city: Sir William Sidney Smith. Since Nelson's historic victory at Trafalgar, he had been serving in the Mediterranean and campaigning vigorously against the treatment of Christian slaves in Ottoman and Barbary captivity. Forever a show-off, he had been living in extravagant fashion but had left England in order to avoid risking a spell in the King's Bench Prison after failing to meet his obligations. In Paris he installed himself at 6 rue d'Anjou, a short walking distance from the restaurant on the rue St-Honoré where he had formerly dined on one of his evening paroles from the Temple prison.[1] He was now in his fifty-second year, and, though having not altogether hung up his sword, he had arrived in the French capital to solve the mystery of his friend's death which, for that brief moment in 1805, had left Europe aghast.

Ten years had passed since Wright had met his tragic end, and it still weighed heavily on Sir Sidney. Like many of his contemporaries, he had never believed that such a brave and deeply religious man would terminate his own life, against the sanctity of his beliefs and in such an appalling fashion. He had read all sorts of exaggerated accounts in the popular press about the manner in which his friend had succumbed: that he had been stretched on the rack, his body pinched with red hot irons; that brandy mixed with gunpowder was infused in his multiple wounds; that in his convulsions he had bitten off his tongue and, seeing no means of obtaining any useful information from him, a gang of Mamelukes had slashed his throat, supposedly the same Mamelukes that had squeezed the last breath from his fellow conspirator, General Charles Pichegru.[2]

Having seen first-hand his handiwork in Jaffa, Smith had no doubt of Napoleon's despotism; however, he gave no countenance to these baseless rumours of torture, which had been calculated to sensationalise his friend's death and stir up the indignation of the British nation. He nevertheless petitioned the government to launch an official enquiry, but on finding no sympathetic ears he conducted his own private investigation. There were many obstacles. The Temple had been demolished on the orders of Napoleon and most of the police files destroyed.[3] In Paris, the Duke of Wellington pretended to open his doors but quickly grew tired of Smith's relentless lobbying, finding him to be undeserving of his reputation, a man 'so silly in all affairs' it was hard to believe he could be a distinguished naval officer.[4] Smith, it is true, was seen as something of a crank, but unlike Wellington, a relic of history, Smith was far ahead of his time, not only presaging T. E. Lawrence but with a predilection for unconventional warfare and weaponry, including submarines and ships firing rockets, which would become key instruments of combat in the twentieth century.[5] Indeed, his expertise in clandestine war, owing much to the encouragement of William Pitt, would eventually inspire the activities of the Secret Intelligence Service and the Special Operations Executive during the Second World War.[6]

Smith was able to rely on former royalists who were now in positions of authority and influence, as well as retired republican officers who had fought opposite him at the Siege of Acre and admired both his valour and the humane treatment which he accorded French prisoners in his captivity. He also found the wife of his former gaoler, Madame Boniface, to be more than forthcoming, her motives actuated by a hatred for the deposed regime, which, in the aftermath of the rue Niçaise bomb attack, had deported her husband to the Seychelles where he soon perished. Understandably, she was only too pleased to assist Smith in uncovering evidence that could embarrass Napoleon, even in exile. Their investigation, however, only deepened the mystery. Most witnesses were certain that Wright was murdered on orders issued by Fouché or Savary on behalf of the emperor, but, due to contradictory statements, unreliable testimony and relapsing memories, none of their suppositions could be proven.

Sir Sidney's devotion to his fallen friend did not end there, and at his own expense he erected a memorial in his honour which to this day is thought to be found at Père Lachaise cemetery, as recorded in the few surviving Temple files. In fact, Wright was buried in Vaugirard cemetery in Paris, as discovered by another friend, W. D. Fellowes, Esq., in 1818 and recorded in his notes on a 'Visit to the Monastery of la Trappe' the year before.[7] The monument was shaped as an obelisk flanked by weeping cherubs and mourning caryatids – Fame and Britannia – holding inverted torches which are extinguished. It was furthermore inscribed with a long epitaph in Latin:

Here lies inhumed

John Wesley Wright, by birth an Englishman, Captain in the British Navy, distinguished both among his own countrymen, and foreigners, for skill and courage; to whom, of those things which lead to the sum and summit of glory nothing was wanting, but opportunity.

His ancestors, whose virtues he inherited, he honoured by his deeds.

Quick in apprehending his orders,

Active and bold in the execution of them.

In success, modest; in adverse circumstances, firm;

In doubtful enterprises, wise and prudent.

Awhile successful in his career, at length, assailed by adverse winds, and on a hostile shore, he was captured, and being soon brought to Paris, was confined in the prison, called the Temple, infamous for midnight-murders, and placed under the most rigid custody. But in bonds, and suffering severities still more oppressive, his fortitude of mind, and fidelity to his country remained unshaken. A short time after he was found in the morning with his throat cut, and dead in his bed.

He died the 28ᵗʰ October 1805, aged 36.

To be lamented by his country-avenged by his God.

William Sidney Smythe, in memory of ancient Friendship, erected this Monument in the year of the Christian Era, 1816.[8]

An engraving of the monument was published in a monthly almanac, *The Naval Chronicle*, and subsequently shown to Napoleon in St Helena, who fulminated that 'Sidney Smith has acted in a manner unworthy of himself ... in the epitaph which he wrote upon Wright'.[9] The implicit accusation evidently preyed on the emperor's mind, and in a series of conversations he returned to the subject, making many feeble attempts to exonerate himself from the crime: 'They accuse me of the death of a poor little post-captain,' he continued. 'If Wright was put to death, it must have been my authority if he was put to death in prison, I ordered it. Fouché, even if so inclined, never would have dared to do it ... But the fact is, Wright killed himself and I do not believe that he was personally ill-treated in prison, Sidney Smith, above all men, knew from having been so long in the Temple that it is impossible to have assassinated a prisoner without the knowledge of such a number of persons as would have made concealment impossible.'[10]

Exiled on one of the most isolated islands in the world, with little to do but count his spoons, Napoleon had time to ruminate. It had been less than a year since he had been transported to that tiny volcanic island in the Atlantic which even the English, with their uninviting climate, hated for its rainy weather. For most of the day, assailed by strong wings, constant rains and dense fogs, he was stuck indoors at his estate in Longwood, a small village pitched on a plain, dotted with indigenous gumwoods and formed on the summit of a mountain approximately 1,800 feet above sea level. He had petitioned the Governor of the Island to be removed to the leeward side of the island, which enjoyed warmer temperatures and was shielded from the piercing south-east wind, but his request was denied and so, away from the prying eyes of the islanders, he occupied several hours of his day reading and sourcing material for a biographical history of his life. When weather permitted, he went horseback riding or raced about in a carriage, accompanied by his generals, before returning indoors to continue dictation. He occasionally played a game of chess or whist or read the works of Corneille aloud. Never losing his appetite, he ate heartily, enjoying a good roasted leg of mutton and the occasional draught of claret in the evening, albeit diluted with water.[11] Although generally in good health, he sometimes complained of being afflicted with catarrhal symptoms for which Dr Barry O'Meara, his Irish physician, recommended the wearing of galoshes. And when not being treated by the latter, he would engage in long discussions on the great events of his past.

Napoleon told O'Meara how he thought Wright's death to be glorious in that he preferred to take his own life than compromise the British government. He invariably flew into a temper when the accusation of foul play was levelled: 'No person asserts positively that he had seen him murdered. If I had acted properly, I should have ordered Wright to be tried by a military commission as a spy and shot within twenty-four hours which by the laws of war I was entitled to do. What would your ministers, or even your Parliament, have done to a French captain that was discovered landing assassins in England to murder King George? ... They would not have been so lenient as I was with Wright, They would have had him tried and executed *sur le champ*.' He made a reasonable argument, but it begs the question (which was not posed by his inquisitive physician): why did he not act 'properly' in the first instance?[12]

Napoleon returned to the matter one morning when he learned that James Wallis, a former lieutenant on board the *Vincejo*, had arrived on the island and had, along with a number of British officers, dined with O'Meara the night before. 'What, is that the Lieutenant who was with Wright?' he asked. 'What does he say about Wright's death?' The doctor replied, 'He states his belief that Wright was murdered by orders of Fouché for the purpose of ingratiating himself to you. That six or seven weeks previous, Wright had told him that he expected to be murdered like Pichegru and begged to him never to believe that he would commit suicide.'[13]

Napoleon also held long conversations with William Warden, the surgeon on board the ship that had transported him to St Helena. He would sometimes speak to him from his bathtub, where he would stew for hours. The surgeon was described by the novelist Stendhal as being a typical Englishman of that age, 'a cold, narrow-minded and honest man who hates Napoleon'.[14] One day, the emperor surprised Warden with an unexpected question: 'He asked me to my great surprise if I remembered the history of Captain Wright. I answered. "Perfectly well and it is a prevailing opinion in England that you ordered him to be murdered in the Temple." With the utmost rapidity, he replied, "For what object? Of all men, he was the person whom I could have most desired to live. Whence could I have procured so valuable evidence as he would have provided on the conspirators in and about Paris?"'[15] His explanation bore little relation to the truth, as Wright had resolutely refused to disclose the particulars of his secret service before, during and after the trial of Georges and Moreau which, moreover, was held the year *before* the prisoner's death.

Napoleon then expounded at length on the 'Great Conspiracy' and the manner of General Charles Pichegru's end. 'The great majority of English people firmly believed,' Warden began, 'that you had him strangled in the Temple.' 'Sheer stupidity!' he snapped back. 'An excellent proof of how passion can blunt that sureness of judgement of which the English are so proud. Why commit a crime by killing a man whom every law of his country would have sent to the scaffold? ... What motive could I have in assassinating Pichegru? A man who was evidently guilty; and whom every proof was ready. No evidence was wanting against him. His condemnation was certain. Perhaps I should have pardoned him.'[16] At this point, Napoleon described the state in which the general had been discovered before making the curious observation that the cause of death being so uncommon was precise proof that he had not been murdered.

What would have been Napoleon's motive for secretly murdering Pichegru? The army's affection for the general had been completely destroyed by a crime which no French patriot forgives: trafficking with the country's enemies. No doubt, a council of war would have pronounced the death penalty on Pichegru for being a traitor to the *patrie* and for having conspired against the government.[17] For unlike in the case of the royalists, who emigrated from France, and whose allegiance under the *ancien régime* was dynastic, not patriotic, Pichegru had originally embraced the principles of the Revolution and had under its colours rapidly attained the highest position to which a soldier could aspire. It was, moreover, just when he held the command of the armies of the Rhine and Moselle that he crossed the Rubicon, driven not exclusively by political principles but supposedly also by personal motives. So, perhaps the old maxim that 'the culprit is the man who profits from the crime' best vindicates Napoleon from the midnight murders in the Temple. Of course, as Stendhal observes, 'is despotism never subject to inexplicable whims?'[18]

NOTES

Prologue

1. Cooper, D., *Talleyrand* (London: Orion Books Ltd, 1997), p. 23.

2. Earl III, J. L., 'Talleyrand in Philadelphia: 1794–1796', *The Pennsylvania Magazine of History and Biography*, Vol. 91, No.3, (1967), pp 282–298.

3. Broglie, A (ed.), *Memoirs of the Prince de Talleyrand*, 5 vols. (London: G. P. Putmam's Sons, 1891–1892), I, p. 172.

4. Earl III, J. L., 'Talleyrand in Philadelphia: 1794–1796', p. 282.

5. Dinwiddy, J. R., *Radicalism and Reform in Britain, 1780–1850* (London: The Hambledon Press, 1992), p. 155.

6. Thale, M. (ed.), *Selections from the Papers of the London Corresponding Society, 1792–1799* (Cambridge: Cambridge University Press, 1983), p. 135.

7. *Ibid*, p. 140.

8. Geoghegan, P. M., *Robert Emmet, A Life* (Michigan: Gill & Macmillan, 2002), p. 138.

9. Wickham, W., *Correspondence of the Right Honorable William Wickham*, 2 vols. (London: R. Bentley, 1870), I. p5.; For a detailed study of the obscure Alien Office, see Sparrow, E., 'The Alien Office 1792–1806', *The Historical Journal*, 33, 02 (1990), pp. 361–384.

10. Mahan, A. T., *The Influence of Sea Power upon the French Revolution and Empire, 1793–1812*, 2 vols. (Boston: Little, Brown, 1892), I, p. 33.

11. Wickham, *Correspondence*, I, p. 5.

12. Mallet, B., *Mallet du Pan and the French Revolution* (London: Longmans, Green, 1902), p. 211.

13. Hall, J., *General Pichegru's Treason* (London: Smith, Elder & Co., 1915), p. 6.

1 Pichegru's Treason

1. Wickham, *Correspondence*, I, pp. 9–10.

2. Galligani, J. A., *Galligani's New Guide of Paris* (Paris: A and W Galligani, 1825), p. xliv.

3. Kennedy, D., *Helen Maria Williams and the Age of Revolution* (USA: Rosemont Publishing, 2002), p. 140.

4. Burke, E (ed.), *Annual Register* (London: 1806) xxxvi, p. 190.

5. Mallet, B., *Mallet du Pan and the French Revolution* (London: Longmans, Green and Co, 1902), p. 210.

6. Hall, p. 8.

7. Wickham, *Correspondence*, I, p. 17.

8. Ministère des Affaires Étrangères, Correspondance Politique 452/453 doss 47.

9. Wickham, *Correspondance*, I, p. 24.

10. Lenôtre, G., *Two Royalist Spies of the French Revolution*, trans. By Bernard Miall (London: T. F. Unwin, 1924), p. 21.

11. Stawell, R., *The Return of Louis XVIII* (New York: Charles Scribner's Sons, 1909), p. 63.

12. Hall, *Pichegru's Treason*, p. 13.; Wickham, *Correspondence*, I, p. 30.

13. Lenôtre, *Two Royalist Spies*, p. 21.

14. Hall, *Pichegru's Treason*, p. 11; Wickham, *Correspondence*, I, pp. 25–30.

15. For Précy's career see Lac. R., *Le Général Comte de Précy: Sa vie militaire, son commandement au siège de Lyon, son émigration* (Paris: H. Champion, 1908).

16. Hall, *Pichegru's Treason*, pp. 13–14.

17. *Ibid*, p. 14.

18. Durey, M., *William Wickham, Master Spy: The Secret War against the French Revolution* (London: Pickering & Chatto, 2009), pp. 64–65.

19. Public Record Office, Foreign Office, 74/7, f.2. William Wickham to Lord Grenville, 10 May 1795.

20. Wickham, *Correspondence*, I, p. 43.

21. Hall, *Pichegru's Treason*, p. 15.

22. *Ibid*, p. 18. FO Switzerland 6, Wickham to Grenville, April 29, 1795; FO Switzerland 20, Wickham to Grenville, March 8, 1797.

23. Ibid, p. 17. W.O 1/169. Duke of York to Henry Dundas, May 23, 1794.

24. For a police description of Fauche-Borel see Archives Nationales, F7 6319.

25. Montgaillard, J. G. M. R., *Mémoire Concernant la Trahison de Pichegru, dans les Années 3,4, 5* (Paris: Imprimerie de la République, an XII), p. 10.

26. Caudrillier, G., *La Trahison de Pichegru et les Intrigues royalistes dans l'Est avant Fructidor* (Paris: Librairies Felix Alcan et Guillaume Réunis, 1908), p. 95.

27. Quoted in Hall, *Pichegru's Treason*, p. 44.

28. D'Avallon, C., *Histoire du Géneral Pichegru, precede d'une Notice sur sa Vie politique et militaire* (Paris: Libraire Barba, 1802), p. 203.

29. Caudrillier, G., *La Trahison de Pichegru*, pp. 50–51; Hall, *Pichegru's Treason*, pp. 46–47.

30. Durey, *William Wickham, Master Spy*, p. 67.

31. Fryer, W. R., *Republic or Restoration in France? 1794–1797: D'André and the Politics of French Royalism* (Manchester: The University Press, 1965), p39.

2 Recalled

1. Lenôtre, *Two Royalist Spies*, p. 56.

2. Popkin, J. D., 'Pamphlet Journalism at the End of the Old Regime', *Eighteenth Century Studies*, 22, No.3, Special Issue: The French Revolution in Culture (1989), pp. 351–367.

3. Godechot, J., *The Counter-revolution: Doctrine and Action, 1789–1804* (London: Routledge & Regan Paul, 1972), p. 369.

4. Mitchell, H., 'Vendémiaire: A Reevalution', *Journal of Modern History*, vol 30 (1958), pp. 191–202 at p. 194.

5. Puisaye, J., *Mémoires du Comte Joseph de Puisaye* (London: D. N. Shury, 1808), p. 540; Lemaître's correspondance was published by the National Convention under the title: *Recueil de la correspondence saisie chez Lemaître* (Paris: Imprimerie. De la République, 1795).

6. Mitchell, Vendémiaire, p. 198. According to William Wickham, Lemaître was betrayed by a double agent named Coleville. FO 74/18 Wickham to Grenville, July 23, 1796.

7. Lyons, M., *France under the Directory* (Cambridge: University Press, 1975), p. 23.

8. Larevellière-Lépeaux, L. M., *Mémoires de Larevellière-Lépeaux: Membre du Directoire Exécutif de la République Française et de l'Institut National*, 3 vols. (Paris: Librairie Plon, 1895), I, p. 321.

9. Barras, P., *Memoirs of Barras: Member of the Directorate*, 4 vols. (New York: Librairie Hachette et Cie, 1895), II, p. 28.

10. Duvergier, J. (ed.), *Collection complète des Lois, Décrets, Ordannances, Réglemens, Avis du Conseil d'État* (Paris: A. Guyot et Scribe, 1828), IX, p. 28; Berland, J., *Les Sentiments des Populations Marnaises à l'égard de L'Angleterre à la fin du XVIIIème siècle et au début du XIXème* (Châlons sur Marne: A. Robat, 1913), p. 48.

11. *Manuel des Commissaires du Directoire Exécutif près les Administrations centrales et municipales* (Paris: Imprimière du Dépôt des Lois, 1799–1800), p. 320. In article 191 of the constitution of *Fructidor an III*, a commissary was to be attached to each departmental and municipal administration.

12. *Ibid*, p. 274.

13. Wickham, *Correspondence*, I, p. 235.

14. *Ibid*, p. 205.

15. Durey, *William Wickham, Master Spy*, p. 66.

16. PRO FO Genoa 13, Drake to Grenville, November 19, 1795 and November 20, 1795.

17. Wickham, *Correspondence*, I, p. 209.

18. Hall, *Pichegru's Treason*, p. 86.

19. Wickham, *Correspondence*, I, p. 242. Wickham to Grenville, 25 November 1795.

20. Debidor, A. (ed.), *Recueil des Registres, Delibérations, Arrêtes, Minutes et Actes du Directoire Exécutif*, 4 vols. (Paris: 1910-1919), pp. 193–4.

21. Hall, *Pichegru's Treason*, p. 99.

22. *Ibid*, pp. 102–104.

23. PRO FO Germany 8, Craufurd to Grenville, December 9, 1795.

24. MAE CP Suisse, vol 456, fol 83, vol 457, fols 28,30; A Debidor, Recueil des Actes, I, pp. 272–3.

25. PRO FO Germany 9, Craufurd to Grenville, January 16, 1796; Hall, p. 110.; Wickham, Correspondence, I, p. 248.

26. PRO FO Switzerland 14, Wickham to Grenville, March 2, 1796; Hall, p. 112.

27. Wickham, I, p. 274.

28. *Correspondance Trouvée le 2 Floréal an 5 à Offembourg, dans les fourgons du Général Klinglin*, 2 vols. (Paris: Imprimerie de la République, 1797), I, p. 32. Translated from 'une exactitue etonnante'.

29. Wickham, *Correspondence*, I, p. 306.

30. Quoted in Durey, *William Wickham, Master Spy*, p. 77.

31. *Ibid*, p. 77.

32. Pitt, W., Hathaway, W. S., *The Speeches of the Right Honorable William Pitt, in the House of Commons,* 3 vols. (London: J. Hatchard, 1808), II, pp. 143–144.

33. *The Scots Magazine or General Repository of Literature, History, and Politics for the year MDCCXCVI*, (Edinburgh: Alex Chapman, 1796), LVIII, p. 272.

34. MAE CP Suisse 456. Rapport du 6 nivôse an IV, 27/12/95.

35. Burke (ed.), *Annual Register*, XXXVIII, p. 125.

36. Wickham, *Correspondence*, I, p. 343.

37. Durey, *William Wickham, Master Spy*, p. 79.

3 The Italian Torrent

1. Bingham, D. A (ed.), *A Selection from the Letters and Despatches of the first Napoleon*, 3 vols. (Cambridge: Cambridge University Press, 2010), I, p. 53.

2. Dwyer, P., *Napoleon: The Path to Power, 1769–1799* (London: Bloomsbury Publishing, 2007), p. 206.

3. *Ibid*, pp. 207–208.

4. Borel, *Two Royalist Spies*, p. 53

5. *Ibid*, p. 8.

6. Wickham, *Correspondence*, I, p. 347.

7. *Ibid*, p. 356.

8. Fryer, *Republic or Restoration*, p. 16.

9. Sparrow, E., *Secret Service: British Agents in France, 1792–1815* (Woodbridge: Boydell & Brewer, 1999), p. 60.

10. Quoted in Hall, *Pichegru's Treason*, p. 134.

11. Sparrow, *Secret Service*, p. 77.

12. Fauche-Borel, L., *Mémoires de Fauche Borel: Agent secret de Louis XVIII*, 4 vols. (Paris: Moutardier Librairie-éditeur, 1829), I, pp. 206–7.

13. Wickham, *Correspondence*, I, p. 501.

14. Quoted in Sparrow, *Secret Service*, p. 81.

15. Wickham, *Correspondence*, I, p. 432.

16. Brown, H. G., *Ending the French Revolution: Violence, Justice and Repression from the Terror to Napoleon* (Charlottesville: University of Virginia Press, 2006), p. 38.

17. Hall, *Pichegru's Treason*, p. 179.

18. Fryer, *Republic or Restoration*, p. 120.

4 *Prisoners*

1. Debrett, J. (ed.), *A Collection of State Papers Relative to the War against France*, 10 vols. (London: John de Brett, 1704–1801), IV, p. 257.

2. Durey, M., 'The British Secret Service and the Escape of Sir Sidney Smith from Paris in 1798', *The Historical Association*, 84, (1999), pp. 437–457 at p. 440.

3. One double agent was the French émigré, Noel Pingent, the Comte de Puisaye's aide de camp. On 13 September 1796, the Govenor of Jersey, the Prince de Bouillon, wrote to Wickham declaring that 'I fear much that Pingent has played a double game'. PRO, FO95 doss. 605; Another source of intelligence was the army commander Lazare Hoche who complained to the Directory that 'Sidney Smith blocks all our ports and vomits on our coasts émigrés, arms, gold. He commands a squadron of four frigates, two brigs and several French luggers.' AN AFIII 362, doss 1734.

4. Durey, M., 'The British Secret Service and the Escape of Sir Sidney Smith from Paris in 1798', p. 439.

5. *Ibid*, p. 440; For more on Sir Sidney Smith's career see Pocock, T., *A Thirst for Glory: The Life of Admiral Sir Sidney Smith* (London: Aurum Press, 1996); Shankland, P., *Beware of Heroes: Admiral Sir Sidney Smith's War against Napoleon* (London: W. Kimber, 1975); Howard, E. G. G., *The Memoirs of Sidney Smith* (London: Richard Bentley, 1839); Russell, E. F. L., *Knight of the*

Sword: The Life and Letters of Admiral Sir Sidney William Smith (London: Victor Gollancz Ltd, 1964).

6. Brenton, E. P., *The Naval History of Great Britain*, 2 vols. (London: C. Rice, 1823), p. 222.

7. Rodger, N. A. M., *The Command of the Ocean. A Naval History of Britain, 1649–1815* (London: 2004), p. 427.

8. *Naval Chronicle*, XXXIV, p. 5.

9. AN F7 6423. Tromelin's Statement, April 1804.

10. *Naval Chronicle*, XXXIV, p. 6.

11. Pocock, *A Thirst for Glory*, p. 45.

12. *Naval Chronicle*, XXXIV, p. 6.

13. This argument is well argued in Durey, M., 'The British Secret Service and the Escape of Sir Sidney Smith from Paris in 1798', *The Historical Association*, 84, (1999), pp. 437–457 at pp. 441–442.

14. Smith, W. S., *The Life of Sir Sidney Smith, His Dreadful Confinement in the French Prison and Escape from Thence; His Defence of Acre against Bonaparte* (Sheffield: W. Todd, 1806), p. 7.

15. Russell, E. F. L., *Knight of the Sword: The Life and Letters of Admiral Sir Sidney William Smith* (London: Victor Gollancz Ltd, 1964), p. 60; Howard, E., *Memoirs of Admiral Sir Sidney Smith*, 2 vols. (London: Richard Bentley, 1839), I, p. 57.

16. 'Biographical Memoirs of Sir William Sidney Smith' in *Naval Chronicle*, IV (1800), p. 459

17. Gifford, W., *The Anti-Jacobin, Or, Weekly Examiner*, 2 vols. (London: J Wright, 1799), II, p. 304; Pocock, *A Thirst for Glory*, p. 47.

18. AN F7 6423 Extract from the registers of the Temple Prison.

19. For information on Temple Prison during this period including a description of its jailor, Citoyen Lasne, see Barbey, F., *La Mort de Pichegru: Biville, Paris, Le Temple* (Paris: Payot, 1909).

20. Wraxall, N. W., *Posthumous Memoirs of His Own Times*, 3 vols. (London: Richard Bentley, 1836), I, pp. 219–220.

21. Barbey, *La Mort de Pichegru*, p. 145.

22. *Ibid*, p. 149

23. *Naval Chronicle*, XXXIV, p. 15.

24. *Ibid*, p. 17.

25. *Ibid*, p. 17.

5 Malmesbury Mission

1. Malmesbury, J. H., *Diaries and Correspondence of James Harris, First Earl of Malmesbury*, 4 vols. (London: Richard Bentley, 1844), III, p. 270.

2. *Ibid*, p. 271.

3. *Ibid*, p. 272.

4. *Ibid*, pp. 273–274.

5. *Ibid*, pp. 277–284.

6. *Ibid*, pp. 290–291.

7. *Ibid*, p. 254.

8. *Ibid*, p. 325; PRO FO 27/46, fo 237, Malmesbury to Grenville, 28 Nov 1796; PRO, FO 27/46, fo.105 Malmesbury to Grenville, 27 Oct 1796.

9. Durey, 'The British Secret Service and the Escape of Sir Sidney Smith from Paris in 1798', p. 446.

10. PRO, FO 27/46, fos. 306–7, Malmesbury to Grenville, 14 Dec 1796.

11. PRO FO 27/46, fos 88.

12. Wickham, *Correspondence*, I, p. 460.

6 The Interrogation

1. The following interrogation is extracted from volume 34 of the Naval Chronicle pages 23–27 and translated from the French by the author.

2. *Naval Chronicle* (40 vols) (London: J. Gold, 1799–1818), XXXIV, p. 179. The Naval Chronicle published a biographical memoir of John Wesley Wright which ran in consecutive issues. For the circumstances of his early life, the publishers sourced the information from his father.

3. Durey, 'The British Secret Service and the Escape of Sir Sidney Smith from Paris in 1798', p. 446.

4. For the operations from Jersey see, for example, Balleine, G. R., *The Tragedy of Phillipe d'Auvergne, Vice Admiral in the Royal Navy and last Duke of Bouillon* (London-Chichester: Phillimore and C, 1973)

5. Broster, D. K., 'An English Sailor among the Chouans', *English Historical Review,* 25, (1910), pp. 129–137 at pp. 132–133.

6. Sparrow, *Secret Service*, p. 88; HRO 9M73 G1802 15.

7. Debidor, (ed.), *Recueil des Actes*, IV, p. 567

8. Barras, Memoirs, II, p. 247

9. Debidor, (ed.), *Recueil des Actes*, IV, p. 567

10. Barras, *Memoirs*, II, p. 247.

11. Barthélemy, F., *Mémoires de Barthélemy, 1768–1819* (Paris: J. de Damierre, 1914), p. 193.

7 Betrayed

1. For a detailed account of Duverne de Presle's career in espionage written by himself, see *Débats de Procès Instruit par le Conseil de Guerre permanent de la XVIIe division militaires* (Paris: Baudouin, 1797),

2. Sparrow, Secret Service, p. 108

3. Lenôtre, *Two Royalist Spies*, pp. 62–63.

4. The police had tracked the Baron de Poly's footsteps from his apartment between eleven o'clock in the morning till ten at night covering a full rotation of shifts. For the surveillance report see AN F7 6151 dossier 7569.

5. During his interrogation Poly explains how persons were enrolled in the royalist cause. They were required to complete the following written statement promising their fealty: 'I the undersigned ... promise and undertake to do my utmost to restore to his throne, Stanislas-Xavier, Louis VIII. I hereby take the oath from Monsieur ... I give my word of honour that I will obey the leaders whom he may make known to me...' *Débats de Procès Instruit par le Conseil de Guerre*, p. 131.

6. Among the pieces seized could be found a plan for bringing about the restoration of the monarchy, the powers given by Louis XVIII to the commissaries, proclamations addressed to the people, the reinstatement of numerous ministers except for the Minister of Interior, Pierre Benezech, the journalists to be arrested and the chouan journalists being retained. AN F7 6351 doss 26 & 27; Barras Memoirs, II, p. 139.

7. Sparrow's extensive research shows that the order of arrest did not emanate from the police Central Bureau nor was it signed by any members of the Directory. In fact, the *Commissaire de Police* who was sent to execute the order, Lambert Becquet, discovered that the agents were already 'prisoners of an armed military posse'. Sparrow, *Secret Service*, p. 107

8. The twenty-three page declaration from Duverne de Presle titled *Sur les motifs de ma Conduite d'auprès aux royalists et à tous les Français* is found among the voluminous correspondence dedicated to this affair in AN F7 6351.

9. Barras, *Memoirs*, II, p. 595; Durey, *William Wickham: Master Spy*, p. 87.

10. For an account of the Duc de la Vauguyon's dismissal see Daudet, E. *Histoire de l'Emigration pendant la Révolution Française*, 3 vols. (Paris: Librairie Hachette et Cie), I, pp. 53–55. Daudet claims that the Duc de la Vauguyon was a victim of court intrigue but recent research from Sparrow reveals his complicity in his son's schemes. Sparrow, E., 'The Swiss and Swabian Agencies, 1795–1801', *The Historical Journal*, 35, 4, (1992), pp. 861–884. at p. 867.

11. Mitchell, H., *The Underground War against Revolutionary France: The Missions of William Wickham, 1794–1800* (Oxford: Clarendon Press, 1965), p. 112.

12. Lenôtre, *Two Royalist Spies*, p. 65.

13. Wickham, *Correspondence*, II, p. 25.

14. *Ibid*, p. 28.

15. Quoted in Fryer, *Republic or Restoration*, p. 207.

16. Durey, *William Wickham, Master Spy*, p. 92.
17. Harvey, R., *The War of Wars: The Epic Struggle between Britain and France, 1789–1815* (London: Constable, 2006), pp. 93–95.
18. Malmesbury, *Diaries and Correspondence*, III, p. 380.
19. *Ibid*, p. 387.
20. Sparrow, E., 'The Swiss and Swabian Agencies, 1795–1801', p. 868.
21. Durey, *William Wickham, Master Spy*, pp. 93–94.

8 Le Comte d'Antraigues' Papers

1. Lenôtre, *Two Royalist Spies*, p. 18.
2. Duckworth, C., *The D'Antraigues Phenomenon: The Making and Breaking of a Revolutionary Royalist Espionage Agent* (Newcastle: Avero Publications Ltd, 1996), p. 215.
3. Aude de l', J. P. F., *Histoire Secrète du Directoire*, 4 vols. (Paris: Ménard Librairie, 1832), II, p. 314.; Fauche Borel claimed that Montgaillard was in secret communications with the Directory from the end of 1795, Sparrow, E., 'The Swiss and Swabian Agencies, 1795–1801', p. 866; Fauche-Borel, L., *Notices sur les Généraux Pichegru et Moreau, par M Louis Fauche Borel* (London: T Harper Young, 1807), pp. 24 & 144.
4. Duckworth, C., *The D'Antraigues Phenomenon*, p. 216.
5. Durey, *William Wickham, Master Spy*, pp. 95.
6. The following interrogation was originally discovered by the historian, Colin Duckworth and published in his excellent biography of the Comte d'Antraigues, pp. 230–38.
7. *Pièces trouvées à Venice dans le portefeuille de d'Entraigues, [sic] portant en tête une conversation avec M. Le Comte de Montgaillard, le 4. Decembre 1796, à six heures après midi jusqu'à minuit.* D'Antraigues Papers, HRO 38M49/1/75.
8. Durey, *William Wickham, Master Spy*, p. 95.
9. Sloane, W. M., *The Life of Napoleon Bonaparte*, 4 vol. (Michigan: Century Company, 1894), I, p. 449.
10. Dumas, A., *The Last Cavalier* (London: Harper Perennial, 2008), p. 5.
11. Sloane, *The Life of Napoleon*, p. 449.
12. Duckworth, C., *The D'Antraigues Phenomenon*, p. 236.

9 Papers

1. Malmesbury, *Diaries and Correspondence*, III, p. 529.
2. Barras, Paul, *Memoirs of Barras: Member of the Directorate*, 4 vols. (New York: McIlvaine, 1895), IV, p. 570
3. Malmesbury, *Diaries and Correspondence*, III, p. 510.

4. Brown, H. G., *Ending the French Revolution: Violence, Justice and Repression from the Terror to Napoleon* (Charlottesville: University of Virginia Press, 2006), p. 247.

5. *Annual Register*, 39, p. 315.

6. Lenôtre, *Two Royalist Spies*, pp. 47–49.

7. *Ibid*, pp. 47–49.

8. Ramel, J. P., *Narrative of the Deportation to Cayenne of Bathélemy, Pichegru, Willot, Marbois, La Rue, Ramel, &c* (London: J. Wright, 1799), p. 20.

9. *Ibid*, p. 28.

10. *Ibid*, p. 33.

11. *Ibid*, p. 48.

12. Peltier, M., *Paris Pendant l'Année 1797* (Paris: Imprimerie de T. Baylis, 1800), XV, pp. 509–524.

13. Debrett, (ed.), *A Collection of State Papers Relative to the War against France*, VII, p. 117.

14. Durey, William Wickham: Master Spy, p. 98.

15. Wickham, *Correspondence*, II, p. 64.

10 Rogue Agent

1. Wickham, *Correspondence*, II, p. 64

2. *Ibid*, p. 67.

3. Durey, M., 'Lord Grenville and the 'Smoking Gun': The Plot to Assassinate the French Directory in 1798–1799 Reconsidered', *The Historical Journal*, 45 (2002), pp. 547–568. at p. 550

4. Bodlean Library, Talbot MSS, c.14, fo.29; Sparrow, E., 'The Swiss and Swabian Agencies, 1795–1801', *The Historical Journal*, 35, 4, (1992), pp. 861–884. at p. 869.

5. Bodlean Library, Talbot MSS, b.21, fos. 71–5.

6. Bodlean MS Talbot, c/14. Talbot to Grenville, 18 Nov. 1797; BL Add Mss. 59011/129–37.

7. *Ibid*.

8. Sparrow, *Secret Service*, pp. 149–150.

9. Durey, 'Lord Grenville and the 'Smoking Gun', p. 558.

10. Quoted in Sparrow, *Secret Service*, p. 155.

11. Durey, 'Lord Grenville and the 'Smoking Gun', p. 559.

12. FO Switzerland 22, Talbot to Canning, November 3, 1798

13. PRO FO 74/22; Sparrow, Elizabeth, 'The Swiss and Swabian Agencies, 1795–1801', p. 875.

14. *Ibid*, p. 875

15. FO Switzerland 74/23, Grenville to Talbot, January 25, 1799.

16. Durey, 'Lord Grenville and the 'Smoking Gun', p. 568.

11 A Simple Plan

1. Lenôtre, *Romances of the French Revolution,* II, p. 42.

2. Shankland, P., *Beware of Heroes: Admiral Sir Sidney Smith's War against Napoleon* (London: W. Kimber, 1975), p. 13.

3. *Ibid,* p. 14

4. Neuville, H., *Memoirs of Baron Hyde de Neuville: Outlaw, Exile, Ambassador* (2 vols.) (London: Sands, 1913), pp. 63–68.

5. Lenôtre, *Romances of the French Revolution,* II, p. 43; See also Neuville de, H., *Mémoires et Souvenirs du Baron Hyde de Neuville* (Paris: Plon, 1912).

6. Lenôtre, *Romances of the French Revolution,* II, pp. 42–44.

7. Shankland, *Beware of Heroes,* p. 15; Pocock, *A Thirst for Glory,* p. 54.

8. Lachouque, H., *Le Général de Tromelin* (Paris: Bloudet Gay, 1968), p. 4

9. For a first hand account of Swinburne's mission see Babeau, A (ed.), *La France et Paris sous le Directoire: Lettres d'un Voyageuse Anglaise, Suivies d'extrait des lettres de Henry Swinburne* (Paris: Librairie de Firmin-Didot et Cte).

10. Swinburne, H. (ed.), *The Courts of Europe at the Close of the Last Century,* 2 vols. (London: Henry Colburn Publisher, 1841), II, p. 205.

11. Shankland, P., *Beware of Heroes,* p. 17.

12. Howard, *Memoirs of Admiral Sir Sidney Smith* II, p. 309.

13. *Naval Chronicle,* 34, pp. 516–519.

14. Sparrow has made this the subject in her most recent path-breaking book, *Phantom of the Guillotine: The Real Scarlet Pimpernel, Louis Bayard- Lewis Duval 1769–1844* (Cornwall: Carn Press, 2013).

15. Anonymous, *The History and Topography of Ashbourn, the Valley of the Dove, and the Adjacent Villages* (New York: Dawson & Hobson, 1839), pp. 47–49.

16. Barras, *Memoirs,* III, p. 186.

17. Shankland, *Beware of Heroes,* p. 19; Pocock, *A Thirst for Glory,* p. 57.

18. Although there exist various accounts of Smith and Wright's famous escape, the following description is principally sourced from Le Menuet de la Jugannière, P. M. J. J. A., *Le Chouan Carlos Sourdat et son Père, l'Agent Royal* (Paris: Firmin-Didot et cie, 1932), pp. 115–119.

19. AN, F7 6150.

20. Howard, *Memoirs of Admiral Sir Sidney Smith* II, p. 390.

21. James, W., *The Naval History of Great Britain,* 6 vols. (London: Harding, 1826), II, p. 299.

22. Anonymous, *The History and Topography of Ashbourne,* p. 50.

23. Lenôtre, *Romances of the French Revolution,* II, p. 51.

24. *Ibid*, p. 51.
25. Sparrow, *Secret Service*, p. 134.
26. *Ibid*, p. 134.; PRO ADM/37852 fol 87.
27. Reynolds, F., *The Life and Times of Frederick Reynolds*, 2 vols. (London: Henry Colburn, 1826), II, p. 224.
28. BL Add. Mss. 37852 fol 83.

12 Desert Tricks

1. Sparrow, *Secret Service*, p. 186.
2. *Ibid*, p. 187.
3. Lachouque, H., *Le Général de Tromelin* (Paris: Bloudet Gay, 1968), p. 75.
4. *The Gentleman's Magazine*, LXXXV, p. 242.
5. *Ibid*, p. 242.
6. *The Naval Chronicle*, XXXIV, p. 371.
7. Quoted in Sparrow, *Secret Service*, p. 187.
8. *Ibid*, p. 189.
9. Historical Manuscripts Commission, *The Manuscripts of J. B. Fortescue, Preserved at Dropmore*, 6 vols. (Dublin: HMSO, 1908), IV, p. 480.
10. BL Add. Mss. 35898.
11. Howard, *The Memoirs of Sir Sidney Smith*, I, p. 81.
12. *Ibid*, p. 81.
13. Pocock, *A Thirst for Glory*, p. 91.
14. Strathern, P., *Napoleon in Egypt* (London: Vintage, 2009), pp. 340-341.
15. *The Naval Chronicle*, XXXIV, p. 203.
16. Howard, *The Memoirs of Sir Sidney Smith*, I, p. 79.
17. BL Add. Mss. 45040 fol 25.
18. *Ibid*.
19. Strathern, *Napoleon in Egypt*, p. 367.
20. Quoted in Strathern, pp. 367–368
21. Sparrow, *Secret Service*, p. 192.
22. Strathern, *Napoleon in Egypt*, p. 399.
23. *Ibid*, p. 399.
24. *Ibid*, pp. 403–406.

13 Georges

1. Sparrow, *Secret Service*, p. 203.
2. *Ibid*, p. 203.
3. Neuville de, H., *Memoirs of Baron Hyde de Neuville: Outlaw, Exile, Ambassador*, 2 vols. (London: Sands, 1913), I, pp. 155.
4. *Ibid*, pp. 155-6.
5. *Ibid*, pp. 130-1.

6. *Ibid*, pp. 133–4.

7. Neuville, *Memoirs*, p. 283.

8. Urban, S. (ed.), *The Gentleman's Magazine* (London: John Bowyer Nichols and Sons, 1856), XLV, p. 340.

9. Neuville de, *Memoirs*, I, p. 160.

10. Cadoudal, L. G., *Georges Cadoudal et La Chouannerie* (Paris: E. Plon, 1887), p. 456.

11. It appears that Duperou was also supplied with a list of police spies by Fouché's private secretary, Villiers du Terrage. Desmarest, P. M., *Temoignages historiques ou Quinze ans de Haute Police sous Napoleon* (Paris: A Levavasseur, 1833); Sparrow, 'The Alien Office', p. 378.; See also the police files AN F7 6245 to F7 6251 for dossiers on the counter police and the *conspiration anglaise* as the 'English Committee' was designated by the French.

12. Michaud, J. F., *Les Adieux à Bonaparte* (Paris: Marchands de Nouveautés, 1800)

13. Sparrow, E., 'The Alien Office 1792–1806', *The Historical Journal*, 33, 02 (1990), pp. 361–384 at p. 377.

14. Tulard, J., *Joseph Fouché*, (Paris: Librairie Arthème Fayard, 1998), p. 137.

15. Sparrow, Secret Service, p. 212.

16. Waresquiel de, E., *Fouché: Les Slences de la Pieuvre* (Paris: Éditions Tallandrier et Librairie Fayard, 2014), p. 288. Sparrow, *Secret Service*, pp. 210-213.

17. See Conseil d'Etat, *Conspiration Anglaise*, 2 vols. (Paris: Imprimerie de la République, 1801).

18. Sparrow, *Secret Service*, p. 213.

19. Bourrienne, L. A., *Mémoires de M de Bourrienne sur Napoléon, le Directoire, le Consulat, l'Empire et la Restauration*, 10 vols. (Brussels: H. Tarlier et Auguste Wahlen, 1829) II, p. 15.

20. FO Army in Switzerland 30, Grenville to Wickham, May 10, 1800; Hall, *Pichegru's Treason*, p. 278.

21. Sparrow, *Secret Service*, p. 215.

22. *Ibid*, pp. 215-216.

23. *Ibid*, p. 216; HRO 38M49/8/2 1August 1800.

24. Fouché, J., *Memoirs relating to Fouché, Minister of Police under Napoleon I* (New York: Sturgis & Walton, 1912), p. 67.

25. Waresquiel de, *Fouché*, p. 329.

26. Lenôtre, *Two Royalist Spies*, p. 97.

27. *Ibid*, p. 329; d'Hauterive, E., *Contre Police Royaliste en 1800* (Paris: Librairie Académique Perrin, 1931)

28. Quoted in Sparrow, *Secret Service*, pp. 216-7.

29. *Ibid*, p. 220.

14 The Rue Niçaise Bomb

1. Lenôtre, G, *Paris Révolutionnaire: Vielles Maisons, Vieux Papiers,* 3 vols. (Paris: Perrin et cie, 1909), III, p. 196.

2. *Ibid,* p. 203.

3. *Ibid,* pp. 204–5.

4. Bourrienne, *Mémoires,* II, p. 26.

5. Dwyer, *Napoleon: Citizen Emperor* (London: Bloomsbury Publishing, 2013), p. 60.

6. For studies dedicated to the rue Niçaise attack see Martel de, A. L. R., Étude sur l'Affaire de la Machine Infernale du 3 nivôse an IX (Paris: E. Lachaud, 1870); Thiry, J., *La Machine Infernale* (Paris: Berger-Levault, 1952); Sydenham, M. J, 'The Crime of Nivôse in Bosher, J. F. (ed.), *French Government and Society, 1500-1850* (London: 1973); Loredan, J., *La Machine Infernale* (Paris: 1924), Darrah, D., *Conspiracy in Paris: The Strange Career of Joseph Picot de Limolean* (New York: Exposition Press, 1953); For police reports housed in the *Archives Nationales,* Paris: AN F7 6271, AN F7 6332, AN F7 3829.

7. Bourrienne, *Mémoires,* II, p. 27.

8. Dwyer, *Napoleon: Citizen Emperor,* p. 69.

9. Sparrow, *Secret Service,* p. 219.

10. Emsley, C., *Napoleon: Conquest, Reform and Reorganisation* (Abingdon: Routledge, 2015), p. 15.

11. Sparrow, *Secret Service,* p. 222

12. Darrah, D., *Conspiracy in Paris,* p. 99.

13. Lenôtre, G., *Paris révolutionnaire,* p. 209.

14. Urban, S. (ed.), *The Gentleman's Magazine,* XLV, p. 346.

15. The other conspirators had a price of 12,000 francs on their heads. Darrah, D., *Conspiracy in Paris,* p. 123.

16. Hall, *Pichegru's Treason,* p. 294.

17. BL Add 37, 9222, Windham's Diary; Hall, *Pichegru's Treason,* p. 294.

18. *Ibid,* p. 294.

19. FO France 56, Windham to Hawkesbury, 25 and 28 March 1801.

20. Hall, *Pichergru's Treason,* p. 297.

15 The Amiens Interlude

1. *The Scot's Magazine,* LXIII, p. 882.

2. Jackson, G., *The Diaries and Letters of Sir George Jackson, K.C.H., From the Peace of Amiens to the Battle of Talavera, 1809–1816* (London: Bentley, 1872), p. 8.

3. *Ibid,* p. 19.

4. *Ibid,* p. 19.

5. *Ibid,* p. 26.

6. *Ibid*, pp. 27–29.

7. *Ibid*, p. 47.

8. Balzac, H., *The Works of Honoré Balzac: And other Stories* (Michigan: Avil Publishing Company, 1901), XVIII, p. 167.

9. Sparrow, *Secret Service*, p. 253.

10. *Ibid*, p. 261; AN F7 6318B does. 6722.

11. *Ibid*, p. 261.

12. Rowan, R. W., *The Story of the Secret Service* (Michigan: Literary Guild of America, 1937), p. 186.

13. Lenôtre, *Two Royalist Spies*, p. 96.

14. Pocock, Tom, *The Terror before Trafalgar: Nelson, Napoleon and the Secret War* (London: John Murray, 2002), p. 62.

15. Trotter, J. B., *Memoirs of the Latter Years of the Rt. Hon. Charles James Fox* (London: R. Phillips, 1811), p. 153.

16. *Ibid*, pp. 266–7.

17. Granville, C. (ed.), *Lord Granville Leveson Gower: Private Correspondence, 1781–1820*, 2 vols. (London: John Murray, 1916), I, p. 355.

18. *Ibid*, p. 355.

19. *Ibid*, p. 355.

20. Quoted in Sparrow, *Secret Service*, p. 263.

16 The Insult

1. Browning, O. (ed.), *England and Napoleon: The Despatches of Lord Whitworth* (London: Royal Historical Society, 1887), pp. 10-11.

2. *Ibid*, pp. 11–12.

3. Johnson, D., 'Amiens 1802: The Phoney Peace', *History Today*, 52 (2002), pp. 20-26 at p. 24.

4. Knight, C., *History of the Peace: Being a History of England from 1816 to 1854*, 8 vols. (Boston: Walker, Wise and Company, 1865), I, p. 57.

5. Malmesbury, *Diaries and Correspondence*, IV, p. 74.

6. Thiers, A., *History of the Consulate and the Empire of France under Napoleon*, 2 vols. (Philadelphia: Carey & Hart, 1845), p. 482.

7. *Annual Register*, XLIV, p. 40.

8. Malmesbury, *Diaries and Correspondence*, IV, p. 208.

9. *Annual Register*, XLIV, p. 40.

10. *Edinburgh Advertiser*, 16 and 17 December, 1802.

11. Quoted in Sparrow, *Secret Service*, p. 263.

12. Kenney, J. J., 'Lord Whitworth and the Conspiracy Against Tsar Paul I: The New Evidence of the Kent Archive' in *Slavic Review*, vol 36, no 2 (June 1977), pp. 205–219 at p. 205.

13. Historical Manuscript Commission, *Report on the Manuscripts of J. B. Fortescue, preserved at Dropmore* (London: 1905), VII, p. 4. Whitworth to Grenville 16 April, 1801.

14. Browning, Oscar, ed., *England and Napoleon,* pp. 4–6.

15. Roberts, W (ed.), *Memoirs of the Life and Correspondence of Mrs Hannah Moore,* 2 vols. (New York: Harper & Brothers, 1851), II, p. 96.

16. Scott, W., *Life of Napoleon Bonaparte,* 2 vols. (Exeter: J & B Williams, 1836), I, p. 375.

17. *Ibid,* p. 375.

18. *Ibid,* p. 376.

19. Browning, (ed.), *England and Napoleon,* p. 79.

20. *Ibid,* p. 84.

21. *Ibid,* p. 119

22. Scott, *Napoleon,* I, p. 376.

23. Argyll, D. (ed.), *George Douglas, 8th Duke of Argyll: Autobiography and Memoirs,* 2 vols. (London: John Murray, 1906), I, p. 36.

24. Scott, *Napoleon,* I, p. 376.

17 An Incident in Calais

1. PRO ADM 36/15008

2. Browning, (ed.), *England and Napoleon,* p. 131.

3. *Ibid,* p. 131.

4. Sparrow, *Secret Service,* p. 267.

5. Browning, (ed.), *England and Napoleon,* p. 227.

6. *Ibid,* p. 240.

7. Cobbett, W., (ed.), *Cobbett's Weekly Register* (London: William Cobbett, 1802–1835), III, p. 647. Oman, C., *Britain against Napoleon* (London: Faber & Faber, 1942), p. 149

8. Sparrow, *Secret Service,* p. 269.

9. Ravenhill, W., 'The Honourable Robert Edward Clifford, 1767–1817: a Cartographer's Response to Napoleon', *The Geographical Journal,* 160, no 2, (1994), pp. 159–172, p. 165; Ravenhill cites Ugbrooke Park Archives, IV/9 I/24, IV/9I/21 and John Graves Simcoe Papers, Archives of Ontario, Series A-4-1.

10. *Ibid,* p. 168.

11. *Ibid,* pp. 165–167.

12. *Ibid,* p. 168; John Graves Simcoe Papers, Loose Correspondence, 23 May 1803

13. Quoted in Sparrow, *Secret Service,* p. 269.

18 The Reconciliation

1. Lenôtre, *Two Royalist Spies,* pp. 78–79.

2. *Ibid,* pp. 80-83.

3. *Ibid*, p83.

4. Sparrow, *Secret Service*, p. 275.

5. David, P. A., *History of Campaigns of General Pichegru: Containing the Operations of the Armies of the North, and of the Sambre and Meuse (London: 1796)*

6. AN F7 6217 dos. 4064, F7 6375 dos.7682

7. Sparrow, *Secret Service*, p. 272.

8. Cadoudal, L. G., *Georges Cadoudal et la Chouannerie* (Paris: E Plon, 1887), p. 296.

9. Madelin, L., *Histoire du Consulat et de l'Empire*, 16 vols. (Paris: Hachette, 1937–1954), V, p. 23; *Acte d'Accusation de Georges, Pichegru, Moreau, et Autres, Prévenus de Conspiration contre la personne du Premier Consul* (Paris: Imprimèrie de C. F. Patris, 1804), p. 47.

10. Lenôtre, G., *The House of the Combrays* (New York: Mead & Company, 1902), p. 21.

11. Sparrow, *Secret Service*, p. 275.

12. Pocock, *The Terror before Trafalgar*, p. 111.

13. Sparrow, *Secret Service*, pp. 274–276.

14. Naval Records Society, *Publications of the Naval Records Society*, 150 vols. (Hants: Naval Records Society, 1893–2006), XCVI, p. 6.

15. *Ibid*, p. 31.

16. Blackwood, W. (ed.), *Blackwoods Edinburgh Magazine* (1817–1980), CCLXX, p. 359.

17. Naval Records Society, XCVI, p. 33.

18. *Ibid*, p. 56.

19. *Ibid*, XVIII p. 31.

20. *Ibid*, XCVI, p. 57.

21. *Ibid*, p. 122.

22. *Ibid*, XVIII p. 141.

23. Thiers, *History of the Consulate*, I, p. 515.

24. Pocock, *The Terror before Trafalgar*, p. 107.

25. Naval Records Society, XCVI, p. 65.

26. *Ibid*, XVIII, p. 137.

27. *Ibid*, p. 137.

28. *Ibid*, p. 137.

29. *Ibid*, p. 140.

30. Thiers, *History of the Consulate*, I, p. 516.

31. *Ibid*, p. 517.

19 Confessions

1. Hall, *Pichegru's Treason*, p. 341; For a balanced view of Méhée de la Touche, consult, Bertaud, J. P., *Bonaparte et le duc d'Enghien: La Duel des Deux France*

(Paris: R. Laffont, 1972); Touche de la, M., *Extrait des Mémoires inédits sur la Révolution française* (Paris: Plancher et Ponthieu, 1823); Touche de la, M., *Alliance des Jacobins de France avec le Ministère anglais* (Paris: Imprimerie de la République, an XII); Cobban, A., 'The Great Mysification of Méhée de la Touche', *Bulletin of the London University Institute of Historical Research*, No.43, (1968), pp. 100–106.

2. Hall, pp. 337–339.

3. *Ibid*, p. 340.

4. *Ibid*, p. 341

5. *Ibid*, p. 341.

6. Cobban, A., 'The Great Mysification of Méhée de la Touche', *Bulletin of the London University Institute of Historical Research*, No.43, (1968), pp. 100–106 at p. 103.

7. Hall, *Pichegru's Treason*, p. 343.

8. Cole, H., Fouché: *The Unprincipled Patriot* (New York: Eyre & Spttiswoode, 1971), p. 147.

9. Cobbetts, W, ed., *Cobbett's Political Register*, V, p. 206.

10. Thiers, Adolphe, *History of the Consulate*, I, p. 519.

11. *Ibid*, p. 519; Meurthe de la, B (ed.), *Correspondance du Duc d'Enghien (1801–1804) et documents sur son enlèvement et mort. Découverte du complot, la sentence de Vincennes, publiés par la Société d'Histoire contemporain*, 2 vols. (Paris: Alphonse Picard et Fils, 1904–1913), II, p. 88.

12. AN F7 3704.

13. Sparrow, Secret Service, p. 284.

14. Barbey, *La Mort de Pichegru*, p. 7.

15. Pocock, *The Terror before Trafalgar*, p. 132.

16. Querelle is described as a 'petit homme au visage grêlé', Barbey, *La Mort de Pichegru*, p. 7.

17. AN AF IV, 1328; Barbey, *La Mort de Pichegru*, p. 18.

18. Lenôtre, G., *Georges Cadoudal* (Paris: Grasset, 1929); Lenôtre, G, *The House of the Combrays* (New York: Mead & Company, 1902); Daudet, E., *La Conjuration de Pichegru et les Complots royalistes du Midi et de l'Est, 1795–7* (Paris: E. Plon, Nourrit et Cie, 1901); Daudet, E., *La Police et Les Chouans sous le Consulat et l'Empire 1800–1815* (Paris, E. Plon, Nourrit et Cie, 1895); Caudrillier, Georges, *La Trahison de Pichegru* (Paris: Alcan, 1908); Anonymous, *Acte d'Accusation de Georges, Pichegru, Moreau, et Autres, Prévenus de Conspiration contre la Personne du Premier Consul* (Paris: Imprimèrie de C. F. Patris, 1804).

19. Lenôtre, *The House of the Combrays*, p. 27.

20. Savary, M., *Memoirs of the Duke of Rovigo, M Savary, Written by Himself, Illustrative of the History of the Emperor Napoleon*, 4 vols. (London: Colburn, 1828), I, pt 11, p. 28.

21. *Ibid*, p. 22.

22. *Ibid*, pp. 22–25.

23. Meurthe de la, B (ed.), *Correspondance du Duc d'Enghien (1801–1804)*, II, p. 119; Bingham, D. A. (ed.), *A Selection from the Letters and Despatches of the First Napoleon* (Cambridge: Cambridge University Press, 2010), p. 66.

24. Thiers, *History of the Consulate*, I, p. 519.

25. *Ibid*, p. 522.

26. *Ibid*, p. 522.

27. Cobbetts, *Cobbett's Political Register*, V, p. 359.

28. Bingham, *A Selection from the Letters and Despatches of the First Napoleon*, p. 64.

29. *Ibid*, p. 64.

30. The police files relating to the hunt for Pichegru and Georges are AN F7 6393–6394; Barbey, *La Mort de Pichegru*, p. 84.

31. *Ibid*, pp. 92–95.

32. *Ibid*, p. 103

33. For an account of Leblanc's duplicity see Grasilier, L., *Par qui fut livré le Général Pichegru* (Paris: Dorbon, 1906); Lenôtre, G., *Vieilles Maisons, Vieux Papiers*, 3 vols. (Paris: Perrin et cie, 1909), III.

34. Anonymous, *Procès Instruit par la Cour de Justice criminelle et speciale du Département de la Seine, séante à Paris, contre Georges, Pichegru et autres*, 2 vols. (Paris: C. F. Patris, 1804), II, pp. 143–145.

35. Barbey, Frédéric, *La Mort de Pichegru*, pp. 121–122.

36. Ségur de, P. P., *An Aide de Camp of Napoleon: Memoirs of General Count de Ségur* (Virginia: Worley Publications, 1995), p. 99.; Pierret, C. M., *Pichegru, Son Procès et son Suicide* (Paris: Imprimerie de Gaultier-Laguionie, 1825), p. 36.

37. Barbey, Frédéric, *La Mort de Pichegru*, p. 127.

38. Anonymous, *Recueil des Interrogatoires subis par le Général Moreau* (Paris: Imprimerie Impériale, 1804), p. 102.

39. Quoted in Lenôtre, *Romances of the French Revolution*, II, p. 192.

40. Lenôtre, *Romances of the French Revolution*, II, p. 191.

41. Cole, Fouché, *The Unprincipled Patriot*, p. 148.

42. Naval Records Society, XXXIX, p. 232.

43. Lenôtre, *Georges Cadoudal*, pp. 140–145.

44. De Polnay, P., *Napoleon's Police* (London: W. H. Allen, 1970)

20 *The d'Enghien Affair*

1. Fay, S. B., 'The Execution of the Duc d'Enghien I', *The American Historical Review*, 3, no 4 (July 1898), pp. 620-640 at 620.

2. Quoted in Boulay de la Meurthre, A., *Les Dernières Années du Duc d'Enghien* (Paris: Hachette, 1886), p. 50.

3. *Ibid*, p. 51.

4. *Ibid*, p. 288.

5. Fay, S. B., 'The Execution of the Duc d'Enghien I', *The American Historical Review*, 3, no 4 (July 1898), pp. 620–640 at 626.

6. Boulay de la Meurthre, *Les Dernières Années du Duc d'Enghien*, p. 127.

7. *Ibid*, p. 127.

8. Savary, *Memoirs of the Duke of Rovigo*, I, p. 36.

9. Boulay de la Meurthre, *Les Dernières Années du Duc d'Enghien*, p. 154.

10. The following narrative of d'Enghien's arrest is sourced from Nougarède de Fayet, A. *Recherches Historiques sur le Procès et la Condamnation du Duc d'Enghien*, 2 vols. (Paris: Comptoir des Imprimeurs-Unis, 1844), I, pp. 28–34 and Anonymous, *Mémoires sur la Révolution Française: La Catastrophe du Duc d'Enghien* (Paris: Baudouin Frères, 1824), pp. 229–233.

11. Charlot's report is quoted at length in *La Catastrophe du Duc d'Enghien*, p. 232.

12. Cole, *Fouché*, p. 149.

13. *Ibid*, p. 149.

14. *Ibid*, p. 149.

15. 'The Murder of The Duke d'Enghien' in *The Living Age* (Boston: T. H. Carter & Co. 1845), I, p. 745.

16. Fay, S. B., 'The Execution of the Duc d'Enghien II', *The American Historical Review*, 4, no 1 (Oct 1898), pp. 21–37 at p. 26; AN AFIV 915.

17. Quoted in Anonymous, *Mémoires sur la Révolution Française: La Catastrophe du Duc d'Enghien*, p. 118.

18. Savary, *Memoirs of the Duke of Rovigo*, I, p. 41.

19. Horne, R. H., *The History of Napoleon*, 2 vols. (New York: A. C. Goodman & Co, 1852), I, p. 323.

20. Dwyer, *Citizen Emperor*, p. 121.

21. Cooper, *Talleyrand*, p. 144.

22. Dwyer, *Citizen Emperor*, p. 122.

23. Boulay de la Meurthre, *Les Dernières Années du Duc d'Enghien*, p. 50.

24. *Ibid*, p. 127.

25. Fisher, H. A. L., *Studies in Napoleonic Statesmanship Germany* (New York: Haskell House Publishers, 1903), p. 74.

26. *Ibid*, p. 76.

27. *Ibid*, p. 77.

28. *Ibid*, pp. 77–78.

21 *Midnight Murder I*

1. AN F7 6391 Rapport de Fauconnier, 11 *ventôse an XII* (2 mars 1804).

2. Anonymous, *Recueil des Interrogatoires subis par le Général Moreau* pp. 102–113.

3. Barbery, F., *La Mort de Pichegru: Biville-Paris-le Temple 1804* (Paris: Perrin et G, 1909), p. 178.

4. Bourrienne, *Mémoires*, II, p. 239.

5. *Ibid*, p. 241.

6. Barbey, F., *La Mort de Pichegru: Biville-Paris-le Temple 1804* (Paris: Perrin et G, 1909), p. 211.; Pierret, C. M., *Pichegru: Son Procès et son Suicide* (Paris: Imprimerie de Gaultier-Laguionne, 1825), pp. 39–42.

7. Savary, M., Mémoire du Duc de Rovigo sur la Mort de Pichegru, du Capitaine Wright, de M Bathurst (Paris: Ponthieu Libraire, 1825), p. 67.

8. *Procés-verbal* is quoted in *Savary, Mémoire*, p. 65; The results of the investigation, such as it was, was formally published by order of the French government under the title *Recueil des Pièces authentiques relatives au Suicide de l'ex-général Pichegru* (Paris: Imprimerie Imperiale, 1804)

9. Pierret, C. M., *Pichegru: Son Procès et son Suicide*, p. 42.

10. Davis, J., *The Life and Campaigns of Victor Moreau* (New York: Southwick & Hardcastle, 1806), p. 266.

11. *Le Moniteur Universel*, 8 April 1804.

12. MacFarlane, C., *The French Revolution*, 4 vols. (London: Charles Knight and Co., 1845), IV, p. 323.

13. Stockdale, J. (ed.), *The Parliamentary Register or an Impartial Report of the Debates that have occurred in the two Houses of Parliament*, 17 vols. (London, 1804), II, p. 488.

14. *The Gentleman's Magazine*, LXXIV, p. 574.

15. Thiers, *History of the Consulate*, I, p. 593.

16. Sparrow, *Secret Service*, p. 292.

17. Bonnet, L. F., *Justification of General Moreau from a Charge of Conspiracy* (London: Longman, Hurst, Rees & Orme, 1804), pp. 16–17.

18. Davis, *The Life and Campaigns of Victor Moreau*, pp. 270–2.

19. *Ibid*, p. 282.

20. *Ibid*, p. 283

21. Ireland, W. H., *France for the Last Seven Years or the Bourbons* (London: G. and W. B. Whittaker, 1822), p. 16.

22. Quoted in Englund, S., *Napoleon: A Political Life* (New York: Scribner, 2004), p. 235.

23. Bingham, D. A (ed.), *A Selection from the Letters and Despatches of the First Napoleon*, p. 53.

24. De Polnay, *Napoleon's Police*, p. 212.

25. Vicomte de Chateaubriand, F. R., *The Memoirs of François Réné, vicomte de Chateaubriand, Sometime Ambassador to England*, 4 vols. (London: Freemantle and Company, 1902), IV, p. 168.

22 *Midnight Murder II*

1. *The Naval Chronicle*, XXXIV, p. 441.

2. *Ibid*, p. 374.

3. *Ibid*, p. 375.

4. James, *The Naval History of Great Britain*, III, p. 220.

5. *The Naval Chronicle*, XXXIV, p. 445.

6. James, *The Naval History of Great Britain*, III, p. 221.

7. Quoted in Brenton, E., *Life and Correspondence of John, Earl St Vincent*, 2 vols. (London: Henry Colburn, 1966), II, p. 143.

8. *The Naval Chronicle*, XXXIV, p. 455.

9. *Ibid*, XII, p. 15.

10. *Ibid*, XXXVI, p. 3.

11. *Ibid*, pp. 4–6.

12. *Ibid*. pp. 6–9.

13. *Ibid*, XXXIV, p. 447.

14. *Ibid*, XXXVI, p. 9.

15. *Ibid*, p. 10.

16. *Ibid*, pp. 12–16.

17. Pocock, *The Terror before Trafalgar*, p. 162.

18. Shankland, P., *Beware of Heroes: Admiral Sir Sidney Smith's War against Napoleon* (London: W. Kimber, 1975), p. 161.

19. *Ibid*, p. 162.

20. Lachouque, *Le Général de Tromelin*, p. 166.

21. *The Naval Chronicle*, XXXIV, p. 446.

22. Quoted in Shankland, *Beware of Heroes: Admiral Sir Sidney Smith's War against Napoleon*, p. 165.

23. Anonymous, *La Revue Hebdomadaire* (Paris, 1922), XXXI, numbers 3 to 4, p. 320; AN F7 6185.

24. *The Naval Chronicle*, XXXIV, p. 448.

25. Cobbetts, William, ed., *Cobbett's Weekly Register*, VIII, p. 412.

26. *The Naval Chronicle*, XXXIV, p. 446.

27. Stockdale, J. (ed.), *The Parliamentary Register*, III, p. 599.

28. Wairy, L. C., *Recollections of the Private Life of Napoleon*, 3 vols. (New York: Saarlfield Publishing, 1904), I, p. 132.

29. Sloane, W. M., *The Life of Napoleon Bonaparte*, 4 vols. (New York: The Century Co., 1906), II, p. 221.

30. AN F7 6319; Lenôtre; *Two Royalist Spies*, p. 99.

31. *Ibid*, p. 100.

32. Pocock, *The Terror before Trafalgar*, p. 163.

33. D'Hauterive, E. (ed.), *La Police Secrète du Premier Empire: Bulletins quotidiens adressés par Fouché à l'Empereur*, 5 vols. (Paris, Perrin, 1908), II, pp. 128–9.

34. Pocock, *The Terror before Trafalgar*, p. 212.

35. Howard, *The Memoirs of Sir Sidney Smith*, II, p. 277; Guy, W., *Principles of Forensic Medicine* (New York: Harper & Brothers, 1845), p. 485.

36. Howard, *The Memoirs of Sir Sidney Smith*, II, p. 300

37. Quoted in Pocock, *The Terror before Trafalgar*, p. 213.

38. *The Times* (7 November 1805).

Epilogue: Private Investigations

1. Barrow, J., *The Life and Correspondence of Admiral Sir William Sidney Smith*, 2 vols. (London: Richard Bentley, 1848), II, p. 496.

2. Goldsmith, L., *Memoirs of the Court of St Cloud: Being Secret Letters from a Gentleman at Paris to a Nobleman in London*, 2 vols. (Boston: The Library of Alexandria, 1900), I, p. 238.

3. AN F7 6185, *Décret de l'Empereur date du Palais des Tuileries, 16 mars 1808*.

4. Pocock, *A Thirst for Glory*, p. 225.

5. Pocock, *The Terror before Trafalgar*, p. 228.

6. *Ibid*, p. 228; Sparrow, Elizabeth, 'The Alien Office 1792–1806', *The Historical Journal*, 33, 02 (1990), pp. 361–384 at p. 362.

7. Fellowes, W. D., *A Visit to the Monastery of La Trappe in 1817* (London: William Stockdale, 1818), p. 163.

8. *Ibid*, p. 164.

9. O'Meara, Barry E., *Napoleon in Exile, or, A Voice from St Helena*, 2 vols. (Philadelphia: H. C. Carey, 1822), II, p. 182.

10. *Ibid*, p. 182.

11. *Ibid*, I, p. 26.

12. *Ibid*, II, p24.

13. *Ibid*, p. 138.

14. Stendhal, *A Life of Napoleon* (Milton Keynes: Open University, 2004), p. 67.

15. Warden, W., *Letters Written on Board His Majesty's Ship Northumberland and at St Helena* (London: R Ackermann, 1816), p. 139.

16. *Ibid*, p. 149.

17. Stendhal, *A Life of Napoleon*, p. 65.

18. *Ibid*, pp. 75–76.

BIBLIOGRAPHY

Archival Sources
AN Archives Nationales, Paris:
F7 Ministère de la Police
AF Bulletins

BL British Library, London:
Additional Manuscripts

HRO Hampshire Record Office, Winchester:
Wickham Mss.

MAE Ministère des Affaires Etrangéres, Paris:
Correspondence Politiques
Mémoires et Documents, France & Switzerland

PRO Public Record Office, Kew Gardens:
Admiralty Papers
Foreign Office Papers
Home Office Papers

Primary Sources

Allonville, A. F., *Mémoires tirés des papiers d'un homme d'état*, 13 vols (Paris: Imprimerie de Paul Dupont, 1828–1838)
Andigné de, G., *Mémoires, 1765–1857*, 2 vols (Paris: E Plon Nourrit, 1900-1901)

Anonymous, *Acte d'Accusation de Georges, Pichegru, Moreau, et Autres, Prévenus de Conspiration contre la personne du Premier Consul* (Paris: Imprimerie de C. F. Patris, 1804)

Anonymous, *Materiaux pour Servir à la Vie Publique et Privée de Joseph Fouché, dit le duc d'Otrante* (Paris: Domère Librairie, 1821)

Anonymous, *Procès Instruit par la cour de justice criminelle et speciale du Département de la Seine, séante à Paris, contre Georges, Pichegru et autres*, 2 vols. (Paris: C. F. Patris, 1804)

Anonymous, *Recueil de la correspondance saisie chez Lemaître et dont la Convention nationale a ordonné l'impression* (Paris: Imprimerie de la République, 1795)

Anonymous, *Recueil des Interrogatoires subis par le Général Moreau* (Paris: Imprimerie Impériale, 1804)

Anonymous, *Recueil des Pièces authentiques relatives au Suicide de l'ex-général Pichegru* (Paris: Imprimerie Imperiale, 1804)

Archives Parlementaires de 1787 à 1860, Recueil Complet des Débats et Législatifs et Politiques des Chambres Françaises (1ère série: 1787–1799), 96 vols. (Paris: 1877–1990)

Argyll, D., (ed.), *George Douglas, 8th Duke of Argyll: Autobiography and Memoirs*, 2 vols. (London: John Murray, 1906)

Aulard, F. A., (ed.), *Paris Pendant La Réaction Thermidorienne et sous le Directoire: Recueil de Documents pour l'histoire et de l'Éspirit public à Paris*, 5 vols. (Paris: AMS Press, 1899)

Aulard, F. A., *Recueil des Actes du Comité de Salut Public avec la Correspondance officielle des Représentants en Mission et le Régistre du Conseil Exécutif Provisioire*, 28 vols. (Paris: Imprimerie Nationale, 1889–1951

Babeau, A (ed.), *La France et Paris sous le Directoire: Lettres d'un Voyageuse Anglaise, Suivies d'extrait des lettres de Henry Swinburne* (Paris: Librairie de Firmin-Didot et Cte)

Barras, P., *Memoirs of Barras: Member of the Directorate*, 4 vols. (New York: Harper & Brothers, 1895)

Barthélemy, F., *Memoires de Barthélemy, 1768–1819*, (Paris: Plon-Nourrit et cie, 1914)

Beville, S. A., Barrière, F (ed.), *Collection des Mémoires relatif à la Révolution Française* (Paris: Imprimerie de Fain, 1827)

Bingham, D. A (ed.), *A Selection from the Letters and Despatches of the First Napoleon* (Cambridge: Cambridge University Press, 2010)

Blackwood, W (ed.), *Blackwoods Edinburgh Magazine* (Edinburgh: William Blackwood, 1817–1980)

Bonnet, L. F., *Justification of General Moreau from a Charge of Conspiracy* (London: Longman, 1804)

Bourrienne, L. A., *Mémoires de M de Bourrienne sur Napoléon, le Directoire, le Consulat, l'Empire et la Restauration,* 10 vols (Brussels: H. Tarlier et Auguste Wahlen, 1829)

Broglie, A (ed.), *Memoirs of the Prince de Talleyrand,* 5 vols. (London: G. P. Putmam's Sons, 1891–1892)

Buchez, P. Roux, P. C., (ed.), *Histoire Parlementaire de la Révolution Française ou Journal des Assemblées Nationales, depuis 1789 jusqu'en 1815* (Paris: Paulin, 1838)

Bury, J. P. T., Barry, J. C., *An Englishman in Paris, 1803: The Journal of Bernie Greatheed* (London: Geoffrey Bles, 1953)

Burke, E., (ed). *Annual Register* (London: J. Wright, 1806)

Cobbett, W., *Cobbett's Weekly Register* (London: William Cobbett, 1802–1835)

Conseil d'Etat, *Conspiration Anglaise,* 2 vols. (Paris: Imprimerie de la République, 1801)

Convention Nationales, Collection générale des Décrets rendus par la Convention Nationale, 52 vols. (Paris: Baudouin Frères, 1794)

Correspondance de Napoleon 1er, 32 vols. (Paris: Imprimerie Impériale, 1858–70)

Correspondance secrète de Charette, Stofflet, Puisaye et autre personnes (Paris: Imprimèrie de la République, 1799)

Correspondance Trouvée le 2 Floréal an 5 à Offembourg, dans les Fourgons du Général Klinglin, 2 vols. (Paris: Imprimèrie de la République, 1797)

Chateaubriand, F. R., *The Memoirs of François Réné, Vicomte de Chateaubriand, Sometime Ambassador to England,* 4 vols. (London: Freemantle and Company, 1902)

David, P. A., *Histoire des Campagnes du General Pichegru: Containing the Operations of the Armies of the North, and of the Sambre and Meuse* (London. 1796)

Debidour, A. (ed.), *Recueil des Actes du Directoire Exécutif: Procès Verbaux, Arêtes,* Instructions, Lettres et A*ctes divers,* 4 vols. (Paris: Imprimerie nationale, 1910–1919)

Debrett, J (ed.), *A Collection of State Papers: Relative to the War against France, Carried on by Great Britain and Several other European Powers,* 10 vols. (London: John de Brett, 1802)

Desmarest, P. M., *Temoignages historiques ou Quinze ans de Haute Police sous Napoleon* (Paris: A Levavasseur, 1833)

D'Hauterive, E. (ed.), *La Police Secrète du Premier Empire: Bulletins quotidiens addressés par Fouché à l'Empereur,* 5 vols. (Paris: Perrin, 1908)

Fauche-Borel, L., *Mémoires de Fauche Borel: Agent secret de Louis XVIII,* 4 vols. (Paris: Moutardier Librairie-éditeur, 1829)

Fauche-Borel, L., *Notices sur les* Généraux Pichegru et Moreau, *par M Louis Fauche Borel* (London: T Harper Young, 1807)

Fellowes, W. D., *A Visit to the Monastery of La Trappe in 1817* (London: William Stockdale, 1818)

Fouché, J., *Ministère de la Police, Rapport fait aux Consuls par le Ministère de la Police, sur l'infâme Complot tendant à assassiner les Consuls ... Correspondance anglaise sur les Conspirateurs ... Liste officiel des Noms, Qualités et Demeurés des chefs de la conspiration de la rue Nicaise, etc* (Paris: Imprimerie de Cornu, 1801)

Fouché, J., *Memoirs relating to Fouché, Minister of Police under Napoleon I* (New York: Sturgis & Walton, 1912)

Fouché, J., *Mémoires de Joseph Fouché, duc d'Otrante,* 2 vols. (Osnabrück: Proff, 1824)

Goldsmith, Lewis, *Memoirs of the Court of St Cloud: Being Secret Letters from a Gentleman at Paris to a Nobleman in London,* 2 vols. (Boston: The Library of Alexandria, 1900)

Granville, Castalia, Countess, ed., *Lord Granville Leveson Gower: Private Correspondence, 1781–1820,* 2 vols. (London: John Murray, 1916)

Harris, J. H, *Diaries and Correspondence of James Harris, First Earl of Malmesbury,* 4 vols. (London: Richard Bentley, 1844)

Historical Manuscripts Commission, *The Manuscripts of J. B. Fortescue, Preserved at Dropmore,* 6 vols. (Dublin: HMSO, 1908)

Hemlow, J. (ed.), *The Journals and Letters of Fanny Burney (Madame D'Arblay),* 12 vols. (Oxford: Oxford University Press, 1972–1984)

Howard, E. G. G., *The Memoirs of Sidney Smith* (London: Richard Bentley, 1839)

Jackson, G., *The Diaries and Letters of Sir George Jackson, K.C.H., From the Peace of Amiens to the Battle of Talavera,1809–1816* (London: Bentley, 1872)

Kaulek, J., *Papiers de Barthélemy,* 4 vols. (Paris: F. Alcan, 1889)

Las Cases, E., *Memoiral de St Helene* (Paris: Gallimard, Pléaide, 1948)

Larevellière-Lépeaux, L. M., *Mémoires de* Larevellière-Lépeaux: *Membre du Directoire Exécutif de la République Français et de l'Institut national* (Paris: E. Plon, Nourrit et cie, 1895)

Lloyd, C. (ed.), *The Keith Papers,* 3 vols. (London: Naval Records Society, 1955)

Londonderry, M. (ed.), *Correspondence, Despatches and Other Papers of Viscount Castlereagh,* 5 vols. (London: John Murray, 1851)

Henri de Bourbon, L. A., *Correspondance du Duc d'Enghien (1801–1804) et documents sur son enlèvement et mort. Découverte du complot, la sentence de Vincennes, publiés par la Société d'Histoire contemporaine, par le Cte Boulay de la Meurthe* (Paris: Alphonse Picard et Fils, 1904–1913)

Michaud, J. F., *Les Adieux à Bonaparte* (Paris: Marchands de Nouveautés, 1800)

Moore, J. C., *The Life of Sir John Moore*, 2 vols. (London: John Murray, 1834)

Naval Records Society, *Publications of the Naval Records Society*, 150 vols. (Hants: Naval Records Society, 1893–2006)

Neuville, H., *Memoirs of Baron Hyde de Neuville: Outlaw, Exile, Ambassador* (2 vols.) (London: Sands, 1913)

O'Meara, B. E., *Napoleon in Exile, or, A Voice from St Helena*, 2 vols. (Philadelphia: H. C. Carey, 1822)

Puisaye de, J., *Mémoires du Comte Joseph de Puisaye* (London: D. N. Shury, 1808)

Ramel, J. P., *Narrative to the Deportation to Cayenne, of Barthélemy, Pichegru etc.* (London: J. Wright, 1799)

Ray, A., *Réimpression de L'Ancien Moniteur: Seule Histoire Authentique*, 32 vols. (Paris, 1843)

Réal, P., *Indiscretions of a Prefect of Police: Anecdotes of Napoleon and the Bourbons from the Papers of Count Réal*, trans. Arthur L Hayward, (London: Cassell and Company, 1929)

Rémusat, C. E., *Mémoires de Madame de Rémusat (1802–1808) publiés par son petit-fils Paul de Remusat*, 2 vols. (Paris: Calmann-Lévy, 1880)

Reynolds, F., *The Life and Times of Frederick Reynolds*, 2 vols. (London: Henry Colburn, 1826)

Roberts, W (ed.), *Memoirs of the Life and Correspondence of Mrs Hannah Moore*, 2 vols. (New York: Harper & Brothers, 1851)

Savary, M., *Memoirs of the Duke of Rovigo, M Savary, Written by Himself, Illustrative of the History of the Emperor Napoleon*, 4 vols. (London: Henry Colburn, 1828)

Savary, M., *Memoire du Duc de Rovigo sur la Mort de Pichegru, du Capitaine Wright, de M Bathurst* (Paris: Ponthieu Libraire, 1825)

Schmidt, A., (ed.), *Paris Pendant La Révolution, d'après les rapports de la police secrète, 1789–1800*, 5 vols. (Paris: Champion, 1880)

Schmidt, A., (ed.), *Tableaux de la Révolution francaise: publies sur les Papiers inédits du département et de la Police secrete de Paris*, 3 vols. (Leipzig: Veit, 1867)

Ségur de, P. P., *An Aide de Camp of Napoleon: Memoirs of General Count de Ségur* (Virginia: Worley Publications, 1995)

Shorter, C. K., (ed.), *Napoleon in his own Defense: Being a Reprint of certain Letters written by Napoleon from St Helena to Lady Clavering* (Michigan: Cassell, 1910)

Smith, W. S., *The Life of Sir Sidney Smith, His Dreadful Confinement in the French Prison and Escape from Thence; His Defence of Acre against Bonaparte* (Sheffield: W. Todd, 1806)

Stockdale, J. (ed.), *The Parliamentary Register or an Impartial report of the Debates that have occurred in the two Houses of Parliament*, 17 vols. (London: Stockdale, 1804)

Thale, M. (ed.), *Selections from the Papers of the London Corresponding Society, 1792–1799* (Cambridge: Cambridge University Press, 1983)

The Gentleman's Magazine: or Monthly Intelligencer (London, 1731–1833)

The Naval Chronicle, 40 vols. (London: J. Gold, 1799–1818)

Trotter, J. B., *Memoirs of the Latter Years of the Rt. Hon. Charles James Fox* (London: R. Phillips, 1811)

Touche de la, M., *Alliance des Jacobins de France avec le Ministère anglais* (Paris: Imprimerie de la République, an XII)

Warden, W., *Letters Written on Board His Majesty's Ship Northumberland and at St Helena* (London: R Ackermann, 1816)

Wickham, W., *Correspondence of the Rt Hon William Wickham*, 2 vols. (London: R. Bentley, 1870)

Windham, W., *The Windham Papers: The Life and Correspondence of Rt. Hon. William Windham*, 2 vols. (London: Herbert Jenkins, 1913)

Wraxall, N. W., *Posthumous Memoirs of His Own Time by Sir N. W. Wraxall*, 2 vols. (London: Richard Bentley, 1836)

Secondary Sources

Alger, J. G., *Napoleon's British Visitors and Captives* (London: Archibald Constable, 1904)

Alger, J. G., *Englishmen in the French Revolution* (London: S. Low, Marston, Searle & Rivington, 1889)

Anonymous, *The History and Topography of Ashbourn, the Valley of the Dove, and the Adjacent Villages* (Ashbourne: Dawson & Hobson, 1839)

Anonymous, *Mémoires sur la Révolution Française: La Catastrophe du Duc d'Enghien* (Paris: Baudouin Frères, 1824)

Arnold, E. A., *Fouché, Napoleon and the General Police* (Washington: University Press of America, 1979)

Aubert, J., *L'État et sa Police en France: 1789–1914* (Geneva: Librairie Droz, 1979)

Aude de l', J. P. F., *Histoire Secrète du Directoire*, 4 vols. (Paris: Ménard Librairie, 1832)

Baines, E., *History of the Wars of the French Revolution*, 2 vols. (London, Longman, 1818)

Balleine, G. R., *The Tragedy of Phillipe d'Auvergne, Vice Admiral in the Royal Navy and last Duke of Bouillon* (London-Chichester: Phillimore and C, 1973)

Balzac, H., *The Works of Honoré de Balzac: And other Stories* (New York: Avil Publishing Co., 2005)

Barbery, F., *La Mort de Pichegru: Biville-Paris-le Temple 1804* (Paris: Perrin et Cie, 1909)

Barrow, J., *The Life and Correspondence of Admiral Sir William Sidney Smith* (London: Richard Bentley, 1848)

Bertaud, J. P., *Bonaparte et le duc d'Enghien: La Duel des Deux France* (Paris: R. Laffont, 1972)

Blanc, O., *L'Espions de la Révolution et de l'Empire* (Paris: Librairie Académique Perrin, 1995)

Boulay de la Meurthre, A. J. C. J. *Les Dernières Années du Duc d'Enghien* (Paris: Hachette, 1886)

Brenton, E. P., *Life and Correspondence of John, Earl St Vincent*, 2 vols. (London: Henry Colburn, 1838)

Brenton, E. P., The Naval History of Great Britain, 2 vols. (London: C. Rice, 1823)

Broster, D. K., 'An English Sailor among the Chouans', *English Historical Review*, 25, (1910), p. 132

Broster, D. K., 'Sir Sidney Smith and Frotté in 1796', *English Historical Review*, 23, (1908), pp. 534–537

Brown, H. G., *Ending the French Revolution: Violence, Justice and Repression from the Terror to Napoleon* (Charlottesville: University of Virginia Press, 2006)

Brown, H. G., *War, Revolution and the Bureaucratic State: Politics and Army Administration in France, 1791–1799* (Oxford: Clarendon Press, 1995)

Brown, H. G., 'The Napoleonic Security State: Special Tribunals', in *Napoleon and his Empire: Europe, 1804–1814*, (eds.) Philip Dwyer and Alan Forrest (New York: Palgrave, 2007)

Browning, O., (ed.), *England and Napoleon: The Despatches of Lord Whitworth* (London: Royal Historical Society, 1887)

Bryant, A., *Years of Victory, 1802–12* (London: Collins, 1944)

Bussey, G. M., *History of Napoleon*, 2 vols. (London: Joseph Thomas, 1811)

Cadoudal, L. G., *Georges Cadoudal et la Chouannerie* (Paris: E Plon, 1887)

Carlyle, T., *The French Revolution* (Oxford: Oxford University Press, 1989)

Caudrillier, G., *La Trahison de Pichegru* (Paris: Alcan, 1908)

Cobban, A., 'British Secret Service in France, 1784–1792', *English Historical Review*, 69, 271 (1954), pp. 226–261.

Cobban, A., 'The Beginning of the Channel Isles Correspondence', 1789–1794, *English Historical Review*, 77, 302 (1962), pp. 38–52.

Cobban, A., 'The Great Mysification of Méhée de la Touche', *Bulletin of the London University Institute of Historical Research*, No. 43, (1968), pp. 100-106.

Cole, H., Fouché, *The Unprincipled Patriot* (New York: McCall, 1971)

Comick, M., Morris, P., *The French Secret Services* (New Jersey: Transaction Publishers, 1993)

Cooper, D. A., *Talleyrand* (London, Orion Books Ltd, 1932)

Darrah, D., *Conspiracy in Paris: The Strange Career of Joseph Picot de Limoelan, Aristocrat, Soldier and Priest, and the Gun Powder Plot against Napoleon on 3 Nivôse, year IX* (New York: Exposition Press, 1953)

Daudet, E., *Histoire de l'émigration: les Émigrés et la seconde coalition, 1797–1800 d'après les documents inédits* (Paris, Librairie illustrée, 1886)

Daudet, E., *La Conjuration de Pichegru et les Complots royalistes du Midi et de l'Est, 1795–7* (Paris: Librairie Plon, 1901)

Daudet, E., *La Police et Les Chouans sous le consulat et l'empire 1800–1815* (Paris: E Plon, Nourrit et cie, 1895)

Davis, J., *The Life and Campaigns of Victor Moreau* (New York: Southwick & Hardcastle, 1806)

De Polnay, P., *Napoleon's Police* (London: W. H. Allen, 1970)

Dinwiddy, J. R., *Radicalism and Reform in Britain, 1780–1850* (London: The Hambledon Press, 1992)

Duckworth, C., *The D'Antraigues Phenomenon* (Newcastle: Avero Publications Ltd, 1986)

Dumas, Alexandre, *The Last Cavalier: Being the Adventures of Count Sainte-Hermine in the Age of Napoleon* (London: Harper Perennial, 2007)

Durey, M., *William Wickham Master Spy: The Secret War Against the French Revolution*, (London: Pickering & Chatto, 2009)

Durey, M., 'Lord Grenville and the 'Smoking Gun': The Plot to Assassinate the French Directory in 1798–1799 Reconsidered', *The Historical Journal*, 45 (2002), pp. 547–668.

Durey, M., 'The British Secret Service and the Escape of Sir Sidney Smith from Paris in 1798', *The Historical Association*, 84, (1999), pp. 437–457.

Dwyer, P., *Citizen Emperor: Napoleon in Power* (London: Bloomsbury Publishing, 2013) Dwyer, P., *Napoleon: The Path to Power* (London: Bloomsbury Publishing, 2008)

Ehrman, J., *The Younger Pitt*, 3 vols (London: Constable, 1996)

Englund, S., *Napoleon: A Political Life* (New York: Scribner, 2004)

Fay, S. B., 'The Execution of the Duc d'Enghien I', *The American Historical Review*, 3, no 4 (July 1898), pp. 620-640.

Fay, S. B., 'The Execution of the Duc d'Enghien II', *The American Historical Review*, 4, no 1 (Oct 1898), pp. 21–37.

Fisher, A. L., *Studies in Napleonic Statesmanship Germany* (New York: Haskell House Publishers, 1903)

Forsyth, W., *History of the Captivity of Napoleon at St Helena* (London: John Murray, 1853)

Glover, R., *Britain at Bay: Defense against Bonaparte, 1803–14* (London: Allen and Unwin, 1974) Godechot, J., *Le Comte d'Antraigues. Un espion dans L'Europe des* émigrés (Paris: Fayard, 1986)

Godechot, J., *The Counter-Revolution: Doctrine and Action, 1789–1804* (London: Routledge & Regan Paul, 1972)

Grainger, J., *The Amiens Truce: Britain and Bonaparte, 1801–1803* (Suffolk: The Boydell Press, 2004)

Grasilier, L., *Par qui fut livré le Général Pichegru* (Paris: Dorbon, 1906)

Guy, W., *Principles of Forensic Medicine* (New York: Harper & Brothers, 1845)

Hall, J., *General Pichegru's Treason* (London: Smith, Elder & Co, 1915)

Harvey, R., *The War of Wars, The Epic Struggle Between Britain and France, 1789–1815* (London: Constable, 2006)

Hazlitt, W., *The Life of Napoleon Buonaparte*, 4 vols. (London: Office of the Illustrated Library, 1852)

Horne, R. H., *The History of Napoleon*, 2 vols. (New York: A. C. Goodman & Co, 1852)

Hutt, M., *Chouannerie and Counter Revolution: Puisaye, The Princes and the British Government in the 1790s*, 2 vols. (Cambridge: Cambridge University Press, 1983)

Hutt, Maurice, 'Spies in France, 1793–1808', *History Today*, 12, (1962), pp. 158–167.

Ireland, W. H., *France for the Last Seven Years or the Bourbons* (London: G. and W. B. Whittaker, 1822)

Ireland, W. H., *The Life of Napoleon Bonaparte*, 4 vols. (London: John Cumberland, 1828)

James, W., *The Naval History of Great Britain*, 6 vols. (London: Harding, 1822–4)

Johnson, D., 'Amiens 1802: The Phoney Peace', *History Today*, 52, (2002), pp. 20–26.

Kennedy, D., *Helen Maria Williams and the Age of Revolution* (New Jersey: Roseman Publishing, 2002)

Kenney, J. J., 'Lord Whitworth and the Conspiracy Against Tsar Paul I: The New Evidence of the Kent Archive' in *Slavic Review*, vol 36, no 2 (June 1977), pp. 205–219

Knight, C., *History of the Peace: Being a History of England from 1816 to 1854*, 8 vols. (Boston: Walker, Wise and Company, 1865),

Lac. R., *Le Général Comte de Précy: Sa vie militaire, son commandement au siège de Lyon, son émigration* (Paris: H. Champion, 1908)

Lachouque, H., *Le Général de Tromelin* (Paris: Bloudet Gay, 1968)

Lefebvre, G., *Le Directoire* (Paris: Armand Colin, 1946)

Le Menuet de la Jugannière, P. M. J. J. A., *Le Chouan Carlos Sourdat et son Père, l'Agent Royal* (Paris: Firmin-Didot et cie, 1932)

Lenôtre, G., *Georges Cadoudal* (Paris: Imprimerie F. Paillart 1929)

Lenôtre, G., *L'Affaire Perlet, Drames policiers* (Lagny: Imprimerie E. Grevin, 1925)

Lenôtre, G., *Paris révolutionnaire: Vielles maisons, vieux papiers* (Paris: Perrin et cie, 1904) Lenôtre, G., *Romances of the French Revolution*, (London: William Heineman, 1908)

Lenôtre, G., *The House of the Combrays* (New York: Mead & Company, 1902)

Littel, E. (ed.), *The Living Age* (Boston: T. H. Carter & Co. 1845)

Loredan, J., *La Machine Infernale* (Paris: 1924)

Lyons, M., *France under the Directory* (Cambridge: Cambridge University Press, 1975)

MacFarlane, C., *The French Revolution*, 4 vols. (London: Charles Knight and Co., 1845)

Madelin, L., *Fouché: Ministre de Police 1759–1820*, 2 vols. (Paris: Plon, 1901)

Madelin, L., *Histoire du Consulat et de l'Empire*, 16 vols. (Paris: Hachette, 1939)

Mallet, B., *Mallet du Pan and the French Revolution* (London: Longmans, Green and Co, 1902)

Martel de, A. L. R., Étude sur l'Affaire de la Machine Infernale du 3 nivôse an IX (Paris: E. Lachaud, 1870)

Mitchell, H., 'Francis Drake and the Comte D'Antraigues: A Study of the Dropmore Bulletins, 1793–1796', *Institute of Historical Research*, 29 (1956), pp. 123–144.

Mitchell, H., *The Underground War against Revolutionary France: The Missions of William Wickham, 1794–1800* (Oxford: Clarendon Press, 1965)

Oman, C., *Britain against Napoleon* (London: Faber & Faber, 1942)

Pierret, C. M, *Pichegru: Son Procès et son Suicide* (Paris: Imprimerie de Gaultier-Laguionie, 1825)

Pocock, T., *A Thirst for Glory: The Life of Admiral Sir Sidney Smith* (London: Aurum Press, 1996) Pocock, T., *The Terror before Trafalgar: Nelson, Napoleon and the Secret War* (London: John Murray, 2002)

Rodger, N. A. M., *The Command of the Ocean. A Naval History of Britain, 1649–1815* (London: 2004)

Russell, E. F. L., *Knight of the Sword: The Life and Letters of Admiral Sir Sidney William Smith* (London: Victor Gollancz Ltd, 1964)

Sardent, M., *La Princess Charlotte de Rohan et Le Duc d'Enghien: Un Roman d'Exil* (Paris: Émile-Paul, 1841)

Schama, S., *Citizens: A Chronicle of the French Revolution* (London: Penguin, 1989

Scott, W., *Life of Napoleon Bonaparte*, 2 vols. (Exeter: J & B Williams, 1836)

Shankland, P., *Beware of Heroes: Admiral Sir Sidney Smith's War against Napoleon* (London: W. Kimber, 1975)

Sinsoilliez, R., *Les Espions du Roi: Histoire de la Correspondance pendant les Guerres de Vendée et de l'Empire* (Louviers: Editions L'Ancre de Marine, 2006)

Sloane, W. M., *The Life of Napoleon Bonaparte*, 4 vols. (Michigan: The Century Co., 1906)

Sparrow, E., *Phantom of the Guillotine: The Real Scarlet Pimpernel, Louis Bayard- Lewis Duval 1769–1844* (Cornwall: Carn Press, 2013)

Sparrow, E., *Secret Service: British Agents in France, 1792–1815* (Woodbridge: Boydell Press, 1999)

Sparrow, E., 'Secret Service under Pitt's Administrations, 1792–1806', *History*, 83, (1998), pp. 280–294.

Sparrow, E., 'The Alien Office 1792–1806', *The Historical Journal*, 33, 02 (1990), pp. 361–384.

Sparrow, E., 'The Swiss and Swabian Agencies, 1795–1801', *The Historical Journal*, 35, 4, (1992), pp. 861–884.

Stawell, R., *The Return of Louis XVIII* (New York: Charles Scribner's Sons, 1909)

Stendhal, *A Life of Napoleon* (Milton Keynes: Open University Press, 2004)

Strathern, P., *Napoleon in Egypt* (London: Vintage, 2009)

Sutherland, D. M. G., *France, 1789–1815: Revolution and Counter-Revolution* (London: Fontana Press, 1985)

Sydenham, M. J, 'The Crime of Nivôse in Bosher, J. F. (ed.), *French Government and Society, 1500–1850* (London: 1973)

Thiers, A., *History of the Consulate and the Empire of France under Napoleon*, 20 vols. (Philadelphia: J B Lippencott & Co, 1861)

Thiry, J., *La Machine Infernale* (Paris: Berger-Levault, 1952)

Wairy, L. C., *Recollections of the Private Life of Napoleon*, 3 vols. (New York: Saarlfield Publishing, 1904)

Waresquiel de, E., *Fouché: Les Silences de la Pieuvre* (Paris: Tallandier-Fayard, 2014)

Bibliography

Wilson, R., *History of the British Expedition to Egypt* (London: C Roworth, 1803)

Zweig, S., *Fouché* (Paris: Grasset & Fasquelle, 1969)

INDEX